*Ecuador*
*Marzo 29, 2011*

# The Amazon, Shamans, God and Ayahuasca

PATRICIO FERNÁNDEZ – SALVADOR TORRES

First Edition, 2006

Paintings and ilustrations by Patricio
Fernández-Salvador Torres
Author Adress: peopleofyage@hotmail.com

Design by Link-Imagen • info@link-imagen.com • -
www.link-imagen.com • Quito - Ecuador.

Author Registration 024381

ISBN - 10: ISBN-9978-45-058-0
ISBN - 13: ISBN-978-9978-45-058-1

Printed by IN - PRESS
Manuel Guzmán 282 y Hugo Moncayo
Quito - Ecuador

• Acknowledgments

In honor to all of the indigenous people in Latin America, Africa, Asia and throughout the rest of the world, who after many years, are still struggling to conserve their land, ancestral ethnic religion and culture from the malicious economical, political and religious attack by modern civilization.

In addition, for my beloved wife Lily and daughter Michelle who have helped me with their continuous support and patience.

# Contents

I believe that it is healthy and God-like for us to be always tolerant and have an open mind, especially concerning all of the diverse cultures and religions that live throughout our planet. As we pass through this life, we will always find people with different religions and cultures, and if we sincerely and openly listen to them, usually we will always learn something, and even if we do not learn anything, let us remember that other people have as much right as we do to a different point of view and to practice a different culture or religion. In the eyes of God, all cultures and all different religions which strive to achieve closeness to God are equal, we are all equal, and we are all children of God. It is only on a personal level where we will find a difference between the Spiritual energy of one person of one religion versus the Spiritual energy and holiness of another person of the same religion or of a different religion.

If in the fifteen hundreds, the Spaniard conquistadors and the Vatican would have been tolerant and had an open mind towards the Incas in Peru, Ecuador and Bolivia, certainly the Spanish would have learned many vital things that could have been useful for them as well as for us today, including something as basic as the Inca stone masonry. The Incas were building many temples with walls made out of huge stone blocks that weighed hundreds of tons and then cutting and fitting these stone blocks together with such precision that today, modern scientists still cannot explain how these walls were built. The advanced engineering and stone masonry technique of the Incas is one of various mysteries in our world that unfortunately has remained forever in the past and just because an incredibly sophisticated civilization was unfortunately conquered by narrow minded people. We should learn from past history and stop making the same stupid mistakes as the Spanish conquistadors, the Vatican, and so many other conquerors and colonizers of our planet.

The South American Amazon is the largest tropical rainforest and most biologically diverse wilderness on the planet. Here we find more species of animals, insects, plants and trees than anywhere in the world. Within this gigantic, prehistoric jungle, we also find the most extensive river system and biggest river. To have a more clear idea of the massive dimension of this rainforest we can picture it to about the same size as continental United States. About twenty-five per cent of the world's supply of oxygen comes from here. Yes, the Amazon jungle is truly a unique, marvelous, beautiful and crucial area of our planet.

For millions of years within this tropical rainforest, the animals and the forest evolved together, developing a close relationship that eventually resulted in a perfect balance. Additionally, for thousands of years the Amazonian native tribes living in this thick jungle learned to live by a simple philosophy that would help to ensure their survival and balance. This philosophy was to love, respect and learn from Pacha Mama (Mother Nature, in the Inca Quechua language) and it is precisely this attitude and behavior which has allowed them to live happily and successfully in
perfect harmony with their habitat. In this manner, the wise, native tribes quickly became an integral part of their ecosystem.

During this time, the Amazonian natives were constantly investigating the jungle plants in order to service their physical needs regarding food, medicine and the manufacturing of tools, weapons, etc... Probably, during this search they accidentally tasted some plants which affected their mind perception and their sense of Spirituality. Once experiencing this new, wonderful Spiritual and mental world, most likely their main interest in life became to investigate more the different plants in order to find the right plants which would help them obtain a maximum communion with this powerful Spiritual and mental energy.

Through their research, one day they found their answers to their religious quest, deep into the roots of God's creation, precisely in the complex, natural chemicals harbored within one of the wondrous Amazonian plants. We cannot begin to imagine how long this pursuit lasted or how many hardships were encountered along the way, but we think that it was at least one-thousand years ago that an enlightened Shaman discovered how to use a unique plant, which has since become the sacred vehicle to transporting millions of Amazonian native people to the beautiful and glorious Amazon Spiritual World, a world which for the ethnic native people is in essence the "real" World.

This unique and remarkable plant is a 7 cm. / 2 in. thick climbing vine which is known as Ayahuasca, it grows only in the upper Amazon of South America and in the Pacific tropical rainforest of Ecuador and Colombia, and then nowhere else in our planet does it grow. The upper Amazon region of South America is the Amazon jungle that is adjacent to the foothills of the Andes; this is the Amazonian tropical rainforest area within the countries of Colombia, Ecuador, Peru and Bolivia. Even though the country of Brazil is not within the upper Amazonian basin, there is evidence that some tribes within the westernmost area of the Brazilian Amazon also used this plant.

For all of the ethnic native tribes, Ayahuasca is considered a sacred plant. A special brew will be made from this plant and will be taken during nocturnal religious ceremonies. The natural chemicals in the brew will act quickly within the physical body to awaken and strengthen the Spiritual body (Soul) of the person, consequently enabling one to reach a maximum level

of Spiritual power with which one can truly relate to and travel to the Spiritual World. This spectacular Spiritual World is filled with tremendous metaphysical energy and beautiful visions where one always achieves a state of oneness with God, and consequently a glorious level of enlightenment. The following day after this marvelous experience, not only will one have strengthened spiritually, but also the rest of one's entire being will have strengthened, this is mentally emotionally and physically.

The Spiritual body or Soul is two different names for exactly the same thing. But how can we define a Spiritual body? For me, the Spiritual body is a part of God, a speck of God's light, a spark of the glorious, eternal energy of God that is naturally inside each one of us. Since we were born, until we "die", our physical body will be constantly changing, this occurs through aging, but our Spiritual body will not change like our physical body, it does not age. Our Spiritual body will not weaken with time and it will not die, because it is eternal.

The Amazonian ethnic natives believe in different states of reincarnation, which depending on their tribe, may vary greatly and be highly complex. In general they believe in different types of re-incarnated souls like; evil spirit demon souls, spirit-souls that are being punished and are suffering of hunger. Butterfly, owl, eagle, dolphin, deer, clouds, and thunder spirit-souls. Also they believe in spirit-souls that are living happily forever with God in the Spiritual World and spirit-souls that are near us and will assist us to reach God.

The ethnic native people believe that all plants have Spirit-souls, and that Ayahuasca in particular has a sacred female-spirit. As a seedling vine, Ayahuasca begins her growth by enthusiastically and rapidly climbing up the trunk of a tree until she reaches the canopy; the highest part of a tree or of the forest. There she vigorously spreads her arms-branches and leaves on top of her host tree as far as possible to benefit from the maximum amount of available sunlight and moonlight.

After at least five years of maturing, she will be ripe enough to provide her noble limbs for the most powerful "Spiritual" and mental experience that can be performed by any human group in our planet.

The ethnic Amazonian tribes believe that there are two worlds, our everyday materialistic world and the eternal, glorious Spiritual World filled with God's divine energy and with complete happiness. Within the everyday material world they can relate to the Spiritual World by means of a persistent invisible force of a powerful energy which they can feel everywhere in Mother Nature; in the forest, in waterfalls, in rivers, in plants, animals, up in the sky and especially inside themselves.

Even though the Spiritual World is so much more beautiful and important, the material world is also very important, because it is in the material world where the God-given tools exist which we can use to prepare our mental, emotional, physical and Spiritual bodies so that our Spiritual-mental body can be transported to the Spiritual World. Also it is in the material world where everyday we will find obstacles and temptations related to the devil, which will have to be overcome in order to strengthen our Spiritual-mental body and consequently strengthen our relationship with God.

Today, the ethnic natives believe that the enlightened Shaman who lived more than one-thousand years ago and first discovered Ayahuasca still lives today as a powerful Spirit within a special dimension or world which is between the Spiritual and material world, but besides believing in this first Shaman powerful-Spirit, they also believe in other powerful spirits which live within the material and Spiritual World. For example they believe that all Harpy eagles according to their individual sex represent a powerful male or female Spirit which controls the sky domains. Also they believe that all jaguars according to their individual sex represent a powerful male or female Spirit which controls the land domains. As well, all anacondas according to their individual sex represent a powerful male or female Spirit which controls the water domains, and all plants, trees and animals have spirits, some spirits are more powerful and or more sacred than others. They also believe that all these different forms of Spiritual energy found in Mother Nature and in different beings are related to more powerful sources of Spiritual energies which live in the Spiritual World.

Undoubtedly, the most powerful Spiritual or material energy that exists is the almighty energy of one supreme God. In their different tribal languages, their name for God is translated to "Father of all", this implies Father of all living and non-living organisms throughout the Spiritual and material worlds. By using the word "Father" does not mean that they believe that God is male; it implies the role of a human family where the Father image is the head of the family. The Shamans that I've met believe that God does not have a sex and that God's divine energy being in perfect wisdom and balance can equally relate to both sexes. The native people believe that God's energy is everywhere and in every living being, but that God personally lives beyond the stars, sun and moon, and this is where we find the heart of the Spiritual World.

In the Amazon, it is the Shamans who are the crucial link between the material world and the Spiritual World. In Ecuador, Colombia and some areas of the Amazon, both women and men can become Shamans. To become a Shaman takes about five years of apprenticeship. During this time from the Spiritual World and from her or his Spiritual body, the apprentices will develop tremendous Spiritual and mental energy. In these ethnic communities it is the most powerful Shaman who will become the Spiritual leader and consequently will also become the political leader.

By using sacred plants and astral flights, the Shamans will guide their people into the Spiritual World. With the use of their own personal holy energy, Shamans are capable of healing people of physical, as well as Spiritual ailments. Shamans have the Spiritual-mental energy to influence or control the behaviour of animals. Of all the people in an ethnic community, the Shamans have the most powerful Spiritual and mental energy and the best knowledge on the medicinal plants. The majority of the Shamans are generous and honest, but unfortunately, there are some Shamans who are evil and can be dangerous.

For at least one thousand years, the Amazon natives lived happily, practicing and perfecting their Spiritual pathway: their true ethnic religion. Throughout this time they never had any contact with white foreigners, but unfortunately for the natives and for the Amazon tropical rainforest, soon that peaceful paradise would change.

After most of South America had won its independence from Spain and Portugal, we begin to see a growing, foreign economical interest from first-world nations in this rich continent. At the beginning this interest was primarily for logging the virgin forests and gold prospecting, but years later it was also for Oil exploitation, mining, and purchasing land to plant valuable export crops.

On a much smaller scale, we also begin to see a genuine scientific interest. Precisely, it is through this scientific interest that we have European and later North American biologists and botanists arriving to South America. Understandably enough, the areas that most attracted them was the Amazon tropical rainforest and the Pacific tropical rainforest of Ecuador and Colombia.

Since many years ago, tropical rainforest native Shamans and healers were generously showing their valuable medicinal plants to foreign scientists for scientific investigations. This is how in 1851 the British schoolteacher Richard Spruce became the first known person to write about Ayahuasca. Unfortunately, Mr. Spruce's personal experience with the sacred brew was disheartening; after drinking the strange potion he got violently sick. Later in 1858, an Ecuadorian geographer called Manuel Villavicencio wrote a more complete description about the native ceremony of drinking Ayahuasca. In summary, Manuel Villavicencio described his personal experiences as amazing as being able to "fly" to far away marvelous places. His writings were published, and at that time won him recognition. Later in 1923, a German chemist called Hans Fischer studied the chemicals in the Ayahuasca vine and was able to isolate an important alkaloid that he named "Telepathine", obviously, because he was convinced of the plant's telepathic property.

Laboratory investigations on Ayahuasca continued by different Botanists and Chemists, isolating diverse alkaloids until eventually it was officially agreed that all these different named alkaloids from Ayahuasca were in reality two highly complex alkaloids called Harmalina and Harmina. Years before, in 1841 the alkaloid Harmalina had been previously located in the Syrian Rue plant. Some scientific investigations believe that the natural chemical of Harmalina has a special and direct effect on our Pineal gland. The Pineal gland is about the size of a pea and is situated at the base of our brain; modern medicine does not know what the function of the Pineal gland is, but within the wise Yoga religious philosophy, it is believed that when the energy in the Pineal gland is activated, then the "Third eye" will be awakened!

In 1927, the French Pharmacologists Perrot and Hamet officially categorized the Ayahuasca vine into the Banisteriopsis genus and into the Caapi species.

Today, scientifically speaking, only a few other Ayahuasca species have been officially classified, even though most of the native Amazonian Shamans assure that in reality at least seven different species of Ayahuasca exist, each one producing a completely distinct Spiritual-visionary experience. What this may probably tell us is that the Amazonian Shamans have an awareness of metaphysical differences in the different species of Ayahuasca vines, which modern day scientists in a laboratory cannot determine.

It is important to note that even though Scientists may some-day be able to chemically synthesize the chemistry of Ayahuasca, the final effects will never be the same as the original Ayahuasca which grows in the Amazon; in addition, most certainly a synthesized, human-made version of Ayahuasca would probably be dangerous and harmful for humans! Ayahuasca is a sacred plant, it is a special gift from God and humans can not duplicate the metaphysical nature of Ayahuasca or any other sacred plant. The metaphysical nature of Ayahuasca is based on a perfectly balanced chemistry which is related to four main elements; first the natural, divine Prana energy of God that is in the Amazon and in the plant, secondly the powerful Spirit of Ayahuasca that is in the plant, thirdly that God picked this plant to grow in the Amazon, and last, all of the religious ritual in handling this sacred plant. All of these conditions will assure the effects which will benefi-cially affect ones Spiritual, mental, emotional and physical bodies.

Scientists have labelled this plant as a "hallucinogenic drug". After drinking Ayahuasca, one will see many things that from a scientific point of view are perceived as not real, because obviously the visions that one sees are not of the material world, so yes from the perspective of the scientific material world Ayahuasca would be a hallucinogen. However from a metaphysical point of view or from the perspective of the Amazonian ethnic religion, Ayahuasca is not a hallucino-gen, the visions that one sees are real for our Spiritual-mental bodies and within the Spiritual World.

A drug is anything that alters one's "normal" state of being. Therefore Ayahuasca is a drug; it will change your "normal" material world state of being, because its main role is to awaken your Spiritual body and safely transport it from this material world to the Spiritual World! But do not be frightened by the word "drug", there are all kinds of drugs, depending on their dosage and how they are used, they can be dangerous, harmless, addicting and non-addicting. Remember, coffee, cigarettes and liquor are also drugs. As long as Ayahuasca is handled and used correctly in the Amazon it will never be dangerous. Ayahuasca can never be considered a dangerous, harmful drug like liquor, cigarettes, Cocaine, Heroin, Marijuana or other hazardous drugs. Also, it is important to note that Ayahuasca is not addicting like most drugs are.

In reality, Ayahuasca is much more than a "hallucinogenic drug". The Amazonian ethnic native tribes and I believe that God intentionally placed this plant in the forest so that humans could benefit from its divine powers.

Since at least one thousand years ago, for the upper Amazonian tribes and the Pacific tropical rainforest tribes of Ecuador and Colombia, Ayahuasca has been the master key to their ethnic religion. The powerful female Spirit of Ayahuasca opens the sacred doorway of the Spiritual World and taking the people by their hands she leads them spiritually and mentally into the beautiful, glorious and enlightened Spiritual World.

Guyana

Surinam

Venezuela

Guyane
(France)

Colombia

Atlantic
Ocean

Ecuador

Peru

Brazil

Pacific
Ocean

Bolivia

Paraguay

Argentina

Chile

Uruguay

Basin of Amazon River is alm
the same size as mainland U.S

Map of South America, giving special emphasis to the countries of Colombia, Ecuador, Peru, Bolivia.

(The ecosystem in this area is quite different to the rest of the eastern Amazonian tropical rainforest.)

The main tributaries with the Amazon River.

PACIFIC TROPICAL RAINFOREST

San Lorenzo

Esmeraldas

Galápagos Islands,
1000 km.

Equator Lat. 0

1 ∧

Ib

Otavalo ∧

5 ∧ ●
Quito

3

∧
6

∧ 8

Manta

**ECUADOR**

*Pacific
Ocean*

Baños

9 ∧

∧

Puyo

Riobamba

10

∧ 11

Guayaquil ●

∧ 12

13 ∧

Cuenca
(Tomebamba)

120 km / 75 miles

Machala

Loja

COLOMBIA

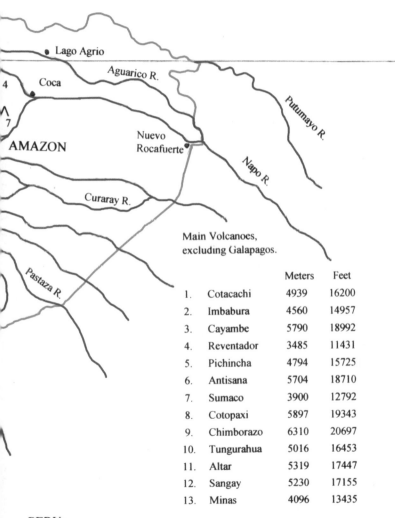

Lago Agrio

Aguarico R.

Coca

4

7

Nuevo
Rocafuerte

AMAZON

Putumayo R.

Napo R.

Curaray R.

Pastaza R.

Main Volcanoes,
excluding Galapagos.

| | | Meters | Feet |
|---|---|---|---|
| 1. | Cotacachi | 4939 | 16200 |
| 2. | Imbabura | 4560 | 14957 |
| 3. | Cayambe | 5790 | 18992 |
| 4. | Reventador | 3485 | 11431 |
| 5. | Pichincha | 4794 | 15725 |
| 6. | Antisana | 5704 | 18710 |
| 7. | Sumaco | 3900 | 12792 |
| 8. | Cotopaxi | 5897 | 19343 |
| 9. | Chimborazo | 6310 | 20697 |
| 10. | Tungurahua | 5016 | 16453 |
| 11. | Altar | 5319 | 17447 |
| 12. | Sangay | 5230 | 17155 |
| 13. | Minas | 4096 | 13435 |

PERU

# CHAPTER 1

# • The Discovery of Ayahuasca

I have heard different stories from Amazonian Shaman friends that I have about how Ayahuasca was discovered. All of the different stories are part of ancient verbal stories that were passed down from generation to generation. Sometimes these stories had varied from Shaman to Shaman or from tribe to tribe, and this is understandable because the Amazon from Colombia to Peru is vast and in many ways the tribes living throughout this area are quite different.

Of all these different legends, the one story that I have heard more often is the following; One day, many years ago, during "Ancient times", this is before the "Times of the Grandparents" (before the time of the arrival of white people); there was an elderly Shaman who went alone deep into the forest. This Shaman was searching for a new medicinal plant that he hoped would be able to cure one of his daughters who was dying of a strange sickness.

While he was in the thick forest examining and collecting different plants, suddenly from within the depths of the jungle he heard the distant angry roaring of a jaguar. Quickly the man looked for a safe place where he could hide. Fortunately, near-by him he found a tall tree that he could easily climb to, in order to seek refuge. With some difficulty because of the sack filled with medicinal plants on his back and because he was holding his long spear, his aged body desperately made it to the highest part of the tree. There out of harm's way, he looked around and he spotted a large branch as thick as his body. He moved cautiously towards the branch until finally he reached it and comfortably lay over it.

Down on the ground he heard the jaguar coming nearer. Hiding behind a group of leaves and branches and careful not to make any noise, he looked down at the forest floor trying to locate the animal. He knew that he was high enough so that the jaguar could not scent his human body smell, but it was imperative for him to keep quiet. The Shaman could not spot the jaguar and realizing that he could be up on that branch for a long time, he decided to wait patiently. He heard the animal moaning and sometimes roaring in anger. By the sound of the jaguar the Shaman was certain that the animal was an adult black male jaguar, the most powerful and dangerous animal in the forest. Besides this, it seemed that the creature was wounded which could make him even more dangerous.

Gradually these frightful sounds became louder, which confirmed to the Shaman that the animal was getting closer. All at once the Shaman felt the intimidating proximity of the jaguar down on the ground. All of the other animals that were within that area of the forest must have also felt the presence of the jaguar, because they suddenly froze into absolute silence.

The Shaman could hear the jaguar's footsteps pressing on leaves and branches and almost at the same time, he distinguished the heavy breathing of the beast. Instinctively he held his spear tighter, and then quietly he looked down, and finally was able to spot the animal. As he had imagined, it was a male black jaguar which was badly
injured; it had part of a broken spear sticking out of one side of its body. The Shaman felt relieved, his tense body recovered its normal, peaceful state. He knew that it was impossible for the wounded animal to climb up the tree. Obviously, it seemed that the animal had been speared by a hunter and had managed to escape; fortunately for the animal its vital organs had not been wounded. The animal had already lost a lot of blood and with that bamboo tip spear in him, he was sure to lose more blood and die. The jaguar approached the base of the large tree where the Shaman was, and then it began sniffing around the buttress root structure, as if it were looking for something special.

The Shaman lay perfectly still with his eyes fixed on the animal, he wondered if the jaguar had scented his presence. Still sniffing among the 2 m. / 6ft. high thick vegetation and at the same time, tearing away branches and leaves with his mighty claws, all at once, underneath all of the torn plants it appeared that the animal had found what it was looking for.

There against the tree the Shaman saw a long, twisting liana (vine), as thick as a fist that was growing from the ground and climbing up. The man's eyes followed the length of the liana and he saw how the plant branched out into an extensive web of many long, thin vines with medium size leaves. All of these vines continued climbing up the branches of the tree until they finally reached the top of the tree. The old Shaman was bewildered; during his lifetime, he had never noticed that strange vine before.

Suddenly the animal grabbed the liana with its strong jaws and grunting in pain he pulled forcefully. The jaguar managed to pull hard again a few more times and with each pull, the Shaman noticed how from the crown of the tree the main vine with the entire web of smaller vines moved. By pulling the plant, the animal was forcing a few meters of the thick vine to lower to the ground. The Shaman could not understand why this animal would invest some of its last physical energy in finding and pulling down a vine.

After this, the jaguar lay down on the ground next to the vine. He was obviously tired, he was panting hard for a few minutes and then he tried to reach the broken spear with his open jaws, but could not, angrily he moaned in great pain. He put his head down to the ground and breathing hard; he closed his eyes and rested. Not finding any other logical reason for the animal's abnormal behavior, the Shaman concluded that probably the jaguar had been speared in mid-air and as it was falling to the ground, it had hit its head against a tree. Surely the blow had injured the animal's brain and had affected its thinking ability.

The man wondered how long he would have to stay in the tree, he looked up at the sky and saw that the sun had well passed mid-day and was already down near the horizon. For a second he thought of throwing his spear at the animal and killing it so that he could quickly take the collected medicinal plants to his daughter, but his people had always felt a natural fear and respect for jaguars. Killing a wounded jaguar in that manner could bring a dangerous curse to him or to his family; it was wiser to let Mother Nature take her natural course. Since it was already late, he would have to wait anyway until the following morning with daylight to be able to continue with his mission. The man knew that by then, the animal would already be dead. After a while the sun began to set and the forest darkened, suddenly diurnal animal and bird calls were less noticeable, while at the same time nocturnal animals began to appear, forcefully claiming the night with their strange, distinct, loud calls.

All at once the Shaman saw the wounded jaguar open its eyes, as if the nocturnal animal sounds had awakened it. With great difficulty the suffering animal stood and looking up to the moon lit sky he made a strenuous roar, the jaguar then staggered to the vine and using its heavy paws, it began to rub off the lichen, moss and algae from the outer bark of the vine, as if it were cleaning it. After this the animal got closer to the plant, he sniffed the part that had been cleaned began eating the strange vine. The Shaman could not believe his eyes, he had never seen or heard of a jaguar eating a plant, jaguars were supposed to be carnivorous. The animal ate about an arm's length of the vine, and then it lay down again and closed its eyes.

The Shaman continued looking at the animal and after a while, he saw a mild iridescent light beginning to emit from the animal's body. The Shaman could not believe what he was seeing, suddenly he felt a peculiar cool breeze coming from the sky and arriving into the higher part of the forest, near to where he was. Carefully he looked around trying to locate the breeze and there on a branch of a nearby tree, he noticed a suspicious movement. Focusing his eyes he looked at the branch and all of a sudden he spotted a powerful, young male-adult, black jaguar staring directly at him. The man had seen many jaguars in his lifetime, but this one was strangely different, it seemed to have come from another world.

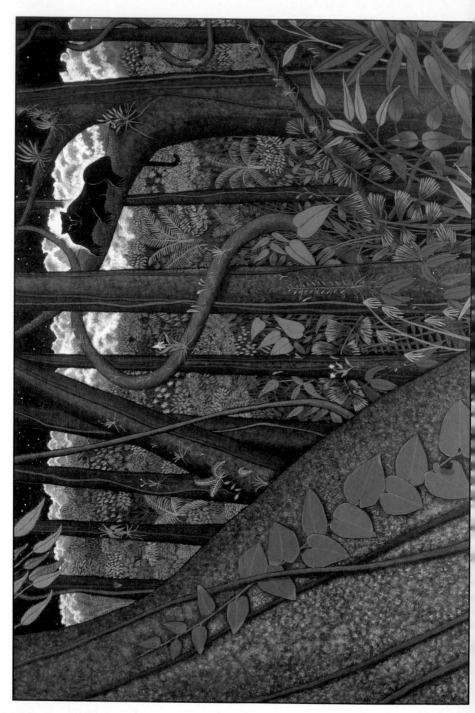

Unexpectedly, this strange animal stood up and leaped down to the ground where it approached the laying body of the wounded jaguar. By this time, the iridescent, radiating light from the injured jaguar's body was much brighter. The wounded animal opened its eyes and looked up at the young jaguar as if it were an old acquaintance. Then the young jaguar grabbed the broken spear in its mouth, and with one swift movement it pulled out the spear and thrust it away. It licked the bleeding hole a few times and almost immediately, the open wound closed. Afterwards, the injured jaguar began to miraculously recover, until finally it lifted its head and stood up. Its wound had completely healed. Its body had fully recuperated its normal strength; it growled and licked the young jaguars face many times. Then the two animals began to play, wrestling and chasing one another among the trees as if they were young cubs. This went on for a short time until gradually they disappeared into the forest.

The old Shaman was perplexed; he could not understand all that he had witnessed. Thinking about the jaguars and the strange plant, he stayed awake for a long time, until gradually he fell asleep. The next morning the man awoke early, he climbed down the tree to the ground and inspecting the area, he found the strange vine. He picked it up and examined it carefully.

He took his sharp hardwood machete and scraped off from a section of the vine all of the lichen, algae and moss, then he smelled the vine trying to identify its chemicals, he chewed a little of the liana and still could not identify the new chemicals. He spat out the bits of vine and then grabbed the vine with his two hands and pulled hard until

more of the plant came down. He cut off a long section of the liana and carefully rolled and tied this special vine into a coiled package, he put it in his sack and quickly carried this new powerful medicine back to his community.

After a few nights of using this liana in different ways, the

Shaman was successful in communicating with Spirits from the Spiritual World, receiving potent Spiritual-healing energy and curing his daughter. The people and other Shamans of the community were amazed to see the extraordinary Spiritual and mental effects produced by this special plant. Together with the elderly Shaman, they helped to select a special site in the forest for planting the stakes of the rest of the vine. They took particular care of these small plants and they spent the rest of their lives experimenting different ways for learning how to perfect the use of this new, powerful, sacred plant.

This legend is one of various ancient stories that fortunately still exist today, and give us an idea of how the ethnic native people believe that Ayahuasca could have been discovered. During my personal experiences drinking Ayahuasca, I have witnessed many strange, scientifically unexplainable events, so I as well as all of the Amazonian ethnic natives (natives still practicing their true ethnic religion) would have no doubt in believing that this legend in reality did happen and consequently is a true story. Similarly, I have heard various other stories told by different Shamans about how they think the discovery of Ayahuasca occurred. I think that all the different legends on the discovery of Ayahuasca are true and maybe they just occurred at different places to different natives.

Whether this legend or another legend is actually true is not important, but what I and all of the ethnic natives of South America do consider important is for modern civilization, especially from first-world nations to acknowledge and give due merit to the ancestors of the Amazonian natives for discovering the sacred vine of Ayahuasca and learning the complicated procedures of handling the vine and cooking the brew. In addition, also important is that the present ethnic Amazonian natives who have kept alive and passed down this valuable information from many generations back, should also be acknowledged and given due merit.

# CHAPTER 2

# • Don Piwali

I was born in Ecuador, South America, when I was six years old my Parents decided to venture with my sister, two brothers and myself to the United States. Our family lived for a few years first in Chicago and later in Los Angeles. I remember that as a child I was always very interested in Ecuador and Latin America. Fortunately, my Father and Mother would always find time to talk with us and tell us different stories about our homeland.

I was grateful for living in the United States and enjoyed very much my new life there, even though at times inside of me it seemed that I was missing something important, something that I was subconsciously searching for but could not find in the vast, beautiful country or modern society of the United States.

Eventually in 1970, my Father and Mother felt homesick and after much deliberation, they decided that it was time to move back to Ecuador. I was looking foreword to this change in my life. However, little did I know that it would be so difficult, mainly because I did not speak enough Spanish, but also because I was a stranger to the Ecuadorian culture.

We lived in the capital city of Quito. After the first few months of settling down and reconnecting with family, I decided to see as much of Ecuador as possible. Therefore I boarded the local buses and trains and traveled on my own throughout the country. Despite Ecuador's small size, it contains more ecological diversity than any other nation in America; North, Central or South. This diversity is based on its geography, ecosystems, flora and fauna; in fact Ecuador is considered one of the ten most biologically diverse countries in the world. The main reason for this country's high diversity is because of different altitudes on the equatorial line.

The small country of Ecuador is made up of four main regions. From west to east, first we have the famous Galapagos Islands, secondly we have the Pacific coast with beautiful beaches and mangroves. In the northern Pacific lowlands we find tropical rainforest and cultivated plantations of coffee, chocolate, rice, bananas pineapples, and many other tropical fruits. On the southern Pacific lowland area we have some tropical rainforest and a semi-desert area. Thirdly, we have the majestic Andes with many sub-tropical valleys, two main Cloud forests, and more than 15 volcanoes averaging 5,195 m. / 17,000 ft., throughout the entire year these volcanoes are covered in ice and snow. The highest peak of Ecuador is the Chimborazo volcano at 6,310 m. / 20,700 ft.

The fourth main region is the vibrant and mysterious Amazon tropical rainforest. Excluding the Galapagos Islands, we find about 25 different native tribes living throughout the country.

All of Ecuador was fascinating to me, but what I became most interested in was the different native tribes, so I decided to take a course in Anthropology and later I studied art at the Government University of Quito.

My enthusiasm for Nature and the native tribes soon provided an invitation to work in tourism. At that time the government did not provide training for tour guides, so it was up to me to investigate and learn all that I possibly could about my country. Unfortunately, my research was not easy because at that time books and information on Ecuador were scarce. Consequently I relied on two main sources; the few historical and scientific books that were available and direct information from the indigenous people of different tribes. Through my relationship with the natives, I developed great admiration for these people and their ancestors. On occasions, I found their information was contradictory but even so, I felt that I have gained much from their wisdom.

As a young child, I had often dreamt of traveling deep into

the Amazon jungle, meeting ethnic native tribes and seeing dangerous animals. One day in 1973, that opportunity arrived. The travel agency assigned me to lead an Amazon excursion to a jungle lodge on the Napo River. I was thrilled and wanted to go, but I did not feel qualified enough to lead a tour to the jungle, I reminded them that I had never before been that far deep into the Amazon. They on the other hand pleaded for me to go, it was just a four-day tour and most importantly the guide who they had previously assigned this tour to was sick, and they simply had no one else to send. They assured me that the lodge had Amazonian native scouts who always assisted the Quito guides. In spite of my overwhelming insecurity about leading this tour, I felt terrible to let the agency down and then also there was that adventurous spirit in me with what seemed the opportunity of a lifetime to fulfill my child-hood dream, so finally I accepted to lead the tour.

Early the following morning I left Quito with eight Canadian tourists in a mini bus. We traveled eastward towards a spectac-ular, warm rising sun, and within an hour we went from a modern asphalt highway to a narrow dirt road, and we began a dramatic climb in altitude. We were actually crossing the east-ern range of the Andes.

Soon we reached the 3,700 m. / 12,200 ft. Paramo (Andean-highland region. At this high altitude, the climate is very strange, most of the time there is a vigorous, cold wind which contrasts with the intense rays of the equatorial sun, and at night there is always frost. These harsh conditions make it an inhospitable place for humans to live, but the vegetation and the animals of course have adopted well. Here there are many bright colored flowers of unique species of plants and trees not found anywhere else in the world.

The good weather allowed us a spectacular view of one of the year round snow covered volcanoes; the 5,700 m. / 18,700 ft. Antisana. We took advantage of the gorgeous scenery to photograph the impressive volcano and to admire the vegetation. As we were walking, I looked up at the volcano and suddenly within a group of clouds near the summit; I spotted a group of very large birds gliding. Not knowing what they were, I went to the driver and pointing to the sky I asked him. Excitedly he said, "Condors!" Quickly I ran to the tour group to show them the birds and happily they photographed five Andean Condors majestically flying overhead. The Andean Condors with a wingspan of about 3 m. / 10 ft. are the world's largest flying birds.

We boarded our mini-bus and continued, the driver turned to me and said "Patricio you have good luck, it's not easy to see Condors, there just aren't too many left anymore."

After we crossed the cold Paramo region, we began to descend in altitude and feeling warmer temperature, we realized that within a few minutes we had actually changed ecosystems. We had entered into the lush semi-tropical Cloud forest. Here practically everyday of the year in the mornings it is clear and sunny, but in the late afternoons and during the night it is always foggy and it drizzles.

Quite often, we stopped in our tracks by the breathtaking scenery to photograph the dozens of waterfalls, streams and rivers traveling down from the year round melting glaciers of the Antisana volcano. These waterways were progressively joining together, holding hands, unknowingly destined to becoming the tributaries to the largest river of our planet, the Amazon River. (The Amazon River is the largest river of our planet, if you put together the next 4 largest rivers in the world; the Amazon is still larger. At the mouth, the river is about 130 km. / 60 miles wide and during the last 1,000 km. / 750 miles it is as deep as a 20 story building. The Nile river is the longest river in the world at 8,000 km. / 4,100 miles long and the Amazon is the second longest at 7,900 / 4,000 miles long, but in volume of water there is no comparison.).

As we continued descending in altitude, the temperature was

rising and within a few hours, the Andes stayed behind us. The landscape was almost flat and the hot temperature and distinctive vegetation of Palm trees and other tropical plants reminded us that we were in the jungle. We were at an altitude of about 1,300 m. / 4,264 ft. Geographically speaking we were already in the Amazon, but as we continued driving further into this ecosystem, I began to feel disillusioned, and the reason is that I was seeing many farms with cultivated fields of chocolate and coffee, huge pastures with cattle, many new adjacent roads and even small towns.

This huge area of the original, prehistoric virgin tropical rainforest had been cleared only since about 1964. The majority of the people living throughout this area were Mestizo settlers and some African-Ecuadorian settlers mainly from the Pacific Coastal tropical rainforest region. The majority of the Ecuadorians, including myself are Mestizos; this means that we have a mixture of Native blood with Spaniard blood. These Amazonian Colonos (settlers, colonizers) arrived years ago and new settlers are still arriving today. But, why did they abandon their agriculturally rich homeland and migrate to the Amazon? There are different reasons, but in the following explanation I shall present the main reasons.

In 1959, we had the revolution in Cuba, and at that time in Ecuador we still had tremendous social, political and economical injustice, about 70% of the population was native and about 5% was African Ecuadorian, these two ethnic groups were still being treated almost as slaves on Haciendas (huge farms and ranches) belonging to wealthy landlords who were part of the governing class families. During those circumstances, if any well organized leftist group would have infiltrated into these two ethnic groups and would have supplied them with sufficient firearms, and showed them the mechanisms for a successful revolution like in Cuba; they together with the leftist groups would have overthrown the military in Ecuador. Precisely, in order to prevent a communist take over, is why in 1963, the Ecuadorian military government puts into effect the Land Agrarian Reform. Once that the poor farmers of the country acquired their own land they would have no need to join an armed leftist revolutionary force.

The Ecuadorian government expropriated land in the Andes and in the Coastal region, but since more land was needed, the government organized the colonization of the Amazon.

The settlers travel in public buses to the Amazon looking for a place to claim their own land and try to raise their poor standard of living. Upon arriving they waste no time in clearing the land, preferably adjacent or near to the new roads that are constantly under construction by the governments. Once the roads connect to major rivers, they begin to claim land, adjacent to these rivers. They invest time, money, hard work and eventually obtain their title deeds from the government or even from another settler who resells his property. As a witness to this massive predatory migration, I had deep concerning thoughts about the certain devastating future that awaits the rest of the virgin South American Amazonian rainforest.

Well finally, around mid-day we arrived to our destination; the Napo River. Of the more than 1,100 tributaries to the Amazon River, the Napo River is one of the biggest. Our mini-bus stopped at the small mestizo settler's town of Misahualli which is right at the junction of the medium-size Misahualli River and the very large Napo River.

The 7-hour journey had been long, dusty and bumpy, but it was well worth it. I escorted the group to a nearby restaurant where they could have lunch; meanwhile I asked around and soon made contact with the pilot of our canoe, then I returned to the restaurant to eat. Afterwards, our bus driver took us to the bank of the river, we unloaded our luggage and immediately two other native employees from the lodge appeared, they placed our luggage into a 15 m. / 47 ft. long, motor powered wooden dug out canoe. They then instructed us to sit in the canoe on wooden benches and to put on our life preservers. At the river our altitude was about 700 m. / 2,295 ft., it was very hot and already there were many small, strange, pestering insects around us. The pilot finally turned on the motor and as we rapidly

parted from the bank we were all relieved, feeling the refreshing breeze against our faces and bodies.

Traveling down river with the fast current was so exciting. The color of the river was dark gray-brown, which is normal. Most of the big Amazonian tributaries are born from the year round melting glaciers of the Andes. The Andean streams and rivers which eventually form Amazonian rivers carry a lot of sediments from the steep Andes. Periodically these Amazonian rivers will flood into the forest, providing rich sediments (vital nutrients) for the poor top soil in the Amazon as well as for the native cultivated fields that are bordering the rivers. As we see, once again Mother Nature is always wise and in perfect balance. However since many years ago, due to government and private companies building roads and deforesting the Andes and the Cloud forests, now there is more erosion, consequently more sediments than normal.

The pilot seemed to know each part of the river by memory; effortlessly he avoided three big whirlpools and many giant fallen trees. The river was about 100 m. / 330 ft. wide. Along both banks the vegetation was impenetrably thick and every once in a while there would appear a small clearing and a few beautiful native, thatch roof huts.

Most of the time the canoe was traveling down the middle of the river, but every time that it would get close to one of the two banks my expectations would grow, I would sit up on the edge of my bench and attentively search into the dense jungle. I was anxiously hoping to spot jaguars, anacondas, caimans, tapirs, wild boars, monkeys or any other large, exciting animals. However, all that I was able to spot were birds and apart from a few groups of vultures, egrets and small parrots the rest of the birds in the opinion of my inexpert eyes were not very spectacular. Anyway, the reality of actually navigating a river in the Amazon, was exciting enough for me and I was very happy.

After one hour, we arrived to our lodge, where ironically enough I was to "conduct" a tour being a foreigner to the jungle myself. It was not an easy tour, but fortunately, the tour group was not scientific. I did the best that I could and considering the situation, I think that it was adequate, with of course a great deal of help from our Amazonian native scout. His name was Remigio Canelos; he was a tall, thin, humble, nice and knowledgeable young man.

At the end of our tour, I returned to Quito with a sense of having done my duty for the travel agency. However, apart from my work as a tour guide, during the third day a very important incident happened to me, and precisely because of this "incident", something distinctive and special had been mentally and spiritually implanted inside of me, which would change my life forever.

On the third day of our tour, after breakfast, we boarded our large dug out canoe and crossed the Napo River to visit a Shaman (Spiritual leader of an ethnic religion). Personally, my expectations were too high and only now do I realize that. For me and for the tour group our experiences with the local native people during the last couple of days had been very disappointing. Since years ago, the native tribes in that area had changed their ethnic lifestyle, they all wore modern style clothing and they had lost practically all of their culture. At that time, I never understood why so many changes had occurred and it appeared to me that no one else really understood.

After crossing the river, we got out of our canoe and began to walk on a narrow footpath. We walked single file, first Remigio, then myself, and behind me the tour group, after about 30 minutes, Remigio turned to me and said "Patricio, all this land for as far as you can see is property of the Shaman." I looked around and to me it seemed that it was quite a large property. We were passing along cultivated fields of cash crops like coffee, cacao (chocolate), and maize (U.S. corn). Also we passed along crops which were important for the daily diet of the native families like; yuca (cassava, manioc, tapioca), bananas, plantains (bananas exclusively used for cooking), oranges, peanuts, limes, pineapples, papayas, Chonta palm nuts and other strange fruits which I had never seen before.

We continued walking under the hot sun until soon we began to hear and see a few groups of chickens with their chicks searching for seeds and insects on the ground.

Further ahead of us, we saw a few pigs lying in mud holes under the protective shadow of large trees. Finally, we came to a small clearing and in the middle was the Shaman's home, I looked at the house and my first impression was of disillusionment. Without knowing any better, I assumed that a "Shaman's" hut would somehow be special and more ethnic looking, but it was not.

Since there was no one in sight, Remigio walked up to the hut and in his native language, raising his voice, he said a few words of greeting. From inside, a woman called back, there was an exchange of words and then we heard laughter from the woman and at least five other people. Remigio came to us and reluctantly told me that we should wait for a while until the Shaman comes out. Unfortunately, as we had to wait, this gave us more time to look around.

The hut was built on six hardwood posts with a bark-wooden floor that was about 2 m. / 7 ft. above the ground. This traditional style of architecture provides many advantages like; a dry storage space for firewood and other materials. A cool protective shady area for some of the farm animals, better air circulation to help keep the hut cooler, better security for the family from snakes and other dangerous animals, better protection for the family from tropical rainstorms and flooding, and a better view from the house to the surrounding area. Only about half of the hut was built with the traditional materials of Toquilla leaves for the thatch roof and long pieces of split-Bamboo for walls. (The Ecuadorian Toquilla palm-like leaves are also used for making the Ecuadorian Panama hats, these famous hats have never been made in Panama.) The rest of the hut was built in the mestizo settler's style with a tin roof and wooden boards. Outside of the hut, within the clearing there were a few wire clotheslines and hanging on them were modern style clothing, which were old, stained and mended.

Scattered on the ground there were some broken pieces of plastic toys and old, blond haired plastic dolls missing arms or legs, these toys obviously belonged to the Shaman's children or his grandchildren. Also there were a few, old leaking batteries of flashlights, worthless old broken aluminum pots, a few empty plastic oil gallons of the outboard motors and to top it all there was a half- starved medium size dog staring right at us. Looking around more carefully I noticed that there were two more dogs lying under the hut. These three poor dogs were without a doubt the skinniest animals that I had ever seen in my life. The two dogs under the hut were in pitiful condition, they were in the shade, protecting themselves from the blazing sun. They had large open scars on their bodies and hundreds of tiny flies feeding on their wounds. The dog that was staring at us had a few large tumors hanging on its scrawny body.

Whispering, without the group noticing, I asked Remigio about the dogs, he whispered back, "They are hunting dogs." I could not believe it; these dogs seemed too weak to hold up their own bodyweight, how could they possibly be hunting dogs? I tried to understand, but unfortunately, at that time Remigio could not explain this to me. I was confused and since I could not think of any logical explanation, I tried to avoid talking to the tour group about the dogs. But of course the subject was unavoidable, they asked and I simply told them that they were hunting dogs; they could not believe it either.

Only years later did I come to understand the reasoning for which the native "hunting dogs" are skinny. The original Amazonian native dog evolved from a special species of a European attack-dog that the Spaniard conquistadors took into the Amazon during the first Spanish expedition into the South American Amazon in 1541, this expedition started in Quito. Most of these original dogs were killed, but some of them were captured by native people and domesticated. Today, the descendants of these dogs are short hair, medium size with a short thin body, very long thin legs, and a long thin tail. They have a thin face with a long pointed snout and long pointed ears. The native hunters prefer for these dogs to be of dark colors, preferably shades of browns or blacks. The senses of sight, hearing and smell of these dogs are incredibly keen, this is so that they can survive in the jungle and easily locate game (wild animals that are hunted for food), as well as also the dogs can sense the presence of dangerous animals which could hurt them. Their long legs allow them to run fast and jump efficiently over fallen trees and because they are skinny, their light body weight allows them to dash quickly on the jungle floor less noticeable to the forest animals.

Until 1963, the population of animals in the Amazon forest was abundant, but because of deforestation, great areas of the virgin forests were destroyed, affecting the normal animal population. This terrible, mass deforestation has caused disastrous ecological, social and health problems for thousands of native families. The native men of these families have especially suffered by not being able to fulfill with one of their traditional duties, which is hunting and providing enough meat (protein) for their families. For the native hunters of each new generation, it just becomes more and more difficult to find game.

In some areas, the deforestation has been worse and especially in those affected areas, the natives purposely keep their dogs more skinny. The usual daily diet of these dogs is bananas, yuca (cassava, manioc, tapioca) and scraps of left over food.

This is cruel, but if on the other hand the dogs were to be well fed, they would lack the motivation to go hunting. Since they are deliberately deprived of meat, when they are taken on a hunt, their craving is so great that they will not be intimidated by jaguars, ocelots, wild boars, snakes, giant armadillos and other dangerous animals that may be lurking in the jungle. Precisely because they are hungry is why they will go hunting, the desperation of these half-starved dogs to eat meat will force them to risk their lives by going into the forest. In addition, once inside the forest, they will overexert themselves to the maximum limit in order to locate any game. Acting together as a group and maintaining a safe distance they will surround the wild animal and bark loudly until the hunters arrive to kill the trapped beast. After this, the native hunters carry all of the dead animals back to the community where the wives will always separate the meat into two groups, one large group of meat will be smoked for the family and another small group of raw meat will be fed to the dogs. This is their reward and this is the only time of the week or month that they are allowed this treat.

Finally, the Shaman came out. He walked down the steps from his hut onto the ground, he was an elderly thin man with medium length gray hair, and I guessed that he was in his mid sixties, but in reality, years later I discovered that he had already been in his eighties. He wore an old, short-sleeve shirt and old, mended trousers, but besides that modern-style clothing, he wore on his head an old, worn-down crown of beautiful colored bird feathers. He was barefoot and as he came closer towards us, we all noticed his friendly smile that combined perfectly with an unusual spark in his eyes. He walked perfectly erect which portrayed a confident, energetic, healthy person. His wrinkled face and smile reflected an inner peace of spirit, emotions, mind and body so great, that I suddenly felt myself in the very presence of peace and wisdom.

Remigio introduced the Shaman to me and to the tour group. His name was Piwali, which in his tribe's language is the name of a special water bird. Instinctively because of the marvelous impression that he had made on me, I felt appropriate to greet him in a special way, so I called him "Don Piwali". From that moment on, I have always addressed him in that way. (In the Spanish language, referring to a person by adding the word Don to the name of a man or Doña to the name of a woman is a traditional way of showing deep respect). Don Piwali was the last true Shaman of the small, disappearing, Yumbo tribe. He did not speak a single word of Spanish, but he was tri-lingual, speaking three different Amazonian native languages.

He spoke to Remigio in his tribal language, then Remigio would translate to me in Spanish and finally I would translate to the tour group in English. The native language sounded musical, Don Piwali and Remigio spoke it slowly as if they had all the time in the world, but with so much enthusiasm and good humor that one knew that the ethnic Amazonian natives are a passionate and happy people. Gesturing with his hands and speaking to us, Don Piwali told us to follow him; we walked across the clearing for about 50 m. / 164 ft. to a large fruit tree.

At the base of this shady tree, there was an old, rustic table and on this table, we saw a display of strange-looking plants. According to Remigio, for Don Piwali these were some of his most important medicinal plants. I estimated that there were about 20 different specimens, made up of whole plants, roots, leaves, vines and barks. Don Piwali proceeded to pick up a sample of each specimen and proudly talk about its medicinal usage, dosage and preparation.

After explaining practically all of the plants, he hesitated and then told us that he would now show us the last, but most important plant. Suddenly I noticed that the expression on his face and body changed as he happily, but solemnly picked up from the table with his two aged hands a dried piece of a twisted vine that was about 40 cm. / 16 in. long and 6 cm. / 2 in. thick. He held it up to us and in a respectful manner, he said "Ayahuasca!" Don Piwali told us that the plant was sacred, it was God's most special plant given to humans as a gift and by drinking a brew made from it, the Spiritual body of the person would leave the physical body and travel to different worlds. By using this plant, the Spirit, mind and body of the person would become healthy and very strong.

Before I realized it, I found myself caught within the magic of the Shaman and the power of his words. Intrigued by the incredible properties of this plant, I personally asked many questions. My obvious interest was noticed and well received by Don Piwali; at the end of our visit we all thanked him. I waited till the end to bid farewell, I said good-bye, shook his hand and was about to let go when suddenly, he took my hand with his other free hand and said a few words to me. Not understanding, I looked at Remigio and he translated. "Do you want to drink the Ayahuasca brew?" I was surprised and was not sure what to say. I paused a few seconds to think and suddenly it seemed that the whole forest with its normal jungle animal sounds were silent as if they were all attentive to my answer. Then suddenly, realizing the unique opportunity that was presented to me, I quickly said, "Yes, yes of course I do!" All at once, we heard a loud sound coming from the top of the tree resembling powerful electric-shavers, it turned out to be a large group of male Cicada insects. The tour group and I were startled by this sound, Don Piwali and Remigio started laughing, and then we all joined in.

Don Piwali was happy, he gave some instructions that Remigio immediately passed onto me; I should not eat lunch, dinner or any other food, I may only drink a little water and shortly after sunset, Don Piwali will go to the hotel to look for me. For the remainder of the day I felt very excited and it seemed to me that it would take forever for the sun to go down.

That afternoon, we went to the small Guambuno River to bathe. I still felt very excited about drinking Ayahuasca. I asked Remigio if he had ever tasted the brew of Ayahuasca, he said "No, of course not!" Jokingly I said to him "Remigio, don't tell me that you are afraid to drink Ayahuasca?" He laughed nervously, then I also laughed and after a short while, he stopped laughing and told me that the young and middle age people of his tribe have never tasted the brew. Only a few elderly natives like Don Piwali still drink it. I could not believe it; I just could not understand how young, intelligent native men and women were not interested in trying a special brew like Ayahuasca. For about ten minutes I tried to convince Remigio and the native boatman to drink Ayahuasca with me, but it was useless, until finally the boatman admitted that he was afraid to drink Ayahuasca and besides that, it was against his and the tribes Protestant-Evangelical religion. Then the boatman looked straight into my eyes and said that I should not drink Ayahuasca because it is the potion of evil, the blood of the devil!

The hours passed and soon it was but a few minutes until sunset, I was ready, waiting outside my cabin within the main garden area of the lodge. I did not have my flashlight because the light bulb had burned out, so in my hand, I was holding a lit candle and as a precaution in my pocket, I had an extra candle and two sets of matches. After about 10 minutes of impatiently waiting, a beautiful orange-red sunset appeared throughout the sky, and almost immediately afterwards, it became dark.

Looking above and all around me I saw the sky covered with the most beautiful, brightly lit exhibit of stars that I had ever seen in my life. The sounds of nocturnal birds, frogs, crickets and other animals that I could not identify were fantastic. Then within the hotel garden area and nearby forest, hundreds of fireflies began to appear emitting a wonderful display of courtship lights. As I entertained my eyes admiring these exquisite, flashing lights of nature, I noticed a distinct, minute non-flashing light in the forest. Soon this light grew in size as it came onto the garden area and then towards me. Suddenly from deep inside my stomach, I began to feel an uneasy sensation growing, as I remembered the native boatman's last comment about the devil. I felt a little nervous, but as I continued observing this light, suddenly I noticed the glowing silhouette of a man; it was Don Piwali's thin figure holding a resin lamp. All of a sudden, the fear was gone.

Don Piwali walked up to me; he said a few words, smiled and bowed his head. I also bowed my head and greeted him, and then he signalled for me to follow him. Walking behind him, we crossed the clearing and passed through a small portion of forest that led to the riverbank. Tied onto a bush was a small dugout canoe about 3 m. / 9 ft. long. He said a few words to me in his native language as he pointed to a tiny wooden board which was on the floor at the bow (front) of the canoe. I imagined that he wanted me to sit there, so I got in and sat on the board. Then he unfastened a thin rope which was holding the canoe onto a small tree and afterwards he gracefully boarded the canoe at the stern (back), he put the resin lamp in front of him, blew the flame out and sat down on another small board. I blew out my candle. Don Piwali then took a small wooden paddle and began to cross the 150 m. / 490 ft. wide Napo River.

There was just enough light to see a little of the river, forest silhouette and riverbank, but besides that, I am sure that

Don Piwali was using his sense of hearing and of course his lifetime experience. The current of this big river was strong. The waves of the river were only about 7 cm. / 3 inches from the top edges of the small canoe. Don Piwali had a perfect balance and control of the canoe, I trusted him, I did not feel at all nervous and because of this, I was able to maintain good balance.

After crossing the river, he jumped out of the canoe and tied it to a small tree. Picking up his lamp he lit the wick with matches and then said something to me, so I got out of the canoe and quickly followed him as he walked into the forest. It seemed to me that in the jungle on this side of the river there were more animal sounds than the forest around the lodge. We were walking on a narrow path that I was sure was the same footpath that I had been on that morning with Remigio and the tour group.

Trying to keep up with the Shaman, I tagged along with difficulty as he was holding his small resin lamp and moving effortlessly through the jungle. Besides the minimum amount of light which shown on the ground in front of Don Piwali, there was a thin glow of light that lit the outer edge of his body and then everything else on the ground and around us was pitch black. Even though my vision was limited, I soon realized that we were in a completely new area. The path we were on was narrower than other paths that we had been on before, there were no cultivated crops and the forest here was thicker.

After walking for about 30 minutes, we arrived to a small clearing. In the middle of the clearing, I could make out a small strange thatch roof hut with bamboo walls. We walked up to the hut and then Don Piwali softly said something towards the inside of the hut, as if he were talking to someone. He unfastened a string holding the bamboo door closed, then he pulled the door open and we walked in. Once inside, I was surprised to see that there was no one there, I was confused wondering to whom he had talked to.

During the few days that I had been in that area, I had never seen a hut like this one. All of the other native huts were built with a palm wooden floor on stilts above the ground, but this hut was built directly on the ground with a dirt floor. The light emitting from Don Piwali's small lamp had a very mild, warm, yellow tone similar to the gentle light of a candle. It helped to create a unique, soothing atmosphere that was beautiful. There was just enough light to comfortably make out all of the different shapes and natural earth tone colors of every object that was inside this small hut. The interior of the hut was made of only one large area; this was a big oval shaped room with about nine wooden posts dug into the ground, which were supporting the beams of the roof. Distributed around the room, I saw about five low wooden stools.

Don Piwali walked to the darkest area of the room, carrying his lamp then; I noticed that there were two old string hammocks tied onto four main posts. Near the hammocks, there were four low benches, and on one of these benches was a large aluminum pot. The pot was covered with an old, worn down dented lid and the outside of the pot it was completely stained with black soot, showing that in the past it had been cooked many times in firewood. Don Piwali took his lamp and carefully hung it onto a large nail that was in one of the beams of the roof. Then he took a couple of steps towards the pot, he smiled, bent forward and lifted the lid from the pot. The light shown inside and I saw that about $\frac{1}{5}$ of the pot was filled with a strange caramel-olive colored liquid. In my life, I had never seen an unusual color like that!

He squatted down next to the pot, slowly he leaned his head closer over the pot and then he breathed in deeply, taking in the full aroma of the brew, he looked up at me and smiling, he said, "Ayahuasca!" I smiled back at him, and then I saw that distinctive spark in his eyes again, as the first time that I had met him. He then stood up and walked a few steps to a string bag that was hanging on one of the posts, he brought the bag to where I was and then he instructed me to sit on one of the benches. Don Piwali then brought a nearby stool and set it next to me; he sat down, put the string bag on his lap and took out a mirror and a small package wrapped in leaves which was about the size of the palm of his hand. After this, he took out a 20 cm. / 8 in. long thin round stick. He opened the leaf package and inside was a strange, hard, dark red color cone shaped object. He wet the dried object with a few drops of his saliva, then he rubbed one end of the thin stick onto it and as he did this, I noticed that a bright red color suddenly appeared on the end of the stick. Then he held the mirror up with one hand and looking into it, with the other hand he started painting unusual, beautiful bright red designs on his face.

These designs were made of fine lines that I imagined were depicting different native motifs. After he finished, he leaned closer to me and began to paint similar designs on my face. Then he reached up and from over one of the ceiling beams, he brought down his old feather crown that he solemnly put on. After this he took out of his string bag another package wrapped in leaves, he opened it and inside were a few hand rolled cigars that looked slightly flattened.

He lit one of these peculiar cigars with the flame from the lamp, and as he puffed, I noticed that the smoke blowing out of his mouth seemed much heavier and whiter than any other cigar or cigarette smoke that I had ever seen before.

Afterwards Don Piwali reached into his string bag and this time he took out a bundle of about 15 fresh palm-like leaves which were tied together at one end. This bundle of leaves was about 50 cm. / 20 in. long. According to the various tribes, these leaves have different names, in Don Piwali's language, which is the Amazonian Quechua, these leaves are called Suri-Panga which means "the leaves that make the sound". All of the upper-Amazonian natives use leaves as a wand for drinking Ayahuasca or for healing.

The last object that he took out of his bag was a bowl made

from a gourd (Amazonian calabash); he put the bowl inside one of the hammocks. Then he walked to the pot with the bunch of leaves in one hand and in the other hand, he held the lit cigar. Suddenly he began to shake the leaves into the air and all over the top of the pot, at the same time I heard him humming loudly. The shaking leaves produced a wind and a beautiful sound that was such a special ingredient to the mystical atmosphere that the Shaman was creating. Don Piwali said a few words to the pot as if the brew was alive and he could communicate with it. Almost immediately he began singing out loud, directing all of his attention to the brew and also up towards the ceiling of the hut, but in a strange way, as if, the ceiling did not exist and he was communicating with someone that was up in the sky.

Occasionally he would puff his cigar and forcefully blow a heavy stream of white smoke to the brew, to the ceiling and occasionally at me. After about 10 minutes of singing, he took the bowl out of the inside of the hammock and dipped it into the pot filling it practically to the rim. Then he lifted it up to his mouth, he said a few words to the brew, he blew air at it and then he slowly drank the brew. After finishing, he walked to the door, opened it and threw outside of the hut, a little bit of brew which had settled in the bottom of the gourd.

Returning to the room, he dipped the bowl again into the pot filling it partway, and then he came towards me. He said a few words and pointed for me to sit on the edge of one of the hammocks. After I sat where he wanted, holding the bowl he moved it to my mouth. Instinctively I took the bowl with my two hands, but then Don Piwali took the bowl away, he frowned and said something referring to my hands. I put my hands down; he approved and again put the bowl up to my mouth. As my lips touched the edge of the gourd, I could not help but notice a weird musk-like odor. I slowly drank 4 mouthfuls and with each gulp I couldn't stop thinking how strange and bitter the flavor of the brew was, but at the same time I convinced myself that the brew was not bad tasting and that I could drink all of it.

I wanted to drink more, but Don Piwali would not let me. He took the gourd away, and then he walked to the door, opened it and threw away the remainder of the liquid that set at the bottom of the gourd. He returned and placed the bowl on the low bench next to the pot. Then he came to me and began to shake the bundle of leaves over my head. He continued puffing his cigar and singing his enchanting song. Since he was singing in his native language, I had no idea what the words meant, they sounded very oriental-like and I really wished that I could have understood their meaning because they must have been very significant for the Shaman and his religion.

After he finished singing, he came to me and began to pass the bundle of leaves with a gentle but firm stroke over my entire body. I had my eyes closed and as he passed the leaves over my forehead, I saw a bright magenta colored light flash in front of me, completely filling my field of vision. This light appeared to me like the peak of a horizontal bright red sunset. Then I heard him get up and go to the door where he said a few words, he opened the door and blowing air, he vigorously shook the leaves outside away from the hut, then he came back to me.

He said a few words, I opened my eyes and he signaled for me to lay back into the hammock. I laid back and while my hammock remained swaying, I admired the marvelous weaving of the thatch roof, and then I closed my eyes and still saw the marvelous magenta color light. I soon felt very strange; my body was being absorbed by the magenta color light and by the mystical, nocturnal Amazonian atmosphere. I was living such a unique moment of peace hearing the beautiful jungle sounds which combined perfectly with Don Piwali's magical singing and the rustling sound of his shaking bundle of leaves.

It seemed that the animal sounds were comfortably louder and I felt as if I was pleasantly falling into a heavy trance. The swaying hammock movement seemed to last for a very strange, long time. I can not say how or when, but the magenta color light, Don Piwali's chanting and the animal sounds gradually faded away and before I knew it, the room was pitch black. Within the darkness of the room and the trance-like state that I was in, I cannot remember whether my eyes were open or closed. However, almost immediately, I began to see a vision which was so vivid and so real, that I can still remember every detail of it, as if I had just seen it a few minutes ago.

I saw myself walking within a lush Amazonian forest. It was daylight and I was on a narrow path about 60 cm. / 23 in. wide, I looked down to the ground and saw that I was barefoot. I looked around at all of the plants and trees and noticed that their flowers were opening as I passed near them. Flying all around me there were hundreds of beautiful colored, harmless insects like butterflies, dragonflies and bees.

Normally walking through the forest I would be wearing knee-high rubber boots, trousers, a shirt and I would be looking out for dangerous insects. Nevertheless, in this vision, I was practically nude like the ancient Amazonian natives, only wearing a loin cloth, I felt so confident believing that there was nothing in the forest which could harm me.

I continued walking and suddenly about 40 m. / 130 ft. ahead of me, I saw a few rays of sunlight passing through the canopy of the giant trees down to the forest floor. As I got closer to the rays of sunlight, I realized that the path was leading to a small clearing that oddly enough, was right in the middle of the jungle. Reaching the clearing, I noticed that all the butterflies, dragonflies and bees that were following me stayed behind in the forest and now 20 cm. / 8 in. wide iridescent blue Morpho butterflies accompanied me.

Suddenly in the middle of the clearing, I saw a giant grasshopper about 8 m. / 25 ft. long. I walked towards this giant insect and noticed that next to it, there was a young native man holding the animal by unusual reins. Looking closer at these reins, I realized that they were the same vine of Ayahuasca that Don Piwali had on his table. Then looking up at the insect's head I saw that I could sit on its back.

At that moment, the grasshopper lowered its head and stretched one of its front legs towards me. I stepped foreword, grabbed the reins firmly with my two hands and then jumping up I mounted the animal. The grasshopper lifted its head and straightening its body, it stood upright.

Then the native man stepped back and I looked at him, he was about thirty year's old, semi-nude but for a loincloth. His body was lean and strong. Around his neck, he wore many necklaces of small black seeds and over them he wore an extraordinary, ivory colored, glowing, jaguar fang necklace. He wore thin cloth bands around his wrists and above his biceps, and fitted underneath these bands were leaves and small, bright purple and yellow flowers. His body was completely decorated in iridescent, red and black vegetable tattoo designs, then he slowly raised his head and looked up at me, I saw that on his face he also had similar tattoos. He had long black shiny hair. His face and entire body had a radiant, oily glow to it, he had no eyebrows and suddenly I noticed a spark in his eyes and at the same time a friendly smile, only then I realized that he was Don Piwali as a  young man. I wanted to talk to him, but at that precise moment, the grasshopper turned his head back towards me. I saw the insects left eye and knew that it was going to start flying, I looked back at Don Piwali and he was no longer there. The Ayahuasca reins had disappeared, so I firmly held onto the grasshopper's mane.

Instantly we ascended to the sky and began flying over the jungle. I looked down to the jungle and saw the winding rivers traveling through the thick forest, there were many spectacular different types of trees, all flowering of different colors. I saw flocks of many colorful species of birds, most of which I had never seen before.

The only birds that I recognized were large green parrots, red and blue Ara Macaws, yellow and blue Ara Macaws and Toucans. In addition, I saw many troops of different species of monkeys walking over and through the canopy layer; they were picking fruits, insects and nuts to eat. Looking down on the rivers, I saw many families of pink and gray dolphins.

All of a sudden I saw a huge white eagle fly next to me. It looked at me, made a soft screech and then dove down towards a troop of large monkeys that were walking over a tree. The leader of the pack screamed and all the monkeys desperately scrambled into the foliage trying to escape. However, with incredible, lightning speed and making a frightful, loud screeching sound, in a split second the bird stretched its huge claws out and grabbed one of the adult monkeys by its shoulders. The terrified monkey screamed and the eagle effortlessly lifted it up to the sky, the monkey continued screaming and was moving frantically trying to break lose. The eagle squeezed its sharp claws into its victim's body until the monkey losing so much blood, eventually remained motionless with its four limbs and head dangling. The eagle circled once over the top of a large Kapoc tree, and then it dropped the dead animal                                        over the thick foliage of the tree. It circled once more and then landed next to its prey. It looked around, and then began eating the monkey. (Only weeks later, I learned that this white eagle that I had seen was a male Harpy eagle, the world's largest eagle and the world's most powerful bird of prey, and the monkey that I had seen was a Spider monkey. An adult spider monkey weighs about 6 kilos / 13 pounds).

We continued flying over the rainforest, and then far ahead of me I saw another clearing in the forest, but much larger. As the grasshopper got closer, I distinguished in the middle of the clearing a huge white pyramid-shape type of structure which looked like a Mayan style of temple that stood above the surrounding jungle.

We descended slowly down to the clearing until we landed right at the foot of this building. The grasshopper stretched its right leg out as it lowered its front body; I dismounted the animal and walked a few steps to the foot of the building. I looked up at the entire temple. It was made of huge white stone blocks. Ahead of me there was a flight of about 300 steps, I started walking up and before I realized it, I had already reached the top. At the top, there was a large flat platform. On the middle of this platform there was a large, one-story, stone, thatch roof rectangular building, then I turned around and saw that the grasshopper was up in the sky flying away.

I walked towards the building and saw a closed stone door without any handle. I pushed hard trying to open it, but nothing happened. All of a sudden I felt the presence of someone behind me, so I turned around, but no one was there. I looked out towards the rainforest, admiring it for a long time. Then again, I felt that someone was on the platform near me, as I turned around, I saw next to me, about 1 m. / 3 ft. away, a group of about twenty dark skin, beautiful young native women standing in a perfect row, side by side. Motionlessly they were looking out at the jungle, their faces were decorated with attractive red and black line designs and they showed a proud, firm stare. Then I looked down at their bodies; they were wearing abundant black seed necklaces that were radiating mild, but stunning color lights, their beautiful breasts were uncovered and as I continued looking down, I saw that they had shiny, black cricket legs. Even though this surprised me, it did not frighten me.

I turned to the forest to try to see what they were looking at, but I did not see anything. I turned back to look at the women, but they had disappeared. Again, I looked back to the forest and looking around more observantly I noticed some small colorful lights radiating from certain trees, vines and plants. At that moment, I thought that those plants must be special. All at once, I felt that I was beginning to levitate, I could not see the jungle anymore, and all I saw was clouds and the sky around me. This sensation seemed to last for a long time, maybe ten minutes until gradually I began to recover my consciousness.

I heard the daybreak jungle sounds of birds. I opened my eyes and there was Don Piwali looking at me. He was sitting in his hammock next to me, his face was clean from the red colored designs, he smiled at me and I smiled back. Don Piwali gave me a small gourd-bowl half filled with an orange-brown colored liquid. I took the gourd and slowly drank the strange beverage; it was bitter but not as bitter as Ayahuasca.

I felt slightly weak and after a few minutes of resting I stood up and feeling a little off balance I carefully walked to the pot and looked inside, it was empty. I looked around at the room and was amazed to see how different it looked and felt from the mystical atmosphere of the previous night. Suddenly I remembered that I had to go back to the hotel, so I signaled to Don Piwali that we should leave, he agreed and we left.

Arriving to the riverbank, I washed the red vegetable tattoo from my face. Then we boarded Don Piwali's canoe and he took me to the other side. I was very grateful to him and I felt that I owed him so much for such a special experience, not sure how to pay him I gave him my Swiss army knife which he gladly accepted. Now looking back on that morning, I wish that I had a worthier gift to give Don Piwali.

That morning after breakfast with the tour group, we left the lodge; we boarded our canoe and traveled upriver to Misahualli. There we got in our minibus and traveled on the dusty road, leaving the jungle and climbing the Andes towards Quito.

Throughout this entire six-hour journey, I thought a lot about my unique and beautiful experience with Don Piwali and Ayahuasca. However, I felt a bit disillusioned, because I realized that I was empty of any particular "enlightenment" as I thought I would have been after drinking a "sacred" brew. I was left with only a vivid memory of an amazing surreal visionary experience, which at times seemed like a dream. Maybe I did not drink enough Ayahuasca.

Only as the months and years passed, did I learn to appreciate more and more my first experience with this sacred plant and with Don Piwali. The reason for this is that with normal dreams one gradually forgets most of, or all of the details, but with that Ayahuasca experience, I have never forgotten any of the details. It is as if that mystical experience of that night had been etched into my mind. What was also special and unexplainable, was that in my vision I saw animals such as the Harpy eagle, Spider monkeys, and other animals that I had never before seen.

Soon I returned to my normal routine of work. I enjoyed anthropology, History, nature and tourism, so I continued leading tours throughout the Andes, Coastal Tropical Rainforest and the Galapagos Islands. Unfortunately, for me at that time there were no tours available to the Amazon.

# CHAPTER 3

## • Reynaldino

Six years had passed since my first Ayahuasca experience. Suddenly one day a travel agency asked me to lead a tour group to the Misahualli area, without hesitation I quickly accepted. I had often thought about Don Piwali and was looking foreword to meeting him and also I was interested in drinking Ayahuasca again.

With the tour group we arrived to the same lodge as my previous trip, but I never got to meet Don Piwali. Regrettably, just a few weeks earlier he had passed away. During the four days that I was in the jungle, I felt terribly sad; I took time to visit his family and to visit his grave. While I was in his community, I had heard that no one had followed his footsteps of Shamanism. I felt disappointed to think that all of his valuable knowledge was not being passed down to younger generations, and were going to be lost forever. I could not understand how it was possible that out of a whole community of about 300 people, not one of them, not even his children or close family had interest in learning something as priceless as their traditional religion.

The fact that no person from Don Piwali's community was interested in the ethnic religion motivated me to try to learn more about the religion and drink Ayahuasca again, so I began to inquire if there was anyone else who knew how to prepare the sacred brew. Unluckily for me, during those days that I was there, Remigio my friend and previous scout was not there, I had been assigned another native scout. I knew that Remigio would not have approved of me drinking Ayahuasca again, but he knew all of the people in the nearby native communities and he could have recommended someone to cook Ayahuasca for me.

During one of the conversations that I had with my new native scout Marcelo, he told me that there was a native man called Carlos who was a Shaman and he knew how to cook Ayahuasca. Conveniently enough, one of the hotel employees was a son of Carlos, so I talked with him and he arranged for his father to come that evening to the lodge.

After dinner I met Carlos, he was a middle-age man, much younger than Don Piwali and he spoke enough Spanish so that we could easily understand one another. He assured me that he knew how to cook Ayahuasca, and that my visions with his cooked brew would excellent. He told me that he could have a bottle of half a liter / about 2 quarts of the Ayahuasca brew ready for the following night and that it would cost me the equivalent in Ecuadorian money of ten U.S. dollars. Even though Carlos was modernized and quite different to Don Piwali, I decided to accept his offer. I asked him if there were any preparations that I should follow or anything that I should avoid doing. He answered, "Just don't eat dinner." However, remembering Don Piwali's advice, on the following day I decided to have a light breakfast, no lunch or dinner and drink only water.

The following night at about six, someone knocked at my cabin door, I opened it and there was Carlos holding a glass bottle of Ayahuasca. He smiled, and handed me the bottle, then he asked for the money, I paid him and asked him where I could drink the brew? He looked into the room and told me to drink it there. I felt disillusioned with his answer, but anyway I thanked him and he left.

I closed the door and went into my candle-lit room where I sat on the edge of my wooden bed. I looked more carefully at the bottle of Ayahuasca, which did not look at all appetizing. Inside the bottle, some of the caramel-olive colored brew had suspiciously stuck onto the glass and as I gently tilted the bottle, I could see tiny pieces of wood, stems and leaves. Since I never got a chance to examine Don Piwali's brew I wondered if all those bits of leaves, stems and pieces of wood should be there.

I carefully unscrewed the cap, and put the bottle and cap on the night table that was next to my bed. Then I took a large glass and filled it halfway, I estimated that that was how much I had drank with Don Piwali. I put the bottle down on the night table and picked up the glass with my two hands. For a moment, I hesitated and started thinking about Don Piwali and how different my experience with him was. But, I was determined to drink the sacred brew, so slowly in a respectful manner, I brought the brew to my mouth, as the edge of the glass touched my lips; I smelled and tasted the brew and instantly my mind and taste buds unmistakably recognized and relived the same strange, smell and taste of Ayahuasca as six years earlier.

At that point, I felt more confident knowing that Carlos's cooked brew looked, smelled and tasted the same as Don Piwali's Ayahuasca. Slowly I drank the brew and then I put the glass down on the night table next to the bottle. I looked at the flame of the candle that was on the night table.

The warm light from the candle illuminated my rustic bamboo room in a mystical manner which reminded me a little of my Ayahuasca experience six years earlier with Don Piwali. I laid back on my bed, closed my eyes and in my mind I remembered part of my beautiful experience with Don Piwali; he was wearing his old crown of feathers, his face was painted with beautiful, red ethnic designs, and then he began painting my face with similar designs. He was blowing his cigar smoke at me and around the room, at the same time he was singing and shaking his bundle of leaves over me and up to the ceiling. Outside of my cabin, I could hear the wonderful jungle night sounds.

About one hour had passed and I still did not feel anything different, so I decided to drink one quarter of a glass more of Ayahuasca. I turned on the candle, drank the brew, and then I turned off the candle and lay back on my bed again and waited. Still after another hour, nothing exciting happened, except that I began to feel nervous! I was not seeing any visions at all and then I felt so bad that I had to get up to the bathroom to throw up. Afterwards I returned to my bed and tried to sleep, but could not. I felt more nervous and that night eventually became terribly long. Two more times I had to get up to vomit and after hours of feeling bad, finally I was able to sleep.

The next morning I felt tired and during the rest of the day I felt weak and disappointed. Because of the dreadful experience of the night before, the following evening before sleeping, I swore that I would never drink Ayahuasca again.

For years, I continued guiding tours throughout different areas of the country. In 1990, a tour company from Quito made me a good offer to lead jungle adventure camping-tours deep into the Ecuadorian Amazon. The areas where these tours were to take place were around the Paña Cocha, Zancudo Cocha, Lagarto Cocha, Garza Cocha, Cuyabeno and Jatun Cocha, lake areas. These areas were reserves that were connecting by small rivers to the Napo or Aguarico rivers; throughout these reserves, there were many species of animals. Just to mention a few animals; there were hundreds of species of exotic birds, at least six different species of monkeys, black and masked caimans (alligators), piranha fish, wild boars, river otters, capybaras, tapirs, anacondas and jaguars. Some of these animals of course were difficult to see, but they lived within the virgin forests in these areas and if my tour group did not see them, usually we were able to spot their fresh tracks. Inclusively at Paña Cocha, Lagarto Cocha, Cuyabeno and at Garza Cocha we practically always saw fresh water dolphins, and quite often we were able to spot the giant Amazonian Paiche fish (Arapaima gigas, the largest freshwater fish in the world, it exceeds 180 kg. / 400 lb. in weight and 4.5 m. / 15 ft. in length.

After months of taking groups into these areas, I met a native man called Reynaldo; he was of the Cofan tribe and was the owner of a motor canoe which we used with the tours. Reynaldo was a very nice, honest, intelligent man of about fifty-five years old, he was married and lived with his family in the native Secoya village of San Pablo de Kantestyaya on the Aguarico River.

Working together on different trips, we soon became very good friends. Reynaldo was a man of many talents, so besides him being an excellent pilot of the river, he was also an excellent scout in the jungle and an admirable human being, who out of kindness I would call him "Reynaldino".

Reynaldo after catching a Piraña fish

I learned a lot from my friend, but what impressed me the most was that often, while we were walking through the jungle with tour groups he would talk to me about a very special plant which he said was the most significant plant for the Kurakas (name in the Cofan language for Shamans).

Reynaldo said that in the past, this plant was the most important plant used by his people. He called this plant Yagé (ja-gé) and he said that drinking a brew made from this plant was the most important training for a person to become a Shaman. He also said that by drinking the brew made from this plant, a person's Spirit could leave the body and would meet other Spirits of animals and people, also he said that a person's physical body would become much stronger and healthier.

I gradually became very much interested in this plant and I asked him if there was any danger drinking Yagé, if there was any side effects or worse if anyone has ever died drinking the brew. He looked at me curiously, laughed and categorically answered "No, never has anything bad ever happened to a person drinking Yagé." Then I asked him if the brew was addicting, again he laughed and said that he had been drinking Yagé since he was about seven years old at least once a month, until he was about seventeen years old and then he completely stopped drinking it. (When Reynaldo was sixteen years old, a group of U.S. Protestant-Evangelical missionaries arrived to his community. They landed in a small hydroplane on a nearby lake and presenting gifts, they were welcomed into the community, eventually after a few months of living in the community they began to preach the Bible to the people. Within ten months, they had convinced Reynaldo and most of the natives to stop drinking Yagé). This as well as many other examples, proves that Yagé and other Amazonian sacred plants are not addicting. Reynaldo's description of this brew sounded very familiar, so one night after dinner, I asked him if this brew or the plant that the brew is made from is called

Ayahuasca. He answered, "No, this brew is not Ayahuasca, it is Yagé."

My interest in the Amazonian ethnic native culture, as well as the trust that I had in my friend induced me to want to try this brew, so I asked Reynaldo if there was any possibility for me to drink the brew. He smiled, made a clicking sound by snapping the tip of his tongue with his palate (roof of the mouth) and excitedly he said, "Of course, in fact my brother Esteban is an expert in cooking Yagé." Whenever Reynaldo was happy, he always made a clicking sound. At that moment I asked Reynaldo if his brother was a Shaman, he answered no, but his brother knew how to cook Yagé because he used to be the official Cooker for Don Fernando; the most powerful Shaman who ever lived on the entire Aguarico river. (A Cooker is a man who in the past used to be a Shaman apprentice and because of this, part of his essential training by his tutor the Shaman, had been precisely to learn how to properly handle and cook the sacred plants. Only men can become Cookers and later I shall explain why).

Reynaldo said that if I was interested, he would tell his brother to cook Yagé for me and that he would bring it for me on our next tour together, I gladly agreed.

Three weeks later, I had a tour again to the jungle with Reynaldo, I was with four middle-age men from the United States. We left Quito by plane and after forty minutes, we landed in the Amazon at the town of Coca. From there we took a bus to the Napo River where Reynaldo with his canoe was waiting for us. Reynaldo was with his seventeen- year old son Marcelino, as soon as we arrived, from his canoe he excitedly told me that he had the bottle of Yagé for me. Then I saw him reaching inside his bag to show me the bottle. Immediately I signaled for him to stop.

At that moment, I did not have time to see the brew, we were already late for traveling down the river and besides that, I did not want the tourists to see the bottle of Yagé.

I was very happy that his brother was able to cook for me, so I told him that I was happy, also I told him not to say anything about Yagé in front of the tourists and that later at the campsite we would have time to see the bottle and talk all about it.

I wanted to reach our campsite before it got dark to avoid traveling on the river at night and so that we would have some daylight to set up camp. Fortunately, Reynaldino knows all of the rivers in the northern and middle Amazon of Ecuador by memory, but sometimes in the rivers there are newly fallen trees and whirlpools, so it is much safer to travel during the day.

We navigated on the river for about three hours until we finally reached a small river which soon took us to a large lake and our campsite. Upon arriving, it was just starting to get dark, so we quickly unloaded the supplies to two thatch roof huts that were in the middle of a big clearing. One of these huts was small which we used as the cooking and dining area, and the other hut was larger which we used as the sleeping area. The two huts did not have any walls and from the interior of any of the two huts, one could look out to the jungle or to the lake. The large hut had a wooden floor made of strips of wood from a tall palm tree known as Pambil. This wooden floor was about 1 m. / 3 ft. off the ground and to get up to the floor and into the hut, there were two sets of steps at each opposite end of the hut. Tied onto the wooden posts of the large hut were two groups of hammocks for sleeping. At one end of the hut were the hammocks for the tourists and at the other end of the hut were the hammocks for the staff, including myself. In the Amazon, I always love to sleep in a hammock because it is the most comfortable and coolest way to sleep.

The small hut was different to the large hut in that it was smaller and had no wooden floor; its floor was the natural ground. At one end of this hut, there was a long table with two benches where we had our meals and nearby was the cooking area. From the grass clearing, there were three different footpaths leading to three different out-houses. About ten kilometers away was the nearest native community.

Once all the luggage was placed in the large hut and the campsite was set up, I showed the campsite facilities to the tour group. Afterwards, the sun set and it quickly got dark, I put on my swim trunk and took a lit candle to the bank of the lake; I placed the candle on the top edge of the canoe and bathed. Meanwhile our cook was already preparing an exquisite dinner. At nighttime because of poor visibility and because of reptiles and other nocturnal water animals, it is not safe to bathe in rivers or lakes. But because I had such a long, tiring day, I needed to refresh myself. The tourists were occupying the camp shower. After my bath, I put on clean clothes and finally there was time to see the brew.

I went to Reynaldo's hammock where he was resting and asked him about the bottle of Yagé, he smiled and made his usual clicking sound with his tongue. (The majority of the native adults are good-natured and they spend most of their lives playing jokes on each other in a wholesome, non-offending manner). Reynaldino turned on his flashlight, reached down into his vinyl bag and pulled out a bottle wrapped in a newspaper.

I took the bottle, took the newspaper off and pointed my flashlight towards the brew. The liquid inside was an olive-caramel color that resembled Ayahuasca. I looked at Reynaldo and said "Reynaldino this looks just like Ayahuasca." He laughed and said, "This is Yagé!" I smiled and asked him when I could drink it. He said that I should skip dinner and that afterwards I can drink it. At that moment, the cook called us for dinner. Reynaldo kept the bottle and we went to the table, I excused myself from eating. During the dinner, I talked about the jungle and about the following day's program. It had been a tiring day, so immediately after our meal the four men took their flashlights and left to their hammocks to prepare for a restful night.

Meanwhile I stayed at the table with Reynaldo, Marcelino, the cook and 2 native helpers. At our campsites the only lighting that we used were candles, I enjoyed this light because it gave a more natural atmosphere. The four tourists were still preparing for the night, but after about ten minutes we saw that all the candles in their sleeping area of the hut were out. Reynaldo quickly went to bring the bottle of Yagé. I was excited, but also I felt a little nervous. After a few    minutes he returned and placed the bottle on the table right in front of me. I looked at him and he smiled, he raised his eyebrows and made his clicking sound. Looking at Reynaldo, I could not help but smile back, instantly he had made me forget that I was nervous.

However, a few seconds later, I looked back at the bottle and at the reality that awaited me, and I said "Dios mio!" (My God!) I could not understand why deep inside of me there existed this interest in trying these strange Amazonian brews. Marcelino got up and brought me a clean stainless steel cup, placed it on the table next to the bottle and smiled at me. Now all eyes were on me and the bottle, I took the bottle, unscrewed the cap and slowly poured the brew halfway into the cup. There were insects flying around us and a few insects walking on the table, I put the cap back on the bottle, picked up the cup and raising it, I brought it to my lips.

Just as my lips made contact with the first drops of the brew, suddenly I recognized the flavor, I was surprised and in disbelief, I looked at my friend and said "Reynaldino, this is Ayahuasca." Confused, he looked at me strangely and said, "No, no, this is Yagé." I felt disappointed; I lowered the cup on the table and sadly looked at the unappetizing brew. All this time I had been thinking that I was going to try something different and better than Ayahuasca.

Then Reynaldo said, "Patricio, drink it, you'll like it, this is good, it's Yagé!" Suddenly from the sky above, flying overhead, we heard the strange call of an unusual bird that I had never heard before. At that instant Reynaldo overcome with excitement said, "Patricio now you have to drink the Yagè, that birdcall is an important sign; it's from a special nighthawk that was sent by the People of Yagé, they want you to drink Ayahuasca, no Yagé." Then we all started laughing and after we finished laughing, I looked at Reynaldo and asked... "Reynaldino, who are the People of Yagé?" Reynaldo kept on smiling and said "The People of Yagé are very good people, they come from the sky, and when a person drinks a lot of Yagé, then that person can see the People of Yagé and they will help one to become a Kuraka." "Are they Spirits?" I asked him. "Yes they are Spirits, but also they are like people because whenever they want they can appear in this world, they are always happy, they are much wiser and better than humans."

I raised the cup, everyone was silent and slowly I drank practically all the brew, except for the granulated material that always stays at the bottom. I asked Reynaldo if I could drink a little more, he smiled, made his clicking sound and nodded yes, so I drank ½ a cup more. Then Reynaldo told me, "Now go wash your mouth with water and then go lay in your hammock to sleep." I bid farewell to all, turned on my flashlight and left for my hammock.

I took my toothbrush, toothpaste, canteen of water and walked to the edge of the wooden bark floor. I sat down and then jumped off to the grass clearing where I walked about thirty steps to the edge of the forest to rinse my mouth. As I was washing out my mouth I was thinking about the brew that I had just drank which definitely was Ayahuasca, the smell and the taste is so unmistakably unique, and also I thought that the only reason why I had decided to drink it was so that my friend would not feel bad. Obviously, Reynaldo's Cofan tribe uses the name Yagé. (A few weeks later after investigating, I discovered that the central Amazonian tribes in Ecuador like the Quichua, Yumbo and Alama use the name "Ayahuasca", whereas in the northern Ecuadorian Amazon; tribes like the Cofan, Secoya and Sione, including a few Amazonian Colombian tribes use the name Yagé. Inclusively the other Amazonian tribes in Ecuador use altogether completely different names).

It was around eight in the evening. The sky was pitch-black, which made it ideal for me to admire the thousands of bright stars, and at the same time, I was entertained by the fantastic orchestra of the nighttime animal sounds. After a few minutes of enjoying the beautiful night atmosphere, I returned to my hammock, took off my boots, my pants and shirt. During those years that I was working in the jungle, I preferred not to sleep without mosquito netting, so I put on my arms, neck, cheeks and feet a small amount of insect repellent and then I got into my hammock. Underneath my hammock, within my reach was my duffel bag, and on it was my sleeping bag and a flashlight. In the Amazon, every night at about four in the morning it always gets cold, so then I would take my sleeping bag.

My hammock was about 5 m. / 16 ft. to the edge of the hut and there was no other hammock between my hammock and the edge. I lay in my hammock and thought in my loving wife Lily, daughter Michelle and the rest of my family. Then I thought about Don Piwali, my friend Reynaldo, the Amazon and the Yagé brew that I just drank. Because it had been such a long day for me, before I realized it, I had dozed off to a deep, profound sleep.

After about an hour, I began to recover my consciousness, but feeling unusually strange. I felt as if my body was gently levitating, but in the same lying down position, also I noticed a persistent, pleasant humming sound all around me, and then I realized that all of the animal jungle sounds were louder. In the past, I had never heard so many nocturnal animal sounds, but these loud animal sounds were not disturbing, in fact they were pleasant. The sounds were of crickets, frogs, owls, nighthawks, nightjars, night herons and other animals that I could not recognize.

I was feeling very strange, but because I was so exhausted, I was still half-asleep. Since it had been such a pleasant rest I wanted to continue sleeping, but suddenly I felt and heard something that moved in my stomach. I didn't want to give any importance to this, but then after a few seconds, I felt whatever it was that was in my stomach begin to move again and this time the movement was with an upward motion.

Immediately I awoke, but I still kept my eyes closed. Just then, I realized that I was having an impulse to throw up. I tried to calm myself and be in command of this unwanted action, so instinctively during a few times I swallowed the saliva that I had in my mouth. By doing this, I was sure that I had my stomach under control. I did not understand why my body would want to vomit; I did not feel any form of stomach pain. I was still amazed to hear so many loud animal sounds and figured that there must be more animals in the area than usual, but why? I tried to fall back to sleep again, but then I felt and heard the same upward impulse in my stomach again and only then I realized that it must be because of the Yagé. I was so tired when I had fallen asleep that I had completely forgotten that I had drunk Yagè. At that second, I regretted having drank the Yagé brew. I still tried to control my stomach but realizing that it was not easy, I began to feel a little nervous. Nothing like this had ever happened to me before. I knew that it would be difficult for me to get out of my hammock, get my flashlight, put on my boots, walk to the edge of the floor, get on to the grass clearing, then walk to the edge of the forest where I could finally throw up. At that moment, I noticed something odd and this was that my stomach felt warm and at the same time my body began to mildly and comfortably tremble at the same rhythm as the jungle animal sounds, which were now louder.

All at once I felt the same impulse, but much stronger and

now in my esophagus (tube from the mouth to the stomach), I could not wait any longer. I desperately grabbed the two edges of my hammock and lifted my body to sit up. Quickly I opened my eyes to get out of the hammock and at that precise second as I had opened my eyes, I heard the jungle animal sounds and the humming sound much louder, and at that exact same instance, I saw in front of me, my first real visions!

I was flabbergasted and completely blown away. I saw in front and all around me millions of tiny, brightly colored small geometrical designs all in a perfect symmetrical pattern resembling butterflies combined with native ethnic motifs, these designs were of all different colors, but mainly in varied tones of purple, pink, yellow, blue, red and orange. The effect of seeing and hearing so much beauty was overwhelming, I could not believe what I was witnessing, and instinctively I opened my eyes   wider. Then slowly I began to turn my head in all directions and I noticed that wherever I looked, for as far as I could see, there were millions of these beautiful colored designs.

The humming sound and other jungle animal sounds were gradually becoming more comfortably intense, I thought of getting out of the hammock to go closer to the jungle, but found it difficult to move. My body felt perfectly content as long as it was still, but if I moved, my body would slightly tremble in an unusual but comfortable manner. I felt strange as if I were in another world or dimension, I had lost my balance, my body muscles and movements had become less coordinated. Oddly enough I did not feel weak, in fact I felt incredibly strong.

With a little bit of difficulty trying to adjust to my new condition, again I grabbed the edges of the hammock and pulled myself up, I managed to get my legs out on one side of the hammock. I sat perfectly still on the edge of the hammock in awe, staring out at all of the gorgeous, colorful geometric designs within the hut as well as within the jungle and sky. They moved gently, all in unison, and then I realized that something extraordinary had happened to my eyesight, about an hour ago when I got into my hammock the interior of the hut was pitch black and now it was beautifully lit, by what appeared to be moonlight. I looked out at the jungle and the same phenomenon was occurring there. Then I realized that there was no moon, my eyes had probably dilated so much, that I had acquired a good degree of night vision.

Looking above and all around me at these colored designs, I suddenly discovered that they were changing. In the most subtle manner, in a fraction of a second, during a blink of an eye, the color combinations were transforming into new, beautiful color variations. New butterfly shapes and new geometrical figures were replacing others, then I blinked my eyes and again everything would change. To me it looked like a perfectly synchronized choreographed slow dance of radiant, stylized geometrical figures. I was completely astonished as I felt that I was truly privileged to witness something so precious and beautiful. For more than one hour, I was calmly admiring and living this wonderful experience.

Then suddenly from the pit of my stomach came that unpleasant sound again, the rumbling. Because I was so distracted admiring the breathtaking visions, I had forgotten about my stomach problem. Promptly I tried to stand up but could not. I tried again, this time I had to make a conscious effort and order my muscles to work. With my hands, I grabbed the hammock as hard as I could and pulled myself up, finally managing to stand up. My legs felt strong, but my knees felt as if they had been locked into a perfectly straight position. I looked sideways to the edge of the hut and decided that I had to walk there. I was barefoot, I took a step foreword and almost fell, fortunately, I had not let go of the hammock, because I realized that, I had absolutely no balance.

It was not a frightful or unpleasant sensation, but at that

moment, it became a problem for me. It seemed to me that my legs were too weak to hold me up. If I would have tried to walk, I think that for sure I would have fallen. Then it occurred to me to crawl to the edge of the hut, so carefully I got down to the bark-floor on my hands and knees and began crawling. The millions of beautifully colored visions were always present in front and all around me. As I was moving my body, I noticed an unusual, dominating force taking over my body. This strange feeling was of a growing confidence combined with the powerful presence of a large animal. My body felt incredibly strong and for a moment, I felt that my physical body had wanted to transform itself into the body of a jaguar.

Crawling slowly and enjoying this new powerful jaguar-like feeling, I reached the edge of the bark-floor. I looked down at the grass and then I looked ahead at the jungle that was about 10 m. / 33 ft. away. From the crawling position I leaned back and rested my buttocks on my heels, my knees stayed on the floor and my arms were straight down in front of me. My back was leaning perfectly straight foreword at a 45-degree angle; at that moment, this kneeling posture seemed to be the most natural and most comfortable for me.

I looked up to the sky and saw the millions of incredibly, beautifully, colored visions moving in the sky, the splendid, brightly colored changing visions were everywhere. The humming and the comfortably loud jungle animal sounds continued. Suddenly after what appeared to be an hour of seeing these beautiful, indescribable visions, I began to feel an unusual, warm sensation like a special energy in the base of my spine; it was like a mild, warm, pleasant electrical current that gradually grew. After a few minutes, I noticed that this sensation was extending slowly up my spine and as this was happening, I found myself responding in an instinctively odd manner.

Without changing my position, I began stretching the muscles of each part of my back simultaneously at the precise moment when I was feeling the warm electrical energy. First, I began stretching my lower spine, then my middle spine, then my upper spine. Simultaneously, this warm sensation began radiating from my spine outwards towards the rest of my body. This new tingling, vivacious energy gradually became so powerful and so alive that I could feel it in each individual cell of my body. Then I felt this pleasant energizing, electrical sensation concentrating again at the base of my spine, but also I began to feel this unique energy also in the tips of my fingers, toes and spreading throughout my brain. Finally, I felt this vibrant force concentrating at the crown of my head. I felt so strong physically, emotionally and mentally and then suddenly I began to feel an awareness of an intense Spiritual nature filling my entire being.

Never before in my life had I felt Spiritual strength; such a new form of energy, which has a divine characteristic and is far more important and powerful than any energy or feeling which exists anywhere in the material world. I was in complete peace, control and had so much confidence in myself. I felt that I was not afraid of anything, not even death. I was looking out at the endless sky and virgin jungle, I was completely absorbed by the indescribable beauty of the colorful visions of this whole new magical environment and I comprehended that it was a wonderful combination of a Spiritual World with the Amazon material world.

At that moment, I was actually living within these two dimensions, two completely different worlds that co-exist in perfect harmony. Absolutely everything in these two worlds was perfectly balanced. I was convinced that because my Spiritual body had been truly awakened was why I could clearly perceive the magnificent, visionary, Spiritual World, which was so beautiful, because it was just a little closer to the actual source of God's energy. I was actually a little closer to God's almighty energy; this was spiritually, mentally, emotionally and physically. Then I thought that if this Spiritual world which I was just barely touching, was so magnificent, then how much greater would the Spiritual world be after a person's physical body dies and one is closer to God's magnificent existence.

Our mind just does not have the capacity to imagine the greatness or beauty of God's true Spiritual world! Moreover, here I was, being so fortunate to actually have an experience within a tiny part of this incredibly magnificent Spiritual world and experience a hint of what God's glorious energy is like.

Here in this Spiritual-material Amazonian world there was no intervention or harmful elements by humans. I felt such a close relationship between the jungle, the visions, the loud animal sounds, the humming in my ears and God. I had actually become an essential part of this unique, metaphysical world. (metaphysical is a science that is abstract, difficult to understand, and deals with everything, which is invisible to the physical senses.) I was entranced and at the same time, I felt that God's Sacred, Supernatural presence had enveloped this entire area of the jungle. It seemed to me that all of the plants and animals were also feeling this divine force. I imagined that this experience was what it must have felt like to be in the Biblical "Garden of Eden." Suddenly in the middle of all of my happiness, I felt and heard from my stomach, again that same retched impulse, but now it was much stronger and faster than before.

This time I could not control it, before I realized what was happening, in less than a second my two hands were firmly grasping the edge of the wooden floor. My whole body contracted and I violently threw up. I vomited out towards the grass about one meter and a half / 5 ft. away, about 4 liters / 1 gal. of brown colored water. I was surprised, but not frightened to see so much quantity of liquid being expelled. After this terribly unpleasant moment, I felt weak, unbearably cold and almost immediately, my whole body began to shiver. I closed my teary eyes, dried my lips with the back of my hand, lowered my head to my knees, rested and continued shivering.

Strangely enough, there was no foul smell, but in my throat and mouth, again I had the bitter taste of Yagé which is so much stronger travelling up the throat than going down. At that moment, I remained motionless, thinking for a while and still could not understand why I threw up and how it was possible for so much liquid to come out after only drinking one cup and a half. I felt disappointed because I had thrown up; I knew that if I would have been able to keep all of the Yagé inside of me, my experience would have been much better. After about five minutes of feeling cold, weak and shivering, gradually I began to feel warm again and I began to feel the comforting, electric-like tingling energy spread throughout my body. Simultaneously I began to recover the extraordinary strength and blissful feeling that previously I had been experiencing. The warm, electric-like tingling sensation felt so good. I slowly raised my head, opened my eyes, smiled and feeling strong and confident again, I continued looking out at the millions of magnificent, colorful, changing visions everywhere.

Soon I began to feel a unique awareness of a mystical, bonding relationship that was developing between the jungle and myself. I sensed that each plant and tree had its own Spiritual energy and were reaching out to communicate with me; they were accompanying me through my Spiritual journey. My mind, eyesight and hearing had become incredibly keen. My eyesight was much better than normal; my eyes became aware of so many minor details of all objects that were at least 6 m. / 20 ft. away in the jungle. Discovering this new aptitude that I had, I began to focus in on each object. I was astonished to see many new things that before I never realized existed. I did not feel at all sleepy which was also very strange because for me, the day before had been dreadfully exhausting.

I stayed in that position for about six hours, even though during the last hour, the visions gradually began to fade away.

There were less animal sounds from the jungle and my hearing began to normalize. Soon afterwards, I felt tired and a little cold, at which point I decided to turn around and silently crawl back to my hammock. My body still had the trembling sensation as I moved and even though I was a little tired, I still felt a tremendous force of energy alive in each cell of my body. Getting into my hammock was not easy, because my body was still lacking its normal balance. Once inside, I reached for my sleeping bag, lay back and covered myself. My experience had been so incredibly wonderful, I was so happy that tears came to my eyes. I thanked God for such an indescribable, wonderful experience. I closed my eyes and I could still see the colorful visions that were gradually fading away, after a while, I inevitably fell asleep.

Within my sleep, I felt my body levitating high up to the sky and at the same time, I felt that I was getting closer to where God's main existence is. I felt the presence of so much energy, love and peace. Then after what appeared to be a long time I began to hear a distant chanting sound coming from the sky. After a long while, this soothing sound blended together with a continuous wind sound that gradually got louder, it stopped, and then after a while it started again. First a series of about six gusts of wind and then one long continuous wind sound. This lasted for about twenty minutes and was progressively getting louder until eventually this unusual sound had made my initial subconscious experience with God's beautiful energy fade away. All that I became aware of was the strong, persistent sound of the gusts of wind. Suddenly, I began to awaken hearing someone call my name. "Patricio, Patricio, wake up, Patricio wake up!" Opening my eyes, I saw Reynaldo, he and everything else in my field of vision
appeared as if they were enveloped in a strange, mystical mist. He was smiling and seemed especially happy, standing next to me and leaning over, he excitedly said, "Patricio, the Cotos have come to see you because last night you drank Yagé."

The wind sound continued and in fact only then I realized that the wind sound that I was hearing in my sleep was the calling of a pack of Cotos (Howler monkeys) and it was much louder now than how I had heard it in my sleep.

During these past seven months that I had been taking tour groups into that area of the jungle and I had never heard the Howler monkeys call so loud and for so long. I was surprised, but could it be true what Reynaldo had just said? Still incredulous, I asked him, "Reynaldino are you sure that the Cotos have come just because I drank Yagé?" "Yes, yes of course." "But why would they come because of that?" Reynaldo answered, "Because they like for the People of Yagé to be happy, so if there are any Cotos in the area, they will always travel during the night towards the person who drank Yagé, then early in the morning they announce their presence to the Spirits of Yagé by making special joyous calls."

Then I asked Reynaldo "Why would the People of Yagé be pleased?" He said, "Because last night you drank Yagé; every time anyone drinks Yagé, they are always pleased." After this, Reynaldo passed me a small gourd-bowl with a bright brown-orange colored liquid to drink; he told me that it would give me energy for the rest of the day. I looked at this brew and saw it similar to what Don Piwali had given me after I drank Ayahuasca, but this tasted slightly different. I asked Reynaldo what it was and he said it was Yoko. (A liana cultivated within the forest, which is used for making a caffeine-rich energy beverage).

As I slowly drank the bitter brew, I was looking at Reynaldo and I noticed that my vision began changing. Before I was seeing everything very hazy, but now my vision was actually improving, even better than my normal eyesight! Everything seemed sharper, there was an unusual shiny, glossy effect and I became noticeably aware of how vivid each different color was. My eyesight had improved because of Yagé. Reynaldo told me how sometimes jaguars, anacondas, howler monkeys, wild boars, dolphins and some hawks and eagles are naturally attracted to a person who has just drank Yagé. "If your experience was good and the People of Yagé are pleased with you, these animals even if they are kilometers away, will travel during the night or early morning to get close to you." I asked him if after drinking Yagè, if a jaguar or an anaconda were to appear, if it would hurt me? He said that after drinking Yagè the jaguar or anaconda would never hurt me, the People of Yagè would always protect me. This all sounded very strange to me, but so many unusual things had already happened to me in such a short time, that I had no reason to doubt what my friend had just told me.

As I was looking at Reynaldo, I noticed that besides my eyesight that had bettered, I had in me a new feeling that was precious and at the same time unusual. I felt in my heart the presence of a sincere, generous kindness and affection, almost like what I naturally always feel for my wife, daughter and the rest of my family. However, this new form of affection that I was now feeling was also for Reynaldo and for anyone else whom I met. I had never before felt this feeling of genuine, honest love towards other people outside of my family.

I knew that this extraordinary and unique feeling of unconditional love was a direct effect of my drinking Yagé and therefore of my true Spiritual awakening and my reaching a closeness to God and consequently achieving a true enlightenment with God's glorious light.

Within me something important which had been dormant for too long had suddenly been awakened, I felt like a new, completely different person. I felt an inner peace like never before in my life. This made me realize how special and priceless the sacred brew of Yagé really is. Then wanting to share my wonderful experience with someone, I said to Reynaldo, "The Yagé that I drank last night was fantastic, it was incredible, it was so beautiful, I saw..." Quickly Reynaldo interrupted me.

"Don't talk, don't say anymore, the people of Yagé don't like for one to talk about their visions. If you talk about your visions this will limit the assistance that you need from them and consequently also it will limit your growth as a Kuraka." I was stunned to hear what Reynaldo had told me, but more so, his reaction, obviously this was a very serious subject. I appreciated his straightforwardness and then I asked him why so much Yagé had come out? He smiled and said, "That's how Yagé always is, it took a lot of water to cook it, some of the water is evaporated and the rest of the water is spiritually assimilated into the brew that one drinks. If one vomits then the water that is in the brew will materialize to its original physical form and if one doesn't vomit then that excess Spiritual water will materialize inside one's body."

The pack of Howler monkeys continued calling and then I asked Reynaldo how much longer he thinks that they will stay there. He turned around towards their direction and said, "They'll stay in that area until you go see them." "It can't be!" I said. "Yes, yes it's true and you're going to see that it's true." I did not believe that that could be possible, so jokingly I said, "Well alright then, I'm going to go bathe in the lake and afterwards we will have breakfast and then we'll go into the forest to find the Cotos." Reynaldo laughing said, "All right, all right, you shall see." I got out of my hammock and immediately my legs felt unstable and a little weak, I felt off balance, similar to the night before.

Mentally, spiritually and physically I felt very strong, which was strange because I had spent most of the night awake, but I did not have good balance. I put on my swim trunk and as I was about to put on my boots, I suddenly had an urge to go barefoot, so for the first time since I had been in the jungle I started walking barefoot within the campsite and most everywhere else.

As I was going to the lake, I could not help but notice how my vision had become so much clearer. Like the night before,

I was noticing minute details wherever I looked, the plants, trees, insects, and even on the ground itself. All of the colors that I was seeing were more vivid and I noticed that my hearing had also improved. I was hearing many new sounds of different birds and even of flying insects that before I just never paid attention to. I wondered how long all these effects would last on me.

When I reached the lake, I walked in and I noticed that the water on my body felt different than on other occasions, it felt surprisingly familiar and welcoming. I noticed that Reynaldo's canoe was not at the bank, so I looked out towards the lake and there about 90 m. / 295 ft. away was the canoe with John, one of the tourists. I waved hi to him, he waved back and then I stepped deeper into the lake until the water reached my waist.

Because I was distracted by all these new feelings, I had forgotten to get a pole or long stick for walking into the lake. (Commonly at the banks of lakes or rivers, camouflaged under the water within the mud or sand there may be fresh-water stingrays. It is always safer to have a long object like a stick, pole or canoe paddle and move it along the ground in front of one as one is walking into a lake or river. This object will hit or touch the dangerous stingray and force it to move away. Obviously, the waters are so dark colored at the bottom of lakes or rivers that one can never see if there are any animals there.) That morning I was lucky I did not touch or step on any animal.

As soon as I felt the water reach my waist, I squatted a little and thrusting myself foreword, I began to swim slowly on the surface. The water felt good and refreshing. As I was calmly swimming, I began to perceive an unusual confidence growing in me. I felt an unusual, new physical strength spreading throughout my body and at the same time, I began to sense in me an instinct of an animal yearning to swim. This instinct in me felt strange, but completely natural. I have never been a good swimmer, so I have always been apprehensive of being in deep water far from the bank. However, that morning I felt so comfortable in the water that I instinctively began to swim away from the bank, out towards the middle of the lake. At that moment as I was swimming, I felt that I was an Amazonian fresh water Dolphin. My movements seemed to be completely natural, fast and perfectly synchronized. I swam out to one side of the lake, past the middle and then around and back towards the canoe.

As I reached the canoe, John had a fishing line in the water. He looked at me and then he asked if it was dangerous for me to be swimming in the lake while he was fishing for piranhas? Amused at his question I laughed and then he laughed. Afterwards I said, "Well my dear amigo John, fortunately for me it's not, because during this time of the year, in this lake the level of the water is high and there are plenty of fish that the piranhas can feed on." Then John commented on how great of a swimmer I was. I smiled at him and then said "Well thank you for saying that, but I am really not a good swimmer, it's just that this morning I feel great." Then I asked him how he was, and I told him that breakfast was ready, so I got into the canoe, picked up another paddle and together we paddled towards the shore. As we were paddling, in the back of my mind I knew that my recently acquired confidence in the water and swimming ability was only because of my drinking Yagé.

My reaction that morning to my particular confidence in the water and to using the abundance of my physical energy was understandable, but months later, I discovered that it is better for one not to waste the special energy of Yagé in physical feats of strength, unless it is really necessary. It is much wiser to reserve that special, divine energy for one's Spiritual growth, that energy will be assimilated by one's Spiritual body and will strengthen it. In addition, it is better for one never to show off one's special Yagé abilities, this will only weaken one's Spiritual body.

After finishing our breakfast, Reynaldo, Marcelino, I and the tour group went into the forest towards the persistent calls of the Howler monkeys. After about five minutes of walking, we spotted the exact tree where they were on. We took out our binoculars and got a much better look at them, they were a troop of nine monkeys, including one baby that was clinging on to the Mother's body. Quietly we approached the tree trying not to startle them. It is practically impossible with a group of tourists to get close to a pack of monkeys without them sensing and fleeing from their worst enemy; humans. However, moving very quietly, we were actually able to reach and stand right under the tree where the monkeys were, we hid behind some branches and leaves, but the monkeys knew that we were there; strangely enough they did not move!

The pack continued howling until the leader, a strong male became obviously upset at us, he and all of the other monkeys were furious. We did not feel that it was necessary to hide anymore, so we came out from under the thick foliage to find better positions to admire and photograph them. Reynaldo took his machete and wandered off into the forest where he began to collect large leaves. After a few minutes, he came back and placed them neatly over an old fallen tree that was almost under the tree of the monkeys. We all sat down on the fresh-cut leaves. Then two of the tourists began changing film in their cameras and taking more pictures until soon afterwards the monkeys started picking nuts or breaking off dried branches and throwing all of this debris at us.

After about thirty minutes of this, we could not help but laugh at the unusually strange behavior of the monkeys. Evidently, they were upset with our presence, so why would they not leave?

The four tourists asked me to explain to them why the monkeys did not leave the tree and move away from us. I told them that I had no idea. Of course, Reynaldo, Marcelino and I knew the real reason for the unusual behavior of the monkeys.

Turning to Reynaldo, I said, "Reynaldino, you were right, this is incredible." He said, "Those poor Cotos can't leave, because the People of Yagé are forcing them to stay there for you." Then I said, "But why would the People of Yagé force them to stay on the tree for me?" Reynaldo then said, "Because they want to give you another sign, so that you will be convinced of the power of Yagé." (The existence of Spirits puzzled me, and it wasn't for at least two more months, during which I was drinking more Yagé and witnessing many more unexplainable events which convinced me that the People of Yagé really do exist).

After the tour was over, I returned to Quito and I realized again that the energy of Yagé is truly potent and this was because even while in Quito, I could still feel the wonderful effects of Yagé in me. I felt lighter, I was sleeping and resting much better, my dreams were more vivid and colorful and the following morning I could remember them much easier. Practically every night my dreams were of me (my Spiritual-mental body) performing beautiful, breathtaking astral flights. In my past dreams I had never experienced such astral flights. In addition, my eyesight, hearing, physical strength, balance and co-ordination had also improved. Also I discovered that during my showers as I rubbed my lower back I could feel a mild, comfortable electrical form of current, similar to what I felt during my Yagé experience in the jungle.

My feeling of unconditional love for all human beings and my internal peace and harmony were still very much alive, and most important was my feeling of closeness to God, which became vital for my daily subsistence. All of these fantastic, new Spiritual-mental, physical and emotional beneficial effects lasted for about thirty days and then they began to gradually wear off. However, there was something that had also happened to me, which was permanent; I had felt a solid Spiritual awareness within me that I had never before experienced in my life.

That night in the jungle I truly felt God's omnipotent glory and presence in and around me, I felt my Spiritual body fully awakened and in a glorious state of happiness. Since that night, I have become a firm believer and follower of God. I have acquired much more self-confidence, past fears disappeared and I have found complete inner peace. It is truly remarkable to think that all of the wonderful effects that I was experiencing were produced by my drinking just one cup and a half of this powerful, sacred brew.

I continued working in tourism, and apart from drinking Yagè during some evenings of my tours, frequently I would go alone deep into the jungle to visit different native friends of different tribes and they in turn would take me deeper in the jungle to introduce me to friends that they had in ethnic native communities. I would stay in those ethnic native communities for a few months, learning from the Shamans and drinking Yagé.

One day Reynaldo invited me to visit his community, he told me that there I could drink very strong Yagé which was prepared by his Father-in-law Don Fernando who was famous for being the most powerful Shaman who ever lived on the entire Aguarico river in Ecuador, as well as in Peru. I soon found time to visit Reynaldo's community. Don Fernando was pleased to meet me; he invited me to stay in his home, where I lived with him for several months. Don Fernando was in his eighties, he did not speak any Spanish, which was common for Amazonian natives of his generation, so to communicate with him I always needed to rely on Marcelino or Reynaldo. Since many years ago, Protestant-Evangelical missionaries from the U.S. had arrived to Don Fernando's community; they had been successful in converting the people, so Don Fernando and the other elders were forced to stop practicing their ethnic religion. During my stay with the Shaman, we secretly drank Yagé many times.

Besides drinking Yagè with Don Fernando, I helped performing the different chores performed by men. I made many new friends in the community, including the children, who were always so open and playful.

The adults and children were just as curious of me as I was of them. Everyday, according to their sex and age the children always had different duties in order to help their Parents. The boys would spend more time helping their Fathers, and the girls would spend more time helping their Mothers. Through the chores, not only were the children physically helping their parents, but also they were learning to become integrated members of their families and communities, also they were learning about responsibility and learning important skills which were vital for them to becoming more independent, prosperous, healthier and happier adults. Both boys and girls would learn about the forest, rivers, and animals, how to cook, how to handle kitchen knives and machetes, how to clear the land and cultivate different crops, how to fish, and also they would learn about different types of medicinal plants and treatments for different sicknesses and injuries.

Specifically, boys would learn how to build thatch roof houses, canoes, tools, weapons, animal traps and make string, weave baskets, hammocks and hunt. Girls would learn how to make pottery, how to make string and make special string bags, a Yuca tapioca chicha drink and Yuca tapioca bread and how to take care of babies. Even though both boys and girls would learn how to cook, the girls would specialize in learning how to cook more varied types of food. The duties that are performed by men/boys or women/girls are based on the ancestral tradition, which is related to the Spiritual energy of both sexes as well as the physical strength or natural aptitudes of both sexes.

Unfortunately because of influences by modern civilization, nowadays women have more work than men, for example because of oil exploitation and deforestation there is less game in the forest, so most men living in affected areas do not go hunting any longer which is one duty less, also because in most native communities the people wear some modern-style clothing, most women spend a lot of time washing the clothes for the family which is one duty more.

After the children finish performing their duties they always are permitted to play. They have different games like climbing trees, practice shooting with small blowpipes and small spears, playing in the Aguarico River; swimming or crossing the river in small dug-out canoes, making balsa wood rafts, playing with different toys which their Parents would make from the natural materials found in the forest. One toy which really called my attention was a unique whistling top, which I have patented because I am sure that it could be used as a model for mass producing a unique, fine quality plastic top. (The profits from the patent and or sales of this Amazonian top will support a foundation which I shall create for the Amazonian ethnic communities which still practice their true ethnic religion.)

Amazon whistling tops

**CHAPTER 4**

# • Shamans and the People of Yagé

In order to introduce their children into the Spiritual World, the ethnic natives practice an important, ancient ritual. When a child is six years old, the parents, together with the most powerful Shaman of the community organize this special ceremony. For this story, let us imagine that the most powerful Shaman is an elderly man.

This ritual always takes place shortly after sunset and during a moonless night, at the communal temple of worship, which is reverently referred to as the Beloved Hut of Yagé (Casita de Yagé in Spanish). This hut is quite simple-looking, but please do not be fooled by its plain appearance; within its interior and surrounding area exists a live metaphysical divine energy that is unique and powerful. The invisible forces of God, the Spirits of sacred plants, Shamans and the Spirits of Yagé are the permanent guardians of this area.

Practically the entire community is present, from children of seven years old till Great Grandparents. All of the people are dressed in their best garments, wearing their special ceremonial Yagé jewelry and using fragrantly scented flowers, leaves or strips of barks. Their faces and bodies are beautifully decorated with brightly colored vegetable-dye tattoos. The Shaman who will lead the ceremony, the Father and Mother with their child, are standing in front of the cooking pot of the brew of Yagé.

The ceremony begins with a special chant sung by the people. In some communities, this chant is accompanied with bamboo flutes, drums and seed rattles. The chant lasts for about twenty minutes, afterwards, the Shaman lights a cigar and smokes while at the same time he is shaking a wand of leaves. He begins to sing one of his personal  chants by which he respectfully summons the blessing and presence of a special group of friendly Spirits that the natives refer to as, the "People of Yagé." After singing, he takes the community gourd-bowl, dips it into the large ceramic pot of cooked Yagé, filling it with the brew, then he pours the brew into his personal bowl and slowly drinks the brew. Immediately afterwards, he pours more brew into the Father and Mother's personal bowls and they drink the brew, the Shaman then pours brew into the child's personal bowl and holding the bowl, the Shaman especially blesses the brew and puts the bowl up to the child's mouth to drink. Afterwards, all the people present, will take turns filling their personal bowls and drinking Yagè. The people may go lay in their hammocks which are set up within the Casita de Yagè, or sit on low benches to smoke and chant.

This significant ceremony introduces the children into the most important aspect of life; the glorious, beautiful Spiritual World. After about three years, there will be another similar ceremony with that child, but then the child would drink more quantity of the brew and after that, the child can drink with the adults as much as and as often as she or he wants. The custom of drinking Yagé is never forced on the children. Living under such a society it is quite normal and understandable that all of the children would want to drink Yagé. Since they were babies, they have seen how their older sisters and brothers, Parents, Grandparents and all other adults had always prepared themselves especially beautiful to cheerfully go to the Beloved Hut of Yagé. Also they remember hearing fascinating stories about how wonderful the Spiritual World is and how after drinking the sacred brew, one benefits in everyday life; spiritually, mentally, emotionally and physically.

Obviously, the children have always imagined the Spiritual World as being fascinating and more beautiful than the material world. Within this type of a cultural and social rearing, practically all of the young people from eleven years of age are seriously interested in becoming Shamans.

Unless one of the parents of a child is a powerful Shaman, when that child wants the tutorship of a Shaman, it is customary for the parents to present forms of gratitude and gifts to the Shaman who has accepted to devote years of his or her lifetime in teaching a child. From ten to twelve years old, a child's heart, mind and Spiritual body are still pure and yielding and it is the best time to learn about Shamanism, God and life. All children of about twelve years old, who want to, may become apprentices, and their training will last about five years, but the sacrifices that are required to become a Shaman are not easy to fulfill. These sacrifices include a diet completely free of spicy hot chili peppers, salt and meat, control of the mind, complete honesty, pure thoughts, no anger, complete celibacy, tolerance, and fasting. Of course the periodic, frequent drinking of Yagè is important in the apprenticeship, but it is not considered a sacrifice.

During the last years of apprenticeship, it is required to drink brews of other sacred plants that are even stronger than Yagé. One of these plants is called Guando or Pejí in the Secoya language, (common name in English; Angel's Trumpet. / Brugmansia x insignis species. / Solanaceac family), this plant is a shrub which typically has beautiful, large white, pink, peach or yellow colored trumpet-like flowers. The effects of the brew of Pejí are so strong that an apprentice needs to have a close friend or relative acting as a guardian to accompany her or him during the entire length of the visionary experience, which could last about twenty hours. This guardian should be a responsible person, who will be attentive and stay near the apprentice throughout the entire visionary experience.

The necessity of a guardian is because quite often the visions are so powerful that the person's laying body may accidentally jump out of the hammock and roll into the forest where obviously it could hurt itself. After the apprentice awakens from their visionary experience, the guardian must also be attentive because even though the person is fully awake and walking around, that person may still be experiencing visions where again the person is in risk of hurting her or himself.

The Pejì visionary experience is much stronger than Yagè and the sacred brew of Pejí can never touch the ground. Where as, the Yagé brew can sometimes touch the ground, even though for apprentices it is not recommended. After drinking Pejì , if one needs to vomit, one has to vomit in one's same personal gourd-bowl, and drink the same brew again, and over again if necessary, until the sacred brew of Pejí stays inside one's stomach. With Yagé one never has to do this. The Pejí sacred plant should not be confused with the Golden Angel's Trumpet, (Brugmansia aurea.) This plant has the flower with a red and yellow color combination and the flower is narrower than the Angel's Trumpet. The Golden Angel's trumpet belongs to the same family as the White, Pink, Yellow or Peach Angel Trumpets and is similar looking, but the Golden Angel's Trumpet is always poisonous. Similarly, if the White, Pink, Yellow or Peach Angel Trumpet plants are not handled, cooked or used correctly, they also will be poisonous and could seriously damage one's physical and or mental health. There are other sacred plants, but these two; Yagè and Pejì are the most commonly used. Because the visionary effects of Pejì are so much stronger than Yagè, most of the people are afraid to drink it. All Amazonian sacred plants should only be prepared in the Amazon by an experienced, responsible, true ethnic Shaman or Cooker.

Once an apprentice has become a Shaman then she or he may marry and have children. However, throughout the rest of a Shaman's life, if the Shaman wants to continue maintaining the same level of Spiritual-mental energy, then the Shaman has to continue practicing similar type of requisites as during apprenticeship. One major difference will of course be the new practice of controlled celibacy instead of complete celibacy.

It is believed that if an apprentice lacks the mental, emotional and physical discipline to fulfill with all of the requirements, then that person will be affected by a more difficult obstacle to overcome; physically not being capable of fully digesting the sacred brew. What this means is that after a while of drinking Yagè, the apprentice throws up, consequently the person's body cannot assimilate the complete chemical dosage of the alkaloids. This difficulty will hinder one's personal advancement in obtaining valuable energy and enlightenment from the Spiritual World, which of course is essential to become a Shaman.

Sometimes for an unknown reason, there are apprentices who have a physical condition in their digestive system that does not allow them to fully digest Yagé. If these frustrating digestive complications persist and the apprentice cannot solve the problem, then it is almost certain that the apprentice will give up their apprenticeship.

Generally, if this happens, the ex-apprentice will soon afterwards marry. They still drink a lot of Yagé and they continue to practice their ethnic religion, but their dream of becoming Shamans has ended. Some of these male, ex-Shaman apprentices decide to become Cookers, where they will be cooking the sacred brews for the Shamans, for themselves as well as for the rest of the community. To be a good Cooker also requires certain lifetime sacrifices, but not as difficult sacrifices as for Shamans.

Within ethnic communities, expert Cookers are among the most admired and respected group of people, they are directly responsible for the proper handling, proper cooking and successful visionary experience of the sacred brews! Cookers have a tremendous responsibility to their religion and to their community. Most ethnic communities are made up of many Shamans, a few cookers, many apprentices and many more ex-apprentices who eventually become the common people of the community. In ethnic communities, usually one out of every four adults is a Shaman.

The Shamans and other apprentices know when an apprentice has become a Shaman because one acquires special Spiritual and mental powers. For example; mental control over animals, healing of people with the exclusive power of one's own personal energy by means of using one's hands, and or by forcefully blowing out air, or sucking in air and then expelling the air. Even though the Shamans have the best knowledge on plants than anyone else in the community, they do not rely exclusively on this form of medicine. Using their powerful Spiritual-mental energy, first they heal a sick person by extracting all of the harmful energy of the sickness, then they balance the overall energy of the person and then afterwards, they may use and prescribe medicinal plants as a therapy.

True Shamans have acquired powerful Spiritual enlightenment, this means that there Spiritual-mental body has actually felt and seen the true light of God, because of this their Spiritual-mental, emotional and physical body has assimilated God's glorious energy and strengthened. Because of their Spiritual enlightenment, they have acquired great energy and wisdom for valuing and incorporating everything important within the Spiritual World and material world. Of vital importance is also that they will be able to guide their people into the Spiritual World.

Shamans are always in absolute control of their minds, in this way they can control the temptations of the flesh and reject any impure thoughts. Control of one's mind is one of the most fundamental requirements for truly strengthening the Spiritual body. Additionally, it seems that whenever people are successfully getting closer to God, those people will become more of a target for the devil and consequently those people will receive more temptations from the devil, so again it becomes vital to control the mind.

Powerful God-like Shamans are modest, generous, loving,

wise, truthful, tolerant, strong of character and physically slender. They are always on a special diet; they fast a lot and drink very strong dosages of Yagé and other sacred plants. For an average person a strong dosage brew of Yagé is quite bitter tasting, but for the experienced powerful Shamans the concentrated brew of Yagè does not taste bitter, in fact, for Powerful Shamans these strong brews taste sweet like honey. After drinking strong dosages and large quantities of brews, the powerful Shamans will never throw up.

Apart from all these signs for one realizing when another person has become a Shaman, there is one other infallible method which the elderly Shamans use. At nighttime, during any ceremony of drinking Yagé, the apprentices and Shamans get out of their hammocks a few times to continue drinking more Yagè. As they are walking around, they cannot help but notice that from each person that has taken Yagé there is a glow of beautiful, colorful lights emitting from their bodies and heads. These colorful lights are the auras of each person.

When advanced apprentices look at each other, they will see that their auras are bright colored, but when they look at Shamans, they will see that the auras of the Shamans are much brighter. Then by comparing the auras among the Shamans, they will see that the auras of the most powerful Shamans are the brightest and most beautiful of all.

The Spiritual World is unlimited and because of this, most of the powerful Shamans will dedicate their entire lives to advancing in their personal quest of strengthening their Spiritual body, obtaining the closest possible relationship to God and receiving the maximum amount of Spiritual-mental energy and enlightenment.

While I was living with Don Fernando, he told me different stories about his youthful days as a powerful Shaman. One of his stories that most impressed me was that one night he drank the strongest and most quantity of Yagè as he could, then as he was travelling in the Spiritual World, he attempted to meet God. He flew as high as he could and reached a new area which was far more beautiful and holy than any other region that he had known in the Spiritual World. As he flew deeper into this beautiful space, he could hear, see and feel much stronger and more beautiful the almighty energy of God. Suddenly, two very holy, powerful Spirits that he had never seen before, appeared before him and stopped him, saying; "You can not go any further, go back, because no human from the material world can get any closer to the Father of all."

For the Amazon ethnic people there is absolutely nothing more important in this life than the development of one's Spiritual-mental body, they are highly mystical people and practically everything that they do in their daily lives is in some way related to their religion.

Everyday the families will awaken around 5:00 and the first thing that each member of a family does while still laying in their hammocks is to take turns sharing with the rest of the family, out loud their dreams. All of the family listens attentively to the dreams which are interpreted either from a Spiritual mystical perception or from a humorous point of view. (The people never try to control their dreams; this form of working the mind will surely interfere with one falling asleep). The people believe that at night while the physical body is sleeping and resting, the Spiritual body is completely awake, receptive to messages from the Spiritual world, but also the people believe that some dreams may be a consequence of something in our everyday lives that has disturbed us.

If a person has prepared herself or himself well, and drinks enough Yagé which has been properly handled and cooked, then that person's Spiritual-mental body will be transported through brightly colored astral flights to far away places in the Spiritual World, within the Amazon or even to other countries.

Sometimes, within the Amazonian Spiritual World if one is even more fortunate, these astral flights may take one to unique communities where native Spirits live. These Spirits live in a similar manner as the native communities that are in the material world. There are children, adolescents and adults of all ages who hunt, fish, build houses, make hammocks, pottery, etc…In these special Amazonian Spiritual Worlds, the forests, rivers and lakes are still virgin, filled with plenty of animals, and the Spirits that live there never suffer from problems, accidents, incurable sicknesses or death. They are always beautifully dressed in their ethnic garments, wearing their Yagé jewelry and decorating their faces and bodies with vegetable-dye tattoos, flowers, leaves and brightly colored bird feathers.

These Spirits are always loving, generous, peaceful and good-humored. The ethnic natives refer to these Holy Spirits as the "People of Yagé", because not only are they so real within the Spiritual World, but also because quite frequently they actually make themselves present either directly or indirectly in the material world.

There are People of Yagé communities living within different areas in the Spiritual World. At times, it seems that these Spiritual Worlds exist at a parallel dimension to our materialistic world. As one advances in the Yagé astral flight experiences one will encounter these different levels or dimensions where the different People of Yagé live. For example there are; People of Yagé of the forest, People of Yagé of the rivers and lakes, People of Yagé of the underworld, People of Yagé of the dry season, People of Yagé of the tree top canopy layer, People of Yagé of the clouds, People of Yagé of the sky, People of Yagé of the stars, etc...

All of these diverse People of Yagé are hospitable, friendly and knowledgeable. Happily they always welcome one who has entered into their worlds and they are always willing to share important, useful information for bettering one's life in the material world. In addition, what is most important is the vital energy and information that they will share with the apprentices concerning the more direct path that should be followed in order to advance more in the Spiritual World. All of the apprentices who are disciplined, persistent and fortunate will meet the People of Yagé, but for non-apprentices it is difficult to make contact with the People of Yagé.

I have five stories to present concerning my experiences with the People of Yagé:

• **1st story)** The first time that I had a personal manifestation from the People of Yagé was about ten years ago. I was with a tour group at a campsite on the bank of the Shushufindi River. Emilio, a good friend of mine from the native village of San Pablo de Kanitzaya was our scout. One night after dinner and after the tour group had gone to sleep, Emilio and I were going to drink Yagé, and so we took our hammocks and set them up about 60 m. / 195 ft. from the campsite by the bank of the river.

We drank Yagé, smoked cigars and lay back in our hammocks. After about one hour I began to see fantastic colorful visions and began to feel the awakening of my Spiritual body, after about another hour of seeing beautiful visions suddenly with my eyes closed I saw and "heard" a huge, colorful, beautiful, soothing, comfortably loud explosion occurring directly in the sky overhead our hammocks. I had never had an experience like that explosion before. I was so taken by the spectacular explosion that I opened my eyes and turning towards Emilio asked him "What was that?" Opening his eyes, he turned his head looking at me, and said, "That explosion came from the World of the People of Yagé." I was so happy and pleased to know that Emilio had also heard the explosion. Also, I was thrilled to hear his explanation because at that time, I had still not made contact with the People of Yagé.

On the following morning, as I was recalling my Yagè experience, another interesting aspect of that fascinating explosion dawned on me. Scientifically speaking how can it be possible that two people, who had taken a supposed "hallucinating" drug and are physically separated with their eyes closed, be able to share the same visual and sound effect that is supposedly a product of a hallucination. Once again, we see a clear example of Yagé's property as a telepathic visionary sacred plant and not a mere "hallucinating" drug. But to leave no doubts concerning this conviction, during breakfast that morning I asked the staff and tour group if they had heard any explosions during the night. (Sometimes, because natives are hunting at night, explosions from shotguns may be heard. Even though, shotgun explosions are so distinct and loud that always the native staff members can recognize them.) However, on that previous night, no one had heard any explosions, except for Emilio and me.

• **2nd story)** On another occasion, I was with Santo, a good friend of mine of the Siona tribe. He is from the ethnic community of Campo Eno. Santo is one of the famous Cookers in his community and was an apprentice to becoming a Shaman. We were together with a tour group in the Lagarto Cocha National Park. One night after the tour group had gone to sleep, Santo and I went to the bank of the Cocha Grande Lake where we set up our hammocks and drank Yagé. We were about 40 m. / 130 ft. from the campsite. We were lying in our hammocks, smoking tobacco and talking. Suddenly I heard from the sky, far away the flapping wings of a medium size bird flying towards us and arriving to the exact spot where we were.

I heard it perch on one of the lower branches of a small tree which was about 6 m. / 19 ft. away from our hammocks. After a few minutes, I heard a loud, unique, enchanting birdcall from that tree.

In the past, the only other times that I had heard that same beautiful birdcall was when I had been drinking Yagé and only during the night. I asked Santo what the name of that bird was and what it looked like. He blew a heavy column of white smoke up to the sky and said, "That bird is a special bird, it is a nighthawk that comes from the World of the People of Yagé." Hearing this I quickly sat up and strained my eyes trying to locate it but it was impossible. I got out of my hammock, stood under the tree looking closer into the foliage, but still could not see the bird. Then it called again its unusual song, the bird was but a few meters away from me. Santo looked at me and laughed, then he said "Patricio, my dear friend you can not see that bird, no one can. Only powerful Shamans can see that bird." On other occasions, I have heard that bird and have asked other ethnic natives about the bird and they have all responded in the same way as Santo.

During that same night with Santo, after about an hour, I was already seeing beautiful, colorful visions and during this entire time, the nighthawk continued making its amusing call. Suddenly during a few long seconds, the forest became unusually silent and all of a sudden, from the sky, I heard a man singing loudly a short beautiful song in a native language. This song came from the sky above us and from a southwest direction! The forest animals continued in complete silence for a few more seconds, and then hastily I sat up and looked at Santo, at the same time he opened his eyes and looked at me, and I asked him who had sung that song? He smiled and said that it was a Person from the People of Yagé! At first, I could not believe it, but then analyzing the song better, I realized that it was so beautiful, so clear, so perfect and celestial sounding, that it could not be from this world. Besides this, we were on a small island and the nearest community to us was about twenty kilometers away. No one else was on that island except for the tour group and our staff who were sleeping. Of our native staff, no one had a voice like of that song. Apart from all of this evidence, Santo and I both clearly heard the song coming from the sky.

I asked Santo what the words meant and he told me that he could not translate the words and that I would have to find out for myself the meaning of the words. (I think that he did not want to talk about the words of the song as a precaution so as not to lose some of his Spiritual energy.) Then I said, "But how can I possibly understand the words of the People of Yagé, if I don't even understand the Siona language?" To this he responded, "Once the People of Yagé make contact with you and start talking to you, you will instantly understand their words and immediately learn the native language that they are talking in. This same statement I have heard a few times in the past from different Shaman friends of other tribes.

Soon afterwards, Santo got up from his hammock to drink more Yagé and then after a while I also got up to drink more. After drinking the brew, he returned to his hammock. I went to the bank of the lake and was looking out at the spectacular visions over the lake, forest and sky. I was feeling especially strong, more so than on other occasions, I started thinking about the Person of Yagé who had just sang that incredibly wonderful song and then I walked into the forest for about 100 m. / 328 ft. I was barefoot which was not a good idea, but I wanted to be alone, thinking that I could make contact with the People of Yagé if I was completely alone. It was completely dark, I had my flashlight on as I was walking, but for a long time as I was standing and sitting on a fallen tree, my flashlight was off, as with other Yagé experiences I had acquired a certain degree of night vision. I stayed in the forest for about an hour but nothing happened, so I decided to go back. I walked into the clearing of the campsite. All of the tourists and the staff were in the hut sleeping and Santo was in his hammock.

Throughout this entire time, as usual, there were millions of brightly colorful visions changing and moving around and these visions were accompanied by the magnificent orchestra of animal sounds from the forest and lake. All at once, I stopped walking because I noticed a strange, distinct loud marching sound. I paid closer attention to this sound, trying to locate it and at that second, I realized that it was coming from the ground right in front of me. I listened more carefully, but did not see anything, so I turned on my flashlight and located where the sound was coming from, it was ahead of me on the ground, but I could not see anything. Looking again more attentively, suddenly I saw about 1m. / 3 ft. in front of my feet a column of one centimeter long / one third of an inch ants making their way through the thick grass of the clearing.

Seeing the ants left me completely overwhelmed. On all other occasions, my hearing had always become keen, but this time there had been such an incredible improvement. I was so surprised and happy to witness this and at the same time, I felt much stronger physically and mentally. At that time I still did not have much experience drinking Yagé, so suddenly I felt an urge to test my strength, I looked at a small tree that was about 10m. / 33 ft. away and forcefully blew air at it. The branches and leaves moved as if a torrential wind had hit them, surprised and pleased to see this extraordinary new energy that I had, I did the same with two other trees and also saw the leaves and branches moving.

Then I looked back and saw Santo sitting on an old fallen tree next to the cooking pot of Yagé, he was drinking more brew and smoking. I went to him, sat down and also drank more Yagé. After he finished drinking Yagé he smiled at me and said, "Patricio, you shouldn't waste your energy on insignificant matters of this material world. If you continue to do that, then you will never become a Shaman. Stay in your hammock, you should not be walking around unless it is to drink more Yagé or to chant out loud or play a musical instrument in honor to God or to the People of Yagé." Santo then smiled, stood up and went to lie in his hammock.

(My friend was right, I had heard this before from Reynaldo

and from other native friends, but at that time I still did not have enough mind-control, it is not easy, the mind wanders off so quickly and takes our senses away with it. I think that especially for people brought up in a modern society, it is more difficult to control the mind. In our modern culture, since we are children, we have daily training to develop our brain and physical body; our minds are constantly flooded by so much information and images from television, movies, videos, etc… Our modern world is very fast with so much information that excites our senses. I think that because of all of this, the great majority of minds from modern societies are much more hyperactive than the minds of the ethnic Amazonian people.)

After a few more minutes of finishing my cup of Yagé, I went to my hammock, lay down, smoked and had another one of many marvelous experiences in the Spiritual World. I was seeing incredibly beautiful colorful visions, and I felt a true strengthening of my Spiritual body and a personal, glorious, intense relationship with God.

The following morning, Santo and I were up early and we went to bathe in the lake. We then took down our hammocks and went to the main hut of the campsite. There was an unusual, heavy mist in the air, quite different to the normal Amazonian atmosphere that I have seen hundreds of times in the past. Everyone was still sleeping and I knew that the previous night with Yagé had been exceptionally unusual for me as well as for that area of the forest, many strange things had happened within the campsite and close to the tourists. Normally, Yagé should be drunk at least 300m. / 990 ft. away from other people who are not drinking the brew. However, on that occasion, Santo and I had no choice, we were on a small island, so we drank the sacred brew as far away as we could from the campsite, but it was still too close. At that moment, I became interested in verifying whether the power of Yagé could affect someone who had not taken the brew, but was nearby another person who had taken the brew.

Soon the cook Carlos and the staff awakened, they bathed and started to prepare breakfast. After a while, my tour group of twelve British also began to awaken and finally after about forty minutes we were all sitting at the table having our breakfast. But at the table there was a peculiar situation because no one had yet said a single word. After about fifteen minutes of complete silence, I decided to break the abnormal serenity and said "Well, how did all of you sleep?" Suddenly all at once, everyone started talking at the same time, they were all telling their dreams. After about a minute, they got organized so that each person could talk at once, strangely enough each member of the tour group began describing their dreams which were unusually bizarre, eventually they all realized and agreed that the night before had certainly been quite strange.

I translated some of these dreams to Santo, until eventually he whispered to my ear that all of these strange dreams were a result of the presence of the Person of Yagé who sang the song. I then got up and went to the kitchen where I asked our cook Carlos and the staff if any of them had heard a man loudly singing a song during the night. No one had heard any song, but then Carlos said something surprising. "Patricio, last night after dinner, Jose and I went to wash the dinner dishes at a fallen tree which is next to the bank, because it was late we were tired and we hadn't finished washing all the dishes, so this morning we went to the same spot to finish washing the dishes and we found a large leaf which had been deliberately folded and placed on the fallen tree. That leaf was not there last night, and I have already inquired with the staff and no one else had gone there during the night or early this morning. For sure, last night someone else apart from our group had been on this island!" (Typically, in the jungle when a native person wants to sit on a fallen tree, log or even on the ground, she or he will collect one or a few fresh, thick, large leaves, turn them backwards, set them down and then sit directly on them. This is done to prevent the dangerous fungus that is always growing on the ground, on fallen trees or logs from coming into contact with the skin and causing a serious skin health problem.)

With the entire staff, which was our cook Carlos Segovia, three natives, Santo and myself we went to investigate the leaf. Seeing the folded 50cm. / 20 in. leaf, we all affirmed that none of us had placed that large leaf there. Santo and the other two natives carefully began to study the leaf and the surrounding area and after a few minutes, they positively confirmed that the previous night a native person had been on the island, placed the leaf there and had been sitting on it. Santo then looked at me and at all of us and said, "Last night, a man from the People of Yagé visited our campsite, first he sang a beautiful song from the sky, and then he made himself physically present here in this area." Then Santo told me that the leaf on the log was in the exact southwest direction from where we had heard the song.

• **3rd story**) On many occasions Reynaldo had talked to me about his experiences with the People of Yagé. His father was a powerful and famous Shaman and since Reynaldo was about twelve years old, he was an apprentice to becoming a Shaman. As an apprentice, he was drinking a lot of Yagé and eventually he travelled to the different Spiritual Worlds of the People of Yagé. Soon all of the People of Yagé that he was meeting became dear friends of his. When Reynaldo was seventeen years old, a group of Protestant-Evangelical missionaries from the U.S. arrived to his village bringing many gifts. After about a year of living in the village, these missionaries eventually convinced practically all of the community, except for Don Fernando and a few elders, to be formally baptized into the Evangelical religion.

Shortly after this event, the missionaries persuaded the natives, including Reynaldo to stop drinking Yagé and other sacred brews. After this, while Reynaldo would go into the forest to collect medicinal plants, hunt or at any time while he was alone, some of the People of Yagé friends would appear to him. They would ask him why he does not drink Yagé anymore, and then they would try to convince him to drink the sacred brews again. On other occasions while Reynaldo was paddling his canoe on a small river, as he turned a bend in the river, there in front of him on the bank he would see a large group of his People of Yagé friends. They were all dressed in their beautiful ethnic dress using their Yagé jewelry, greeting him and pleading for him to visit them. These numerous encounters with the People of Yagé went on for many months until eventually one day they stopped visiting him.

• **4th story)**  My dear Shaman friends have always taught me that the People of Yagé like very much for one to use the Yagé jewelry when drinking the sacred brews, and very important is that no other person should ever touch one's personal Yagé jewelry. One day as I had just arrived to Quito from the jungle and was unpacking my bags, my wife Lily saw one of my Yagè seed necklaces and commented on how beautiful and unique of a necklace it was. Then I saw her wanting to pick it up, so quickly I explained to her about the peculiar metaphysical energy of Yagé, and begged her not to touch the necklace. However, she did not pay attention to me and said that I should not be so superstitious; she said that she just wanted to admire it better. She picked up the necklace and walked to the sunlit window where she looked at it closer and then she went to a nearby mirror on the wall and put the necklace around her neck.

Almost instantly, upon putting it on, she was startled, she protested and quickly took off the necklace throwing it down to the floor. I asked her what was wrong and she said that the necklace had suddenly smelled terribly bad and that she felt it vibrating on her skin. After some time I went back to the jungle and told this story to my Shaman friends. They laughed saying that my wife was highly receptive and that she would make a good Shaman, also they said that this happened to her because of the powerful energy of the Spirit of Yagé as well as also because of the powerful energy of the People of Yagé.

• **5th story)** Included in my personal Yagé jewelry I use a special gift which was given to me by my dear native friend Esteban. This gift is a unique large seed about 4cm. / one and a half inch long. This beautiful seed has a natural shape of a trumpet. Esteban personally received this seed as gift from one of the Persons of Yagè while he was visiting one of the People of Yagé communities in the Spiritual World. In some People of Yagé communities, the People use these seeds as whistles to call the Guangana wild boars, these white lipped peccaries have always been one of the favorite meats for all Amazonian tribes.

During Esteban's Yagé experience, by which he received the seed, he returned to the material world. Still laying in his hammock he gradually recovered full consciousness. He could still feel the large seed in his hand which he had so dearly protected during the night. Slowly he opened his eyes, carefully he opened his hand and there in the palm of his hand was the valuable treasure.

After years of visiting the People of Yagé communities, Esteban had eventually acquired a few of these seed whistles. After he gave me one of his whistles, he told me that whenever I am near any native community and after I drink Yagé I should blow the whistle a few times during the night to call the Guangana wild boars.

It is not necessary for the whistle to sound loud because the energy of Yagé combined with the energy of the People of Yagé would force the metaphysical sound of the whistle to travel far away, deep into the forest to locate any nearby pack of wild boars.

Trumpet shaped whistling seed from the World of Yagè

According to Esteban and my Shamans friends, after the leader of the pack of wild boars heard the whistle, he would always travel during the night, leading his pack towards the area where the whistle sound came from. Each time that I'm going to drink Yagé, the natives of the area where I am going to drink Yagè and who know that I have this special whistle will organize a hunting party for early the following morning. In the majority of the cases where this has happened, the native men were able to hunt wild boars somewhere near to where I drank Yagé. Unfortunately, because of Oil exploitation, deforestation, African palm oil plantations and road building, today there are not as many packs of wild boars as in the past.

Whenever I use my Yagé necklace and meet new Amazonian ethnic communities or even modernized native communities, the natives, particularly the elders always look especially attentive at the Yagé trumpet-seed that is around my neck. After a few minutes of observing it carefully, they are always astonished by it, because they know that it does not come from this materialistic world, it comes from one of the Spiritual Worlds of the People of Yagé. Apart from these types of special trumpet-seed whistles, the People of Yagé give other unique object gifts to fortunate natives.

For many years, I have witnessed abundant, unusual, supernatural events caused by the People of Yagé. These events have occurred directly to me, as well as also to many of my native friends.

All of what one sees in the Amazon Spiritual World should be kept as a personal religious experience. To reveal ones Spiritual state, expands ones Spiritual energy, which consequently weakens it.

Because of this, I should not give anymore information about the People of Yagè and I cannot explain the role they play in the Yagé Spiritual World, or the mysterious relationship that exists between them, God, the Sacred plant of Yagé and the Amazonian ethnic religion, but I have no doubt that they really do exist. What is difficult to believe, but it is true is that they have the power to manifest their influence, or personally appear in our material world.

**CHAPTER 5**

## • Evil Shamans and the Devil

$A$s in the Chinese philosophy of Yin and Yang: the forces of negative and positive, feminine and masculine, night and day, life and death, moon and sun, unconscious and conscious, etc., are always present and necessary in a co-existing relationship. All two opposite forces need of each other for their mutual existence, and only by the two existing, can we fully understand and appreciate them. If it were not for darkness, we would not be able to understand and appreciate lightness, and vice versa. In the heart of each is the seed of the other, and precisely this is why they exist in balance. We should accept the natural, necessary existence of any two opposite forces; this is in accordance with the laws of God.

In this unjust, complicated world, the best way for us to try to achieve a healthy balance is never to get fanatical with any extremist opposite forces. We should try and always practice mind control, unconditional love for all, honesty, generosity, tolerance and humbleness. Many Holy people throughout history have emphasized the importance of being tolerant, not criticizing or judging and of finding a middle point between two extreme opposite forces.

In the Gospel of Thomas, there is an important message by Jesus in relation to Polarity:

*Jesus said to them:*
*When you can make the two as one,*
*and you make the inner as the outer*
*and the outer as the inner, and the above*
*as the below, and when you make the male and*
*the female as a single one; so that the male*
*is not male and the female is not female,*

*when you make eyes in place of an eye,*
*and a hand in place of a hand, and a foot in*
*place of a foot, and an image in place of an image,*
*then you will enter the kingdom.*

The Amazon ethnic natives believe that the most powerful opposite forces of energy that exist in our universe are God and the devil. Before Catholic or Protestant Evangelical missionaries ever-stepped foot into South America or the Amazon, the ethnic natives already believed in the existence of God and the devil.

The Shamans and the ethnic natives believe that the devil with its evil energy is present here in this material world as well as within the Spiritual World. They also believe that in general, between the Spiritual and the material worlds, God's energy exists in perfect balance to the devil's energy, but in the end, the energy of God is much more powerful than the energy of the devil.

Unless one has the aid of a powerful, Spiritual tool like Yagé, the existence of God as well as the existence of the devil is difficult for most humans to accept as true. Through Yagé, one will be transported to the Spiritual World where one will see and feel the true glorious energy of God, and eventually after months of drinking more Yagè one will perceive the wicked energy of the devil.

All people who drink a lot of Yagé will eventually see demons. The first time that I saw demons was fifteen years ago, along the Putumayo River. This important tributary to the Amazon River is a natural geographical boundary between the Amazon jungle of Ecuador and Colombia.

I was on a visit to a Colombian Cofan community of Shamans. During one night of drinking Yagé with my friends and after a few hours of having seeing many beautiful visions, I opened my eyes to get out of my hammock. Suddenly in the distance, I noticed up in the sky together with the rest of my visions, a strange looking face.

This face called my attention, because in all my past Yagé experiences I had never before seen an unusual face like that. I decided to investigate this vision so I lay back in my hammock, closed my eyes and still seeing the face, I began to analyze it. Almost immediately, the face became clearer. It had been looking to one side, but as I observed it more attentively, it changed from abnormally strange to very ugly and at the same time it began to turn its neck until it was looking directly at me and then it smiled at me.

The sudden appearance of this grotesque face puzzled me. Where had it come from and why was it there? In the past, each detail of my visions had always been incredibly beautiful, and in this vision, every aspect was beautiful, with the exception of this horrific face. Looking around at the rest of the vision that was all around me, I suddenly noticed that there were two other similar-looking ugly faces looking at me and smiling.

Even though I felt uneasy with these three ugly faces, I did not feel at all frightened. After drinking Yagé, the Spiritual body will strengthen so much that one always feels confident and spiritually, mentally, emotionally and physically strong. It is as if God were holding one by the hand and in such a circumstance, one will never be afraid of anything horrible or terrifying that can exist in the universe.

Not knowing what these faces meant was confusing to me, but I was certain that they could not be from a good source, so I decided to ignore them. After a while, I went to the pot of Yagé and drank more. I smoked and returned to my hammock, closed my eyes and realized that the three faces had disappeared.

The following morning I mentioned these faces to my Shaman friends, and smiling they said, "Patricio, those faces are of devils. They sometimes appear and they will do their best to convert you and all people to their world." Hearing this shocked me, in the past I had never believed that the devil could exist. Then I asked, "What should I do if they present themselves again?" They said, "Nothing can be done to stop them from appearing, but once they are present, you can either ignore them or if you feel that you're strong enough, you can pay attention to them and they will make contact with you." Not understanding, I then said, "But why would I want to make contact with them?" They then said, "Patricio, if you want to become a very powerful Shaman you have to make contact with them, learn of their world, and then you would have more knowledge of the entire Spiritual World."

Obviously, my friends were giving me recommendations to become a powerful God-like Shaman that would use the devil only as an educational experience and not for forming alliances with the devil as evil Shamans do.

Talking with other Shamans about the devil, I have concluded that for apprentices it is better not to make contact with the devil, the chances of this relationship becoming dangerous for the apprentice are too high. Most people, even powerful apprentices will become easy prey to the dominant, evil energy of the devil. The majority of the Shamans are God-like, but there are also some Shamans who should never be trusted, they are evil and dangerous. These evil Shamans drink Yagé, but they have allied with the devil, they perform witchcraft by which they harm and kill people!

In most cases, apprentices become evil Shamans because their teachers were evil Shamans, but it is also possible that an apprentice may have had the tutorship of a God-like Shaman and that during the Yagé visionary experiences, the apprentice made contact with the devil. The temptation that the devil offers to attract people is an immediate acquisition of supernatural powers. All apprentices who become God-like Shamans eventually acquire great supernatural powers but the hardships that must be endured during the estimated five year apprenticeship are difficult and some people are not success-ful, precisely this is when the devil has an opportunity of recruiting people.

The devil is more astute and more powerful than most humans and soon obtains complete control over the weak mind of its victim. The apprentice will begin to receive direct apprenticeship from the devil and will eventually become an eternal servant of the devil. The apprentice has to do many strange things to feed her or his growing evil energy, for example the apprentice has to go into the forest at night and catch live lizards, frogs, spiders and other small animals and swallow them whole. Also the apprentice has to go into the forest and search for a special black and white, iridescent night frog that is calling loudly from a hollow tree. This frog is only a few centimeters in size, yet it needs to compete with all the other nocturnal animal sounds. By calling from inside a hollow tree with water in its base, the frog is able to produce one of the loudest animal calls in the Amazon.

At night, the apprentice will follow the call of the frog, find the hollow tree and looking inside the tree's base, the appren-tice will see water with many small animals that live there, as well as also the droppings of bats, snakes, iguanas, rats, weasels and corpses of decomposed animals. The apprentice has to collect and drink a gourd full of this rotten water.

Digesting so many inhuman, unnatural things will act meta-physically in the apprentice's mental, physical, emotional and Spiritual bodies. These abnormal horrifying acts will feed the evil energy that is growing and gradually taking over the apprentice.

This malevolent energy that is living inside the apprentice will actually begin to materialize itself in the apprentice's stomach by means of iridescent white or lime-green witchcraft darts that are used each time that the evil apprentice or evil Shaman wants to defend her or himself from witchcraft or wants to cast a harmful or deadly spell. As these darts are being used, the evil apprentices or evil Shamans have to be continuously renewing their malicious energy, these magical witchcraft darts may also be obtained directly from another Shaman. Evil Shamans may regurgitate these witchcraft darts onto the palm of their hand and give them to a person in exchange for something valuable; the person that receives these darts must immediately swallow them.

As the apprentices of evil energy acquire supernatural powers, they will begin to change in accordance to the strengthening of the evil energy that is growing inside of them. Frequently their faces will take on harsh, unattractive features and their voices will become deeper or strangely different. They enjoy killing, not only hunting for food, but more so for personal pleasure. Usually their physical bodies will acquire a sulfur type of odor. In time, when the family or close friends become aware of these changes, the family and others will develop a more distant relationship with the apprentice.

The powerful God-like Shamans have two different methods by which they can tell if an apprentice or Shaman has allied with the devil. The first method occurs during nocturnal astral flights in the jungle where they may observe a person suspiciously collecting small animals. The second method is if a God-like Shaman sees the aura of the apprentice, after she or he has taken Yagé. After drinking Yagé or any of the other sacred brews, the light and colors of that person's aura will always be revealed to all Shamans and advanced apprentices. All people who follow the glorious Spiritual path to God always have beautifully rainbow colored auras, but if a person has an aura which looks like a blinding white light, similar to looking directly at the sun, then that person is in alliance with the devil. Soon after the God-like Shamans discover this, they will spread the word among the community and out of fear; the people will begin to isolate that evil apprentice. Eventually the majority of the native families will force that person to abandon the community, either alone or with her or his family.

Criminal, evil Shamans have caused much harm to many innocent and honest Amazonian people. Throughout centuries, many deaths, family feuds, inter –community or inter-tribal wars and in general, much suffering has occurred because of witchcraft. If a person dies because of witchcraft and the victim's family catches the evil Shaman, most certainly they will try to kill the evil Shaman.

Unfortunately, this terrible situation of evil Shamans may get worse because there are dishonest Shamans or imposter Shamans who may feed on the fear that people have concerning witchcraft. They take advantage of trust of their patients and because of their inefficiency in detecting the true source of the sickness or because they want to make more of a profit, they may diagnose an ailment as a product of witchcraft. They go as far as to lie to their patients by telling them the name of the "supposed" person who cast the spell! The name could be of any evil Shaman who they know or they may accuse any innocent person who they dislike. With this type of diagnose, typically the patient or patient's family want revenge and may contract the same dishonest Shaman to send a deadly spell to the person supposedly responsible for the witchcraft.

Something in relation to witchcraft once happened to me about eight years ago. I was traveling in a canoe on the Aguarico River with a group of native friends. One of my good friends was Emilio, whom I had known for years, our friendship was so strong, that we had often drank Yagé together. He was feeling sick those days and decided that he would like to stop at a "famous" Shaman's house along the river. Soon we arrived to the Shaman's property, we tied the canoe to a tree and we accompanied Emilio.

Emilio went inside the Shamans hut, while we waited outside. After about an hour Emilio came out of the hut visibly worried, he did not say a word. We boarded our canoe and left.

I noticed that Emilio looked upset, so I asked him what the Shaman had said. He did not answer and was reluctant to talk, finally after much persistence by me, he said, "The Shaman told me that you had cast an evil spell on me." I could not believe what I had heard, I had personally known this Shaman for a long time and I always thought that he was an honest person. Since the first day that I began going to the jungle, I have always had an honest, generous relationship and friendship with all native people, including Emilio. Fortunately, because of this, I was able to convince my friend, that this Shaman was a liar.

A powerful spell of witchcraft killed Marcelino a dear friend of mine who was Reynaldo's oldest son. In addition, out of revenge, Genaro another dear friend of the Siona tribe was killed because he had been dishonestly accused of casting a spell of witchcraft to another native. Typically, in the Amazon, after a person dies of witchcraft, a dark mark in the shape of a dart or a spear appears on the skin, usually across the chest or back. Fortunately, it was only once that I had a harmful spell of witchcraft cast against me by an evil Shaman, which a Shaman friend cured.

It is distressing to think that innocent people in the Amazon may become victims of cowardly, dishonest, evil Shamans or evil apprentices. Yes, the devil is at the source of all evil and witchcraft; however, the devil is not only in the Amazon with the ethnic native people, the devil is present throughout the entire world. The devil is actively at work, lurking through all human societies trying to spread its evil force to each person on this planet.

In reality, the devil's influence is much more successful in modern societies than in the Amazonian ethnic communities. In these small communities, you rarely find so much dishonesty, hypocrisy, injustice, and violence as you always find in modern societies.

In the Amazon, we find Shamans who have chosen to

become evil, this is wrong, but that does not give us the right to generalize and condemn the wonderful Amazonian ethnic religion. Even in some highly organized religions from modern societies, we find dishonest leaders who have sided with the evil energy of the devil. This is the case with the televangelist preacher Jimmy Swaggart who in 1987 was caught committing adultery and having sexual relations with prostitutes in motels, or also the discovered cases of pedophilia that were performed by different priests of the Catholic church from 1995 till 2002.

In 2005, the famous U.S. televangelist preacher and religious leader Pat Robertson (Club 700) expressed the need for the U.S. government to kill the President of Venezuela Hugo Chavez. One of God's most important laws, which is accepted by all religions, is that humans do not have the right to kill. Certainly, Mr. Robertson has read the "Ten Commandments", however it is obvious that he has never had a true Spiritual awakening of his Soul and of course has never experienced a true closeness with the glorious energy of God; otherwise, he would have never declared such an immoral, devil-like, political statement.

Throughout the Amazon material world, as in all materialistic societies in the world, the devil is invisible to the human eye, but in the Amazon Spiritual World, the devil cannot hide itself. All people who begin to drink Yagé will see and feel the powerful, divine energy of God, and then much later after drinking more Yagè they will see the devil. Precisely because of these encounters, all of the ethnic natives believe that the devil exists and the majority of them will reject the devil and its evil energy. However, in modern societies, since people are not able to see the devil, they cannot relate to the devil and consequently the majority of people do not believe that the devil exists. This situation of course becomes a great advantage for the devil and its energy.

For the same reason, since most of the people in modern

societies have not personally felt God's divine energy, the majority of them do not believe in God's existence. Then also, there are people who say they "believe in God", but since they have never truly felt God's divine energy, they do not give much importance to their conduct. If I had not experienced a true and personal relationship with God's divine energy, surely my philosophy and behavior would be different to what it is now.

In the eyes of God, each human being is equal. After our physical body dies; our religion, race, nationality or culture will not matter. God will judge us by looking into our heart and seeing how much unconditional love we have transmitted to others during our life, and also God will evaluate the strength of our Spiritual body, as well as also evaluate each good and bad deed that we have created here in this material world according to our possibilities.

After you have truly awakened your Spiritual body with Yagè or with another effective religious pathway, you will have a profound desire to communicate with God. By doing so, you will be enriching more your Spiritual body with God's energy.

By communicating as much as you can, every day with God and by practicing every minute of your lives unconditional love for all, tolerance, honesty, generosity and humbleness, you will find a personal balance, which will help you live in peace, wisdom, good health and happiness in this modern, material world, where unfortunately the devil's evil energy is so successful.

CHAPTER 6

# • My Spiritual Pathway

As a child, my inherited Spiritual path was the Catholic religion, the day I received my first communion, was one of the happiest days at that time in my life. I remember doing my best to practice my religion. With my sister and two brothers, we studied in Catholic elementary and high schools in the United States. Every Sunday we accompanied our Mother to Mass, but as I grew older, I became disillusioned with the Catholic religion because my Spirituality was not growing. I never felt a personal awareness of my Spiritual body existing.

Disappointed with this lack of Spiritual identity, I soon found myself questioning different aspects of how the Catholic Church was practicing the religion. Not convinced by the answers that I received, I experienced an unpleasant gap growing between the Catholic Church and myself. Years of misunderstanding, frustrations and lacking a true Spiritual awareness became so traumatic that by twenty years old, I had became an atheist.

Initially it was an interest in Anthropology and Tourism, which motivated me to investigate and learn about the native cultures. This is why I drank Yagè with Don Piwali and later, why I drank Yagè with Reynaldo. However little did I imagine that this plant would have such a powerful effect on me. Immediately, my original interest in Anthropology and Tourism changed into something much more significant; a personal quest to strengthen my Spirituality.

My life took on a new meaning and consequently after years of research, I created my own, unique, personal Spiritual path that has enabled me to strengthen as much as possible my Spiritual body and feel God's true, magnificent energy alive within me. I shall always be grateful to God and to my dear friends Reynaldo and Esteban for allowing me the opportunity of discovering the magnificent Amazon Spiritual World, through which I have become a healthier, happier, more complete and balanced person.

Since fifteen years ago, I have personally adopted this valuable, ancestral South American religion of Yagè as the most important part of my religion. Part of my Spiritual philosophy also includes certain beliefs and practices of Yoga and the teachings of Jesus Christ.

In this chapter, I shall be presenting certain aspects of my philosophy about Spirituality. In addition, I shall be presenting different practices, which have helped me and I am sure will help you in your Spiritual growth, regardless of which religion you practice.

When God made humans to his-her image, it means that God made us to his-her Spiritual image, not physical image. Unfortunately, many years ago the Vatican, as well as some Christian Churches have distorted this essential nature of God. Within their little minds, they actually transformed the almighty, glorious, universal existence and energy of God into a human being. They gave God a race, "obviously" the white race, and then they gave God a sex, "obviously" the male sex. During hundreds of years, this terrible falsehood has deprived millions of followers from obtaining a true, direct, personal, Spiritual relationship with God, a sacred right that has naturally always existed inside everyone. What is terrible also is that for hundreds of years, this dishonest interpretation of God has subconsciously fed the dreadful, stupid, racist feeling of "white superiority".

In reality, God's divine Spiritual energy has always been inside the Spiritual body of each person here on Earth; therefore, since we have inside of us the same holy nature as God, then as God, we are sacred beings. This is magnificent, but there is one minor problem, and this is that we cannot feel this sacred Spiritual energy of God in us, unless we truly awaken our Spiritual body. Only then will we feel this powerful, vibrantly live sacred, Spiritual energy of God within ourselves, as well as also, we will be able to perceive this glorious energy of God within other humans and all other living species in this world.

Your Spiritual body is composed of sacred energy that derives from the same divine, sacred energy of God: just a tiny spark from the magnificent light and energy of God.
Within your physical body, this sacred energy is concentrated in your seven chakras and your Spiritual-mental body. However, for most of us brought up in a modern, western type of society, throughout nearly all of our lifetime, our chakras and Spiritual body have lived in a sad, weakened state of dormancy.

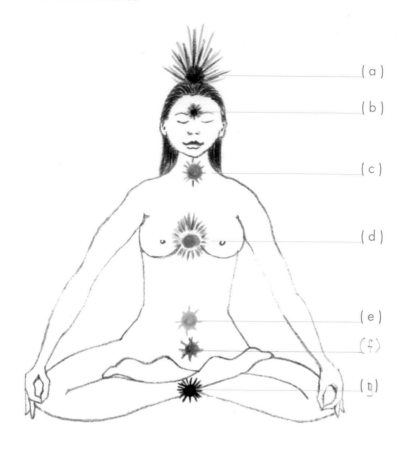

( a ) Sahasrara
( b ) Ajna
( c ) Visuddha
( d ) Anahata
( e ) Manioura
( f ) Svadhisthana
( g ) Muladhara

For your Spiritual body to truly awaken, you have to first awaken your chakras. The chakras are seven special, metaphysical energy points in the human body that were first recorded by enlightened, holy, Asiatic religious leaders and philosophers, centuries ago. At the birth of our physical body, God assured that our chakras and Spiritual body were fully awakened; because of this, our Spiritual-mental-emotional and physical bodies were equally balanced and integrated. This wonderful, perfectly balanced relationship between our four bodies existed until we were about six years old, then gradually this balance and integration began to deteriorate.

This occurred because of three reasons; first, no one ever taught us how to strengthen our chakras and Spiritual body, our parents and family did not know how. Secondly, our parents and family were too preoccupied on developing our mental and physical bodies. Thirdly, many different biased political, economical and social points of view began to come into our mind, influencing us in a harmful manner, affecting our point of view, our character and the health of our equally balanced Spiritual, mental, emotional and physical body. In general, these points of view were coming from different sources of our society, like our Parents, classmates, teachers, government leaders, church leaders, television, news media, etc.

All of this harmful energy that we were assimilating, influenced our young, innocent mental and emotional bodies. Consequently as children, we began to create our own non-tolerant and hostile energy like; criticizing and judging other people, cultures, races, nations, religions, styles of dress, physical appearances, etc… This type of harmful energy that we were producing was weakening more our naturally awakened Spiritual, God-like body. This has brought upon us terrible consequences that affected us at that moment in our lives, but also have developed into serious problems, which have effected our adulthood.

Since early childhood years; our Great-Grandparents, Grandparents, and Parents have been victims of the same type of modern society social pressures influencing and molding their philosophy and character, but also they have been victims of simply not knowing how to truly strengthen and or awaken their Spiritual bodies.

Our parents taught us from their point of view, what they considered the best philosophy and behavior for living this life. Unfortunately, some of what we have learned from them, as well some of what we have learned from our teachers, church leaders, and certainly from our government or television as "right or wrong", "good or bad", "normal or abnormal" was almost certainly inaccurate. These polarized ways of looking at life and the action of criticizing or judging is terribly harmful for our Spiritual, mental, emotional and physical bodies and will only push us further away from God.

Years of polarized thoughts, harmful words and actions, violent images coming into your mind especially from television have gradually covered your naturally awakened, God-like Spiritual-mental body with an accumulation of damaging energy that has suffocated the light of God that is in your Spiritual body.

If you do not take-off that harmful energy and allow the light and energy of your Spiritual body to illuminate freely within your interior and within your lives, then the sacred energy of God will weaken so much, that it will exist only in a pathetic state of suffering. Its desperation will be screaming out at your mind, claiming its natural birthright existence, but its frail voice is being unnoticed by your ignorance, loud noises and harmful pleasures of your flesh.

Only, when your Spiritual body is truly awakened and strengthened, will your four bodies become one, then and only then, will you be complete. As it states in the wise Yoga philosophy, when a person's four bodies are in balance, then that person will become one with God. Obviously, this condition of oneness with God will fill your lives with complete harmony and happiness.

In our modern society, the easiest way for you to start awakening your chakras and Spiritual body is by first getting rid of the years of accumulated harmful energy. To do this, first, you should objectively analyze all of your perspectives on life, and avoiding all extremist positions, you should consciously change your point of view and learn to control your mind, emotions and actions, so that they will be in accordance to God's energy. As I have often heard the dear, wise, enlightened, international Holy lecturer, healer and teacher Axel Rudin say, "You have to change the hard disc that has been previously placed into your brain, and then on a minute-to-minute basis, you have to become conscious creators of your lives." And starting all over again, you should consciously practice what you have not practiced sufficient of during your past lifetime: total mind control, unconditional love for all beings, complete honesty, tolerance, generosity and humbleness. This vital step of changing your perspective on life and acting according to God's benevolent energy has to be undertaken as soon as possible. This will not only help you to get rid of the past, accumulated, harmful energy that is overpowering your sacred God-like energy and destroying your health, but also this vital step will begin to awaken again God's divine energy in your Spiritual body. This is most helpful for preparing you to drink Yagé and / or for following any other Spiritual pathway that is effective in truly strengthening your Spiritual body.

You should never criticize or judge and if you have nothing nice or pleasant to say about someone or something, it is healthier for you to keep silent. You should always attempt to transmit cheerful, loving, friendly, harmonious energy to all people. If you have a past grudge with someone, you should sincerely forgive that person and forget the fault that the person committed against you. In the same way, you should look into your past and if you have acted wrong against someone, then you should ask that person for forgiveness and make up for your fault. This will be healthier for you and for other people who are involved. It is much better for you to make up for your mistakes as soon as possible here in this material world and not in your next life.

On a minute-to-minute basis, you should practice mental control; this is an important way of strengthening your Spiritual body. You should never get angry and you should never permit evil thoughts to enter your mind, you should only permit righteous thoughts to enter your mind. The mind is a powerful form of energy, by learning to control your mind you can obtain great benefits. Do not waste the valuable, powerful energy of your mind on absurd fits of anger or bad thoughts. If you do not control your mind, then you will be losing much valuable, powerful mental energy and your overall Spiritual, mental, emotional and physical health will weaken

During every second of your lives, by means of your thoughts, emotions and deeds, you are creating energy. The energy that you create will act like a magnet, in the sense that all of the good energy that you produce here in this material world will always attract more good energy, either in this material world and or in your next life. Similarly, all of the harmful energy that you produce here in this material world will attract more harmful energy that will affect you here in this material world and or in your next life.

If you are loving, humble, honest, generous, tolerant, forgiving etc., then this energy through other people or God will someday come back to you. However, if on the other hand, you are dishonest, aggressive, non-tolerant, greedy, stingy, etc., then this energy that you have produced will also someday come back to you. Whether you believe in God or not may not matter to you at this moment, but for sure someday, you will have to pay for any harmful energy that you created here in this life.

The light of God is in each atom and in each living being in this universe, and precisely because of this, if you harm others, you harm God.

When your physical body dies, automatically your Spiritual-mental body will awaken and be completely alive in its glorious, powerful, God-like state; this will be a moment of great ecstasy for you. Finally your Spiritual-mental body will be completely liberated from this material world, your Spiritual-mental body will begin a marvelous, glorious life in the Spiritual world with God's powerful, divine energy and with the presence of your deceased dear ones. This magnificent, eternal life is your reward for having awakened and strengthened your Spiritual body during your difficult existence in this material world. Because of this, you should never be afraid of the death of your physical body.

Remember, energy never dies, your Spiritual-mental body will take on a new life, either joining permanently with God in the Spiritual world or reincarnating back to this material world in another physical body. Which of two paths your Spiritual-mental body takes, depends on first,     how strong your Spiritual body was at the time of your physical body's death, secondly what deeds and how many good or bad deeds you performed in this material world according to your possibilities.

Your life in this material world will pass by so fast, that it will be equivalent to a split second, compared to the eternal Spiritual life, which awaits you with God and your deceased dear ones, if you only awaken and strengthen your Spiritual body and strengthen your relationship with God. So, what are you waiting for? Please act now, before it is too late. None of us know, when our physical body will pass-away.

I think that the following phrase written by a wise, enlightened, holy person is important for us to remember:

*Sikhs scriptures:*
*You who waste the nights dreaming,*
*the days in filling your stomachs.*
*This life as valuable as a jewel is sacrificed for a trinket.*
*Ignorant fools, you who have never achieved the name of God,*
*at the end of your life, you will be sorry.*

Throughout the day, as much as possible, you should communicate with God and God's energy that is inside of you. One of the admirable aspects of the Islam religion is that at least five times a day, millions of Muslim people around the world stop their normal activities and pray to God. Every day, you should thank God for your water, food and all you have, and ask God to bless you and to bless all of the hungry, unemployed, poor, suffering and needy people throughout the world.

Within the upper Amazonian ethnic religion to obtain, a true Spiritual awakening is not difficult. However, what is essential is a controlled diet and a series of important metaphysical practices for the correct preparation of the sacred brew. Additionally, for an optimum Spiritual experience, one should also incorporate all, which I have mentioned, including other recommendations that I shall present.

It only takes one to three sessions of drinking the sacred brew of Yagé to feel the powerful, newly awakened energy of one's Spiritual body, in all its grandeur and mystical force. This may sound too good to be true, but it is true and as with everything that is important in life, there are certain sacrifices which should be made and also some precautions which should be considered.

Based on years of personal investigation, it is my intention to convey the most complete information possible concerning the best and safest procedures for practicing this unique religion. For me this investigation has been difficult and this is because of the following reasons; the handling and preparation of Yagé sometimes varies from tribe to tribe or even within the same tribe, from Shaman to Shaman. In addition to this and more importantly is that because of years of intrusive foreign missionaries, a lot of valuable information concerning Yagé has been lost.

For me it is important to clarify that the upper Amazonian ethnic native tribes have always used Yagé and all other sacred plants, with utmost respect and exclusively for religious reasons, never for recreational purposes. It is essential to bear this in mind, because, if these potent sacred brews are not used correctly for a religious purpose, their effects could be dangerous to one's health!

When I first became interested in this Amazonian religion, I asked Don Piwali as well as other Shamans about any secondary effects or dangers that could occur to a person who drinks Yagé. For example if there has ever been any case of brain damage, addiction, or any other form of harmful effects. All of the Shaman's whom I have inquired, have assured me that there is no danger involved in drinking Yagé, as long as the plants have been properly handled and properly cooked. I trusted my friends and my instinct, for me, at that moment in my life that was all that I needed to hear.

Today, I still have absolute confidence in what my Shaman friends tell me and I would not hesitate in drinking other sacred brews, which are much stronger than Yagé, but I would never recommend to any non-native person to drink Yagé or any other sacred brews. The main reason for this is that an ethnic Amazonian native and a person brought up in a modern society can physically be different. The Amazonian natives have never had operations, x-rays, removal or transplant of organs, or any other form of artificial medical interventions. All humans in all societies have problems, but as bad as they could be for the ethnic Amazonian natives, their emotional problems rarely develop into psychopathic disorders, as unfortunately happens so frequently in modern societies.

However, if you, a non-native person are determined in drinking Yagé, then you should consider all of the recommendations that I have given, including the following ones. First, without any influence by anyone else, you alone should make the final decision of drinking Yagé. Secondly, at least two months in advance you should prepare yourself mentally, emotionally, physically and Spiritually. Last, the person you contract to cook Yagé should be an experienced, honest and responsible Shaman, or an experienced, honest and responsible Cooker.

For many years, as I was searching to learn more about this ethnic religion, I encountered many problems, for example; the great majority of the natives that I would meet did not know about Yagé or were of the Protestant-Evangelical religion, which of course meant they were firmly against the practice of their ancestral religion. Another difficulty that I encountered was that after I would finally meet a person who called himself a Shaman; I would contract that Shaman to cook Yagé for me, and after drinking the brew, I would physically suffer and have frightening visionary experiences. Of course, this happened because the Shaman was an imposter or the Yagé plant had not been properly handled and or properly cooked. One should never contract a person to cook Yagé, just because natives or mestizos call that person a Shaman or a Cooker, or because that person calls herself or himself a Shaman or a Cooker.

About ten years ago, I had one particularly bad experience. Early one morning I was with my friend Reynaldo in his motor powered dugout canoe in the
Cuyabeno lake area. As we were crossing one of the lakes, we met a small paddle canoe and in it was an old acquaintance of Reynaldo. The man was a native of the Cofan tribe who was with his family fishing in the lakes. This man and Reynaldo started talking in their native language about different things

and eventually they began talking about Yagé, then after a while, I heard Reynaldo say to this man that I like to drink Yagé. Suddenly this man turned to me and in Spanish, he said that he was an experienced Cooker and that if I wanted; he could cook Yagé for me. Not knowing this man, I told him that I would think it over and let him know later. Reynaldo and his friend talked for a few more minutes and then the man left. Immediately I asked Reynaldo what he thought about his old acquaintance cooking Yagé for me. In the past, Reynaldo had heard about his friend whom years ago was training to become a Shaman, but he had not heard anything recent about him, so he was not sure. Then after a few minutes of thinking it over, he changed his mind and said "Patricio, I think that it would be alright for him to cook Yagé for you." Hearing this I signaled to Reynaldo to turn the canoe around and follow his friend.

In a few minutes, we caught up with the Cofan native and I asked him if he could cook Yagé for me. He looked up at the sun and said that he could have the cooked Yagé ready for me that evening.

A couple of hours after sunset, the native man paddled in his small canoe across the Cocha Grande lake to our campsite, he gave me the bottle with the cooked brew, it was so fresh that it still felt warm. I paid him his money and he stayed talking for a while with Reynaldo, then he left. Since it was already late, I said good night to Reynaldo and taking my flashlight, I walked far away from our campsite to my hammock, which for that night I had tied onto two large trees in the forest. It was a tranquil, beautiful night, the jungle sounds in the Cuyabeno lake area sounded magical. There were thousands of crickets, frogs, nightjars, owls, nighthawks, and occasionally I heard the loud splashing in the water of Black Caimans, snapping their giant jaws as they were hunting in the lake. (Black Caimans are an Amazonian species of alligator; adults reach a length of 4 m. / 13 ft.)

Reynaldo is a dear friend of mine, but he is a Protestant-Evangelical and since many years ago, he had stopped drinking Yagé. Even until today, I have never been able to convince him to drink Yagé with me.

I took out of my duffle bag a small block of hardened red Achiote vegetable dye, a thin stick, and a small mirror and with the dim light of a lit candle, I began to paint special, ethnic designs on my face. After this, I put on my native Yagé jewelry that is made of three different necklaces. First, is a necklace of abundant natural black colored seeds, then over that necklace I put on another necklace of abundant, different colored glass beads and finally over that necklace I put on my special necklace made of Guangana fangs. (The largest species of Amazonian wild boars (white lipped peccaries), nowadays because jaguars are scarce, many native people make their Yagè jewelry from the fangs of these animals.)

Then I took the bottle of Yagé and poured the liquid into my personal cup. I said a prayer to God and to the People of Yagé and then slowly I drank the sacred brew, it tasted normal. I washed my mouth out with water and lay into my hammock. I closed my eyes and slept. Always when the effects begin, I hear a pleasant humming sound, then I feel a tingling warm sensation starting in my lower back and gradually extending throughout my spinal column and rest of my body and almost at the same time, my hearing becomes keen and the beautiful color visions begin. Most of the time these effects start after about an hour of drinking the brew, but on that particular night I was about to have an unexpected, different experience.

After about two hours, I woke up feeling an uncontrollable anxiety building up inside of me and spreading viciously throughout all of my body. I did not feel or see any of the normal, beautiful, colorful, Yagè effects. I began to feel cold and restless, something was terribly wrong. Everything gradually began to turn black with the exception of eerie flashing, gray and white shadows. I began to hear very strange far away

sounds that I had never heard before. These unpleasant noises were gradually getting louder until they eventually smothered out all of the normal animal jungle sounds. Hearing these unidentifiable sounds get louder made me more nervous.

After about one hour of hearing these sounds, suddenly I realized that they were coming from inside my own body. My functioning internal organs were actually making these sounds. Then after a few minutes, I began to hear a distant pounding sound, which gradually got louder until it prevailed over all of the other sounds. After hearing this sound for a few minutes, I suddenly realized that this pounding sound was coming from my heart.

I did my best to control my mind and keep calm, but my nervousness grew. I remembered Don Piwali's words; "No one has ever died or become sick by drinking Yagé." As much as I tried to convince myself that Don Piwali's words were true, during a few times that night I actually thought that I would be the first exception to that rule. The last thing that I remember

was begging God to protect me and then afterwards I lost consciousness.

The following morning I awoke to the most beautiful bird sounds that I had ever heard in my life, a colony of Crested Oropendulas. I opened my eyes, it was already sunrise, quickly I touched my heart, it felt healthy and strong, then I gave a deep sigh of relief and looking up to the beautiful sky, beyond the clouds and the sun, I gave thanks to God. I felt very tired, so I stayed a while longer in the hammock. After about thirty minutes, I walked to the campsite and spotting Reynaldo who was fishing from his canoe, I sat on a log and waited for him to return.

Upon returning, Reynaldo gave me a gourd with the bitter Yoko brew to drink and then he asked me how my Yagè experience was. I told him it was dreadful. He nodded his head in disappointment. Obviously, the Yagé had not been properly handled, and or cooked. Throughout the rest of the morning, I felt weak, so I stayed in my hammock sleeping. Finally, during the late afternoon, I felt better and moved my hammock to the campsite. That night after I ate a delicious fish dinner that Reynaldo had prepared, I said goodnight to him and eagerly went to sleep in my hammock. I looked up at the millions of fantastically bright stars that filled the black sky above me. As my hammock continued swaying side to side for a few minutes, I thought about God, the People of Yagé, and the majestic Amazon rainforest and then about what had happened to me the night before. I was so exhausted that before I realized it, I had fallen asleep.

That night I had a strange, but very pleasant dream with Don Piwali. As in my first vision with Ayahuasca, I saw him as a young man with his body fully decorated, using his Yagé jewelry, leaves, flowers and vegetable dye tattoos. He was in a sacred ceremonial hut of Yagé, sitting on a low bench and cooking something in a large ceramic pot. I walked up to him, he smiled at me and then as usual, I could see a beautiful spark in his eyes. I sat down on a low stool next to him, and he started shaking his bundle of leaves over the pot and at the same time, he began singing. Looking into the pot, I saw the vines and leaves of Yagé. Then he stopped singing and he picked up a gourd bowl, he filled it with Yagé and gave it to me. I drank the brew and gave him back the gourd; he then dipped it into the pot, filling it with Yagé. He then raised the gourd bowl to his lips and drank the brew.

Suddenly, I heard the beautiful, humming Yagé sound and looking at the cooking pot, I saw colorful Yagé visions coming out of the pot and flooding the area. Then I looked at Don Piwali and I saw him singing aloud, then I noticed many colorful Yagé visions coming out of his mouth. Initially I did not understand the words of his song because he was singing in his native language, but, near to the end of his song, I suddenly began to understandthe words. It was a truly beautiful and very real dream.

Upon awakening the following morning, I kept my eyes closed and began recollecting my dream. Suddenly I remembered the whole dream and understood it. Don Piwali had explained to me a method that would help me to prevent having more bad Yagé experiences. This method was that I should never again contract an unknown Shaman or Cooker to cook Yagé for me, unless that "supposed" Shaman or Cooker would also drink at least the same amount of his cooked Yagé with me.

By applying this new method, I was drinking less Yagé, but I never again suffered with bad experiences of improperly handled or improperly cooked Yagé. Eventually among all the Shamans or Cookers who accepted to drink their brew with me, finally I was lucky to find a few excellent Shamans who prepared good Yagé and who eventually become my Spiritual guides as well as my good friends. This method is another important recommendation for anyone who is planning to drink Yagé from an unknown Shaman or Cooker.

There are many mystical aspects of this religion, which many people from modern societies may consider absurd, superstitious and impossible to believe. This of course is understandable and just shows how different our modern, materialistic culture is to these ancient, mystical, ethnic native cultures. When I first began inquiring from the Shamans about their religion, I heard many stories that to me seemed superstitious. However, as time passed and I drank more Yagé, I gradually verified for myself that absolutely every story that my Shaman friends had been telling me was in fact true.

Today when I hear new stories, they may seem a little strange to me, but I never doubt their credibility.

In all of the ethnic native communities, there exist six essential rules that each adolescent and adult person has to know about and live by. These rules are associated to the religion, and since the religion is so important for the people, these rules play a vital role within a family and community. Specifically the rules apply to all people who are in any direct or indirect form of contact with the planting, handling, cooking or drinking of Yagé. These rules are important to follow, in order to obtain a better Yagé Spiritual experience, or in order not to harm other people who drink the sacred brews.

The first rule is regarding diet; Those native people who are interested in obtaining a better Yagé experience should abstain from eating salt, spicy hot chili peppers, fish and all types of meat for at least fourteen days prior to drinking Yagè. For mestizos or foreigners, I would recommend at least thirty days in advance a vegetarian diet free of fish, chicken and all types of meat, white bread, waxed cheese, chocolate, mustard, sugar, soft drinks or colas, liquor, coffee or tea with caffeine, chili peppers, candies and pastry. Additionally, I will say to avoid the direct consumption of eggs, and to eat the minimum amount of salt, if you can avoid salt completely, that would be better.

Drinks should never accompany a meal and if you want a drink, then I would recommend warm or hot drinks at least thirty minutes before or after the meal. Ice cold drinks cause difficulty to your digestion and all soft-drinks (colas) should be avoided, they are terribly unhealthy.

Eating meat of any animal will always complicate the proper digestion of Yagé. Apart from this reason, most animals from modern societies are bred in factory farms; they are physically and psychologically mistreated in many ways. They spend their entire life indoors without receiving the sun, they are purposely placed in tiny spaces so that they will not move, without anesthesia they are castrated and or parts of their bodies are cut off, they are forced to eat an unnatural diet which will fatten them as soon as possible. These animals are not healthy! Energy never dies, it transforms, so if you eat the meat of these unhealthy, stressed animals; you will be assimilating not only the protein and vitamin content of the meat, but also their poor health and terrible stress, which will produce a harmful effect on your Spiritual, mental, emotional and physical health. After your Yagè experience, if you cannot give up eating meat, I think the least harmful meat is fish that is free of chemical pollution and free-range chickens.

Even when native men are building the ceremonial religious Hut of Yagé, at least eight days prior to building the hut and throughout the entire construction, these men will abstain from eating meat, salt and chili peppers. Deep in the forest, are a few species of birds, which are the only meat that Shamans can eat. God-like Shamans and apprentices always abstain from eating meat, spicy hot chili peppers and salt. A few days before cooking Yagè, Cookers will abstain from eating salt, chili peppers and meat.

Your diet plays an important role in order to achieve internal purity, which will be more acceptable for God's energy in you and for the Spirit of Yagè that you will ingest. Additionally for providing, the optimum conditions so that your digestive organs may work at their best.

The second rule refers to pure thoughts. It is vital to control your mind in everything that you think, say or do. You should never have impure thoughts like; egoism, envy, jealousy, hatred, or anger, and you should never have sexual thoughts about another man or woman that is not your husband or wife. You should never lie, steal, commit adultery or perform any type of dishonest act.

The third rule is about celibacy. To control your sexual activity to the maximum length of time will greatly benefit the awakening and strengthening of your Spiritual body, as well as also the Yagé Spiritual-visionary experience. Married couples should try to restrain from too much sexual activity. What is important also, is that the beautiful, energetic act of sexual intercourse should be performed only with whom there exists an emotion of true love.

The over-indulgence of sex weakens your Spiritual energy because it affects your first two chakras, your first chakra is at the tip of your spinal column and your second chakra is just above your sexual organ. It seems that because of their proximity to your sexual organ is why they are directly effected and they lose vital energy each time that there is sexual intercourse. By practicing celibacy, your first two chakras will be able to respond more effectively for its awakening and consequently this will make much easier the subsequent awakening of the other five charkas. Only after your seventh chakra has awakened, can you experience the true, blissful awakening of your Spiritual-mental body.

According to the wise Yoga philosophy, the sexual fluid in the body is an important part of the life of a person; it should be preserved as much as possible for the energy of the Spiritual body. The practice of celibacy is most beneficial for those who are following a Spiritual path. Precisely these are the main reasons why many ancient religions have always expected the practice of celibacy from their Spiritual leaders. It seems that in this material world, sex and food are the two main weaknesses for the physical body, so here we find these two major sacrifices which we should fulfill in order to be more worthy of God.

(For mestizos or foreigners I would recommend celibacy at least thirty days prior to drinking Yagé.)

The fourth rule refers to menstruation. It is always important to abide by the natural laws of God and Pacha Mama (Mother Nature) and particularly, concerning the perfect balance of opposite forces that always exist. It is believed that Yagé and the other sacred plants have female Spirits. Consequently, the female Spiritual energy of these plants will reject the female energy-nature in women because there is not a balance.

For adolescent girls and women, their menstruation can

create a conflict of energies, between the metaphysical energy that exists in their female nature and the sacred plant's female Spirit nature. This conflict would occur if there were to be physical contact between a woman that is menstruating and Yagé. For the Amazonian ethnic native religion, the act of menstruation is not only a physical act, but also it is a metaphysical act, which the powerful female Spirit of the sacred plant of Yagé is able to perceive.

Before menstruation begins, the adolescent girl's body or the woman's body had been preparing itself to create life, since that did not happen, blood is released, but also what is being released is the invisible, metaphysical, Spiritual energy that was being created. The blood of menstruation or this metaphysical Spiritual energy is not bad, but it is of a powerful, female life origin and only because of this, it
conflicts with the powerful, female Spirits of Yagé and other sacred plants. This metaphysical, Spiritual energy of menstruation does exist, even though in modern science or in modern cultures it is unknown. However, since centuries, the wise Amazonian Shamans can perceive it.

Years ago, something happened to me concerning the metaphysical energies of menstruation and Yagé. One day I was with my Cofan and Secoya native friends Reynaldo, Esteban, Delfin and Emilio, we were traveling in Reynaldo's dugout motor canoe on the Putumayo River, this famous river forms the natural boundary line between the Ecuadorian and Colombian Amazon. We stayed three days with a Colombian Shaman, during that time, I drank Yagé and my Spiritual-visionary experiences were excellent. Therefore, when we left the Shaman's house, I carefully placed the left over, half-full bottle of cooked Yagé into my backpack, because I was planning to drink it that night.

We traveled all day, stopping only twice to fish and rest. We wanted to arrive to a Colombian Cofan native village before nighttime, but as we were still on the river suddenly, Reynaldo realized that a tropical rainstorm was heading towards us. Quickly we scanned the two riverbanks, looking for a place where we could protect ourselves from the storm. Ahead of us, Esteban spotted a house, so we arrived to the front of it and tied our canoe to a large tree. Then we promptly got our bags, tents and cooking supplies and ran for cover. A few angry, barking dogs met us and forced us to stop in our tracks. Almost immediately, the owner who was a mestizo man came out and gladly received us, he welcomed us to wait under his porch roof to protect ourselves from the rain. The mestizo man was called Jose; he had a large family made up of many children and a few adult women. We waited for the torrential storm to pass and meanwhile we were talking with Jose. Forty minutes passed and we realized that it was already too late to continue down the river so fortunately Jose suggested that we set up our tents on his clearing to spend the night there. We thanked Jose for his generosity and after the rain passed, we set up the tents.

Since I was planning to drink Yagé, I went in the forest as far away from the house as possible, to set up my hammock and nylon tarp roof covering. Suddenly I realized that I had forgotten my backpack in the porch area of the house. Quickly I raced back to the house and found it in the same room, but in a different spot from where I had left it. At that moment, I did not give any importance to this.

Later that night I excused myself from eating dinner and I went into the forest to my hammock, I prepared myself and drank Yagé. The previous night I had an incredibly beautiful Yagé experience, so I was looking forward to another wonderful experience, but when my visions began, all I saw for six hours were black and white unrecognizable images, which were continuously flashing on and off, similar to a strobe light in a discotheque.

The following morning I woke up very tired and with an

unusual headache. I went to see my friends, and told them about my awful experience. Immediately Reynaldo asked me if anyone else had touched the bottle of Yagé or my backpack. I told him that for twenty minutes I had left my backpack unattended and that I had found it in a different place. Reynaldo, Emilio, Esteban and Delfin then said, "The black and white colorless visions accompanied by a headache, is always because a woman who is menstruating had touched something of the person who is drinking Yagé. Surely, one of the mestizo women of this house was menstruating and she touched your backpack."

All adolescent girls and boys who want to, may train to become Shamans. However, for the girl apprentices, their training is slightly different and this is because of the natural conflict between the sacred plants Spirit female energy and the girl apprentice's female energy. Girls that are apprentices as well as all women can never touch the Yagé vines and they can never go near to the area where the cultivated vines of Yagé or other sacred plants are. Since they cannot touch the sacred plants, they cannot become Cookers. For the women Shamans, their only inconvenience is that they can never cook their own Yagé or other sacred brews, so they will always have to rely on a male Cooker. Women cannot build the religious Hut of Yagé and while they are menstruating, they cannot drink the brew of any sacred plant or go near to the area where the sacred Hut of Yagé stands. Inclusively during these days, they cannot have any personal contact with any person that is planning to drink Yagé, not even with members of their own family.

In the ethnic native communities, adjacent to each family hut there is a smaller hut with its own thatch roof and own exclusive steps to enter or leave the hut. During the days that the adolescent girls or women of the family are having their period, they will take to this small hut their hammock and other personal belongings that they may need during those few days. The wooden floors of both, the large family hut and the women's small hut are exactly at the same level and between the two huts; there is a separation of only a few centimeters. This special hut, as well as the family hut, has no walls, so if the husband and children are in the main family hut and the wife is in the special hut, they can easily talk between one another. These women cannot have any physical contact with anyone who drinks Yagé. The babies obviously do not drink Yagé, so they may be with the Mother, especially for breast-feeding.

Within this special hut, the women or the adolescent girls rest in their hammocks whenever they like, when they want they may walk outside of the hut to go into the forest or to wash or bathe in the nearby river. Frequently each day, neighbors, friends or family arrive to the main family hut to visit and they converse with the women or adolescent girls that are in the small hut. During these days, the father cooks for the entire family. In addition, he performs all of the normal daily chores of his wife and takes care of the family's small children.

For the women or for the adolescent girls, this time of the month becomes a pleasant time to have a break. Evidently, they do not mind at all to have this well deserved time to rest, especially during those particular days of the month.

However, the main reason why the ethnic natives have this wise custom is not necessarily, so that the women can rest. This custom exists because, if a woman were having her period and if she would cook, or accidentally manipulate food or water which her children or husband would eat or drink, or if she would touch them or they would touch her. Then when the rest of the family drink Yagé, they would have a bad Yagé experience, and for a couple of days they could suffer from headaches or nose bleeding. If a woman, who is menstruating, accidentally does any of these things, she would lose some of her own Spiritual energy.

Whenever I am going to drink Yagé I always make sure to protect all of my Yagé items, including the cooked brew from any person touching them, especially women. Inclusively I completely avoid shaking hands with anyone, especially women.

Because of this rule, if there are any women who are planning a visit to the Amazon to drink Yagé, they should organize their schedule so that while they are in the Amazon, they will not be having their period. Alternatively, they could be on a flexible schedule, so that while they are in the Amazon, they can wait until their period ends, to drink Yagé.

The fifth rule is regarding the custom of shaking hands. In the center of our palms are important receptors and transmitters of our Spiritual energy. It is not wise to shake the hand of a stranger, who could have some harmful metaphysical energy that could affect the health of our personal energy. Within the ethnic native culture, apart from the intimate family, people do not touch each other and people never have the modern-society custom of shaking hands. In non-ethnic native communities, all of the natives will shake hands. However, the majority of the elders and all women will shake hands in a different manner. They extend their open hand and gently touch their fingers of their open hand to the fingers of the other person's hand. They never give a firm handshake.

In relation to this rule, it is improper for men outside of the family, to look directly into the eyes of an adolescent girl or woman. Also, it is offensive for men outside of the family to over-converse or affectionately converse with adolescent girls or women, this is considered flirting, and in the case of single woman, it could lead to a misunderstanding of one's interest in marriage. If the woman is married, obviously it could lead to a response of violence by the jealous husband.

The sixth rule is concerning the respect for the privacy of all personal Yagé items belonging to other people. It is forbidden to touch the personal Yagé items of another person. These items may include anything that is used during the ceremony of drinking Yagé. For example; the ceramic or gourd bowl for drinking the sacred brews, all of the seed or glass beads, feathers, flowers, jaguar or wild boar fang jewelry, musical instruments, cloth wrist and arm bands, fresh or dried leaves, "Mame Koko" bundles of leaves and the hammock that a person uses for the Yagé ceremony. Therefore, if you ever arrive to a native home, you should always ask the father or Mother of the family if it is permitted to lie in an empty hammock.

All of these different items have special, personal Yagé energy that is essential for the owner. This energy becomes an important part of the Spiritual identity and Spiritual energy of a person in the Spiritual world, as well as also the Spiritual relationship between the person and the People of Yagé. Only the owner may touch her or his Yagé items and clean them when necessary. Always, the natives who drink Yagé keep their personal Yagé items wrapped in a cloth package that is stored within the beams of the thatch roof.

Part of this sixth rule also, is that once a person is fully dressed with their special Yagé garments and jewelry, one should never touch that person, the person's jewelry or anything else that the person may have. These six rules are important to know, especially if a mestizo or foreigner is visiting an ethnic native family or community.

Apart from these six rules, I shall now present other recommendations:

## PRANA

In Yoga, Prana means life; it is the sacred energy of God that is everywhere, including the air. By the regular practice of Yoga breathing exercises known as Pranayama, through your thought you will be able to control the Prana that functions within you, as well as all around you. This is obtained by daily practice of deep breathing Pranayama exercises and mind control.

Everyday, as many times as possible you should practice deep breathing exercises and especially so, during a fast. During your everyday normal breathing, you should remember to inhale and exhale only through the nose.

You should learn the following basic Yoga Pranayama breathing exercise; Assume a Yoga meditation pose or simply sit with your spine erect, put your hands on our knees, with your palms facing up. First, exhale as much air as you comfortably can, then as you inhale, you should start by gradually expanding your stomach as much as you comfortably can, and as you do this, you should gradually raise your collarbones. Breathe in as much air as you comfortably can. When you exhale you should start by gradually lowering your collarbones and end by contracting your stomach as much as you comfortably can. By learning this method of breathing, you will be allowing more space in your lungs to take in more oxygen and you will be able to expel more stale oxygen.

In modern, western type of societies, most adults inhale and exhale only about half a liter (1 pint) of air, but the average adult lungs have a capacity for five liters (10 pints) of air.

By breathing correctly through your nose and by performing deep breathing exercises throughout your everyday life, you will supply your blood and body with more oxygen that is equivalent to healthier blood, more energy and more life. This breathing exercise is the simplest of the Yoga "Pranayama" exercises. Advanced Pranayama breathing exercises will strengthen more your Spiritual-mental energy and the powerful energy of Prana that is inside of you.

Within the wise Yoga philosophy, for the Spiritual body to awaken and strengthen, first it is necessary for the physical, mental and emotional bodies to be in a high level of good health. Consequently, in Yoga, there exist many excellent exercises for improving one's physical, emotional, mental health, as well as for acquiring Spiritual awareness through meditation.

## WATER

After Prana and air, water is the most important element for your daily subsistence. About seventy per cent of our planet is water, and about seventy per cent of the average human body is made-up of water. Because so much of your health is dependant on water, you should give more importance to this precious liquid of life.

Yes, most of us know how important it is to drink sufficient pure water on a daily basis, but I recommend also, to thank God and ask God to bless the water each time before you drink it, just as you should with food. In addition, I recommend each time that you get wet in rain, or each time you bathe in a shower, in the ocean, river or lake, you imagine that the water you are in is a beautiful gift from God, a magnificent light coming from God, which truly nourishes you.

## COLD WATER SHOWERS

Cold-water showers are most beneficial for your blood circulation, nervous system, digestion and general health. However, the water should not be ice-cold temperature and you should never take a cold-water shower while you are with a pinched nerve or coming down with a flu or cold. To take your cold-water shower you should never be with a full stomach, preferably after nature calls in the mornings or thirty minutes before a meal, or at least two hours after a meal. Your body should be warm.

With the shower on, you should apply soap to all your body,

then wash your face with cold water, and then in sequence under the cold-water shower; first wet the front part of your right foot and up your right leg until your right shoulder, then the left foot and up until your left shoulder.

Next, turn around and from the back of your right foot up until your right shoulder, then from your left foot up until your left shoulder, then from your buttocks up your spinal column until the beginning of your neck.

Turn sideways and from the right side of your right foot shower up until the right side of your torso and armpit, then turn sideways again and from the left side of your left foot shower up until the left side of your torso and armpit. Then turn forward and the middle front part of your body, from the feet up to your collarbone.

Never shower your head or neck with cold water. With a warm, wet hand towel, you may wash your neck, and on the days, that you wash your hair you can bathe in warm-hot water and afterwards you can finish your shower with only cold water. Never jump into a cold-water pool; you should go in gradually. During the days that women are having their period they should not take cold-water showers.

Cold-water towel compresses is excellent for lowering a fever of an adult or a child. A towel wet with cold water should be partially ringed so that the water is not dripping and then it is applied over the stomach of the sick person that is in a laying down position. After a minute, the towel should be turned over to the other side and then after another minute, the towel should be washed out again in cold water and the process repeated. In about fifteen minutes, the fever will drop to normal.

**Fasting**
One of the most important practices performed by apprentices and Shamans is fasting. Periodic fasting will strengthen

the health of your Spiritual body, but also it will strengthen the health of your emotional, mental and physical bodies.

• Mohammed the Holy and wise prophet once stated; Praying will take you the first half of the way to God and fasting will take you the second half of the way to God and to the open doors of Heaven.

• In the Bible, there is an important story that we do not hear very often. It is of the Essenes, who are one day with Jesus and they are persistently begging him to talk to them about the laws of life, which can heal a sick body. Finally
Jesus responded to them:
"You do not understand any longer the words of life, because you are dead. If you want to live the word of God and if you want God's power to enter into you, do not soil your body and your Spirit, because the body is the temple of the Spirit and the Spirit is the temple of God. Purify the temple so that God will live in it and will occupy the place that is meant for the Lord. Protect yourselves with God's divine heaven so that you can ward off all temptations of the body and Spirit that proceed from Satan. Renovate and fast. Because in truth I tell you, that Satan and his legions will only be expelled by means of fasting and prayer. Remain alone and fast, and do not show your fast to others, God will see it and your reward shall be magnificent."

Living in modern societies, most of us do not do enough exercise in relation to the amount of food that we eat, so most of the time we are overeating. Apart from this imbalance, most of our food has harmful chemicals or little nutrition and we do not eat enough vegetables and fruits. Because of all of this, our elimination process is deficient.

As the years pass, throughout the interior of our body we become overloaded with unnecessary fat and dangerous toxins. This condition takes energy and health away from us and is one of the main causes for most sicknesses.

The main benefit of a fast is that your body will be able to rest from the permanent, forced work of digestion, and during this important rest period, each cell in your body will work intuitively to eliminate all toxic and unnecessary matter.

The type of fast that you decide to follow depends on different factors, but in general, I would recommend a fast-diet of one kind of fresh fruit throughout one day of the week or a few continuous days. To start the fast it would be better if you can take a Lower Bowel Tonic or something similar to help clean your intestinal tract. Personally, I take two teaspoons of castor oil in a glass of fruit juice. Remember that taking castor oil or something similar means that you need to be near to a bathroom for at least six hours after taking the laxative.

A fast of three or four oranges a day or two or three grape vines a day is sufficient to supply an adult with enough energy to perform most forms of mild work.

Children should never be forced to eat; parents should respect a child's desire when they say that they are not hungry. When the child feels hungry again, which of course should never be more than one day, the child should eat fresh fruit as the first meal and afterwards, as the child recovers her or his normal appetite, a nutritious, balanced, healthy diet should try to be undertaken.

Only adults can fast exclusively with water or natural fruit juices. Especially for long fasts, these should be of fresh fruits or fresh vegetables and not only of water or juices.

Regardless of what type of fast you choose, it is important to drink sufficient water during the fast. It is better for your health, if whenever you drink liquids, these liquids should be warm or room temperature, but not ice cold. You should always drink all liquids very slowly, slightly chewing and taking small sips, instead of large gulps.

If you are considering a fast for a long period, then you should consult a nutritionist. Remember also that during your fast, you should avoid performing strenuous work. All forms of fasting are favorable and longer periods of fasting of up to twenty days are even more favorable.

It is important to remember that when you break your fast, this should be gradual, and once you have changed over to your everyday diet, it should be as healthy as possible.

In preparation for drinking Yagé, I would recommend at least thirty days before a diet of: fresh vegetables, fresh fruit, beans, grains, cooked potatoes, unrefined rice, soybeans, Quinoa Andean grain, peanuts, honey and olive oil. This diet should be practiced until three days before drinking Yagé and then a fast-diet of only one type of fruit until lunchtime of the day of drinking Yagé. After one's Yagé experience, then one can gradually include in their normal everyday diet; soy cheese or non-aged (non-waxed) mozzarella type of cheese, mayonnaise, butter and non-yeast bread. Pineapple is high in acidity, it is an excellent fruit to eat alone, but it is not recommended to eat it together with other fruits.

All food and all liquids including the brew of Yagé, should be eaten or drank slowly and chewed as much as possible. We should never eat until we are full. We should replace refined sugar for honey or brown sugar and try to lower our salt consumption as much as possible.

Upon getting out of bed in the mornings, we should slowly drink a glass of warm water, preferably with a few drops of lemon to facilitate our digestion. If we have difficulty to evacuate the bowels, then we can give the abdomen a gentle massage with one hand, but after periodic fasts and a healthy diet accompanied with sufficient warm water and exercise, we should not suffer from constipation. Correct posture as we sit or stand is very important for good blood circulation and proper digestion.

## SUNBATHS

When you are not sick with a cold, and avoiding the strong mid-day sun, you should try to take sunbaths, you should keep your head under a shade. In addition, it is good for your health if you can walk barefoot on a clean natural surface like grass or dirt, the surface should be free of pesticides, chemicals, animal droppings or sharp objects. The best time for this exercise is early in the morning.


## SMOKING

Smoking is dangerously addictive and destructive for your blood circulation, nervous system, digestion and the general health of your entire body. However, all of the Amazonian Shamans smoke hand rolled tobacco cigars during Yagé ceremonies or during healing sessions. Tobacco is native to tropical Latin America and it enhances the Yagé visionary experience, so I highly recommend for you to smoke after you drink Yagé. When I drink Yagé, is the only time that I will ever smoke. Unfortunately, some Amazonian ethnic natives have acquired the habit of smoking a little every day while not drinking Yagé, consequently they have become addicted to this dangerous drug.


## FLEXIBILITY

Our brain and spinal column contain the central nervous system of our body, and within our central nervous system we find the most valuable and powerful source of physical energy that exists in our physical body. It is because of the vital energy that is in our central nervous system that we can make all physical movements.

I recommend learning Yoga and Tái Chi for maintaining a flexible and healthy spinal column and body. Within the wise Yoga philosophy, it is believed that the age of a person is partly determined on how healthy and flexible the spinal column is. All babies are born with flexible and healthy spinal columns, this is why typically many adults playing with a baby laying on a bed can gently take the babies feet and raise them until the feet touch the baby's ears. Unfortunately, because of lack of adequate exercises, the natural flexibility that we as babies were all born with begins to stiffen and as we get older, the stiffening of the back and body gets worse. Our physical body should always be as flexible as possible, and likewise our points of view, our perspective on different issues and on life should be flexible.

## TELEVISION

It will be much easier for you to awaken and strengthen your Spiritual body if you stop watching television and its news programs. Because of the violent or polarized images of television coming into your mind, the constant thinking action of your mind, gossip, and the unstoppable human conversations, your God-like internal voice, is unperceived by you.

## MEDITATION

Most of us in modern societies do not set aside time in order to communicate with the God-like internal energy and voice that is inside of us. Every day for at least an hour, you should find time to remain in total silence, completely quiet your mind, meditate and listen to the internal voice of your Spiritual body. If you can take a course with an experienced Yoga meditation teacher, it will be better. Your meditation will be helpful if you ever decide to drink Yagé, but also it will be rewarding for every day of your entire life.

## HARMFUL ENERGY & CANDLES

Remember that energy never dies, and that humans are constantly creating energy, because of this, we should try to protect ourselves from this energy.

Fire is an important element in Mother Nature, fire and the flame of candles purifies energy, so we should always have a supply of candles and incense, and use them at least once every day when we pray and meditate, and always when strangers or guests come to our house. We should always light the candles if an unpleasant moment or discussion is starting or has already occurred, and if someone is sick.

If you can buy a natural non-synthetic quartz crystal, this would be more helpful for protecting your home and yourselves. During the nights of the full moons, you should leave the quartz crystal outside of your house, under the moon light, so that the moon can purify it of harmful energy and regenerate its strength.

The day that you effectively awaken your Spiritual body, you will truly feel the live energy of God within yourself, and because of this, you will become enlightened. This means that you will have seen and felt the powerful, divine energy and light of God, consequently your Spiritual-mental body and brain will be enlightened and keener, in this way, you will be able to understand life from a more insightful perspective. In addition, you will discover that your most prized fortune here in this material world is your divine relationship with God and the strengthening of your Spirituality. As you realize this, you will also discover amazing Spiritual powers that we all keep deep in the most remote corner of our brain and mind. You will feel a new, potent flow of Spiritual energy that will radiate within yourself and you will instinctively yearn to transmit sincere unconditional love, generosity and respect to all humans, as well as to all other beings. The reason for this sudden desire to give unconditional love to all is because by truly awakening your Spiritual body, at the same time, you have awakened the powerful energy of God in yourself and God is the maximum expression of love that exists in the universe.

The Spiritual-mental body that has never been enlightened by God's energy cannot understand or describe God, and even the human mind that has been enlightened is still limited in trying to understand and describe God. Based on my Spiritual experiences, I with much respect will attempt to present a humble description of God:

God is the maximum expression of unconditional love, life, peace, tolerance, purity, wisdom, mental control, honesty, generosity, humbleness, beauty and ecstasy. God is the most powerful manifestation of energy, light and sound that exists in the universe. God is all; God is within each natural particle that exists in the universe, God is the Master of the universe, God always existed, God is eternal.

Each time that I drink Yagé, I personally feel the almighty presence of God and of course, because of this perception, I know that God exists. I do not believe, as some Christian church leaders affirm that we have to rely on "faith" to be convinced that God exists. During my teen-age years as a Catholic, for me to have had to rely on "mere faith" in order to convince myself that God exists was not sufficient. For years, I practiced the Catholic religion, but never experienced a personal, glorious Spiritual communication with God. It was only in the Amazon, after my third experience with Yagé that I truly felt Gods divine, powerful energy. This glorious experience with Yagè convinced me that God truly exists, and my belief had absolutely nothing to do with faith, because at that time when I drank Yagè, I was an atheist.

CHAPTER 7

## • Preparing and drinking Yagé

So that you will understand and appreciate more the final product of the cooked sacred brew of Yagè, I shall present basic information on its cultivation and cooking: Since at least one-thousand years ago, Amazonian Shamans began to domesticate Yagé. Initially, wild sacred plants were transplanted from a virgin forest to a clearing which days before had been previously prepared. This clearing is nearer to the ceremonial hut of Yagé than to the community, but it is still far, at least two kilometers (1 mile) away to the community or to any native dwelling or navigable river. The reason why the vines of Yagé are planted in such a secluded area is to protect the live Spiritual energy of the Spirits of the plants from any harmful or conflicting human energy.

Transplants are always performed during a new moon and never during the start of the driest months of the year. At least seven days before transplanting, the site will be selected and prepared, within this site, medium size trees have been selected for acting as host trees for the vines. Large trees have been cut down to allow more sunlight into the clearing. About three meters (10 ft.) around the host trees, the vegetation is burned, by doing this the vegetable matter is forced to release nitrogen to the top soil, which will benefit the Yagé cuttings. The cuttings are then cut at 45° angles and in an inclined position are pushed into the ground next to the host trees and facing the trees. For the Yagé plants, those host trees will act as thrones for them to reach up to the sky where during the day they will receive important energy from the sun, and during the night, they will receive important metaphysical energy from the moon, stars and the Spiritual world of Yagé. For the Amazonian Shamans, during the nighttime there is much more metaphysical-Spiritual energy in the air than during daytime.

After transplanting, the Shamans and apprentices will inform all the people exactly where the Yagé plants have been planted. This site is sacred, only male Shamans, Cookers or male apprentices can go to the site to check on the young plants and later to collect the Yagé vines for cooking the brew, no other person is permitted to go near to the site. Usually, one would have to wait about five years until the planted vines are mature enough to be harvested.

If at any time, wild Yagé vines are found in the virgin forests, these would be collected and used for a session of cooking and drinking Yagé. The brew that is made from wild Yagé is considered more potent and consequently produces a better Spiritual and visionary experience.

Besides where Yagé is planted, the only other sacred place is the "Casita de Yagé" ceremonial hut. This hut is at least 400mt. (1,300 ft.) away from the community. Its floor is directly on the ground, this is quite different to the native houses, where     the floor is usually above the ground on posts. This simple looking religious temple is used only for the cooking and drinking of the sacred brews. No person is ever permitted to enter this area, unless it is to take part in cooking or drinking the sacred brews.

For the actual day of drinking Yagé, the water that is used for cooking the brew, as well as for drinking water has to be pure water. The natives use virgin, spring water, which should not have been touched by humans within the past twelve hours.

On the day of drinking Yagè, upon arising, most of the people will drink a warm, mild purgative to clean the digestive system. (For non-natives I recommend for you to bring your own natural purgative to use that morning).

Now, let us imagine that a Cooker and his assistant are going to cook Yagè; Around 5:30 in the morning, after drinking the purgative, the Cooker and his assistant get together their machetes, hammocks and anything else that they would need to take to the ceremonial hut of Yagé. The large ceramic cooking pot and some other important Yagé items are already at the ceremonial hut; stored on shelves that are within the ceiling beams. The two men, carrying their belongings and holding their lit resin lamps meet and start walking on a narrow footpath to the ceremonial hut. In silence, they are mentally asking God and the People of Yagé to help ward-off any evil or harmful spirits from their bodies, the path, the clearing and the Casita de Yagé.

Arriving, they put everything on low benches, the Cooker brings down from the beams of the ceiling the ceramic cooking pot and places it face down on one of the benches. This special cooking pot and other Yagé items should not touch the ground. The Cooker takes his lit resin lamp and machete and leaves the hut; he crosses the clearing and enters the forest. Walking quickly, he goes to the cultivated site of Yagé, it is better to get there before the sunrays touch the vines. Meanwhile, the assistant is collecting sufficient virgin water and lighting the firewood which days before he had already collected.

When the Cooker arrives to the cultivated site, he asks permission to the Spirits of the sacred plants to allow him to enter into their area. Then the Cooker walks into the sacred field, where he checks out each Yagé vine, until he selects the thicker vine to use. The thicker that the vine is, the older that it is, this means that it is more mature, wiser, and with more Spiritual sacred energy, consequently the Spiritual and visionary effects will better. After selecting the vine, he asks permission to the Spirit of the Yagé vine that he has selected, for touching it and for harvesting part of it. After this, sufficient secondary vines are pulled down, cut and tied together.

Then the Cooker finds the other important sacred plant (Psychotria viridis), which he needs. In the Siona and Secoya language, this shrub is called Yagé Oko. The vine of Yagè and the thin vines and leaves of Yagè Oko are the chemical plant ingredients for making Yagè. Some Shamans or Cookers will also use another sacred plant admixture. The harvested vines are tied together, after this, the Cooker will respectfully thank the Spirits of the sacred plants, the People of Yagé, and then he will leave. Carrying the two types of sacred plants, he eventually arrives to the ceremonial hut and puts the plants on one of the benches.

The assistant already has the cooking pot filled with enough virgin water and by now, the water is beginning to boil. The Cooker rests for a few minutes and drinks some of the collected spring water.

The preparation and the cooking of the sacred plants always occurs at the east end of the hut, when the ceremonial hut was built, it was purposely built with its axis on the most exact east to west orientation. The Shamans believe that special metaphysical energies from the Spiritual World and Pacha Mama will first reach the hut from the east. The Shamans have many important beliefs regarding the essential metaphysical energies and laws that exist within our planet. For millennia, the Amazonian Shamans have been living their daily lives in relation to God, the devil, the Spiritual World, Mother Nature, the People of Yagé, the Sun, and the Moon.

After the Cooker finishes his short rest, the two men carefully put the Yagé vines on one of the low stools, and begin to chant special songs in honor to the Spirits of the sacred plants and to the People of Yagé. They take the Yagé vines and using their machetes, begin to clean the bark of the vines from as much algae, lichens, moss, dirt, etc.... The chanting continues and now the vines will be pounded with wooden clubs in order to split them open, then the crushed vines are rolled into a circle about 40 cm. (15 in.) in diameter and are then tied. The Yagé Oko vines are also cleaned, pounded, folded and tied into a rectangular 20 cm. (8 in.) package. During this process, the two sets of vines should not touch the ground, so all of this is being done on the low benches and or on wooden boards that are on the ground.

The rectangular package of Yagé Oko vines and leaves is reverently placed in the middle of the Yagé vines. Then, this one bundle of the two types of plants is placed inside the boiling water, most of the plants will sink, but looking inside the pot, one will always see some of the vines and leaves floating on the surface of the water. With this final step, the actual cooking begins.

During the time that it takes to cook the brew, the two men are resting in their hammocks and are taking turns adding firewood. Because of the possibility of evil energy or demons attempting to enter into the clearing and ceremonial hut, it is imperative that once in a while, the men take turns chanting, to ward off any harmful forces.

In the cooking pot, the water is continuously boiling  and gradually it is reducing in quantity. At the same time the potent, psychoactive chemicals and the live Spirits of these two sacred plants is metaphysically fusing together, creating one of the most powerful, Supernatural, sacred potions, which exist anywhere in our planet!

After about eight hours of cooking, the boiling water will change into a vibrant orange-brown color, upon seeing this unique color, the Cooker knows that the brew has begun an important stage, at this point, the brew is referred to as "Wea Yagé", which in the Secoya and Siona language means Maize Yagè (U.S. corn Yagè.) Respectfully the Cooker takes out of the pot the rectangular package of the Yagé Oko vines and places it on the ground, near to the pot. The cooking will now continue for about one more hour, only with the Yagè vines.

After this, the color of the brew gets a little darker, the lit firewood is removed and the roll of Yagé vines is gently taken out of the pot and placed on the ground over the Yagé Oko vines. Now the sacred brew will naturally cool off, without any disturbance or movement. After the used vines have cooled off, the apprentice will take them into the virgin forest and will thank them for their vital service, then he will leave them on the ground so that they will be recycled back to Pacha Mama.

Most of the Shamans prefer Yagé to be thick, usually the thicker brews will produce a better Spiritual and visionary experience. The only inconvenience is that, generally the thicker brews are bitterer. While the brew cools off, the two men take turns supervising the area and preparing themselves for the religious ceremony. Usually the Cooker prepares himself first by going to a nearby river or lake to bathe.

After the brew has cooled off, the assistant takes down from within the beams of the ceiling, three hardwood sticks about one meter (3 ft.) long. These sticks typically made of Pambil palm wood will be pounded into the ground near to the pot of Yagé to form a tripod; they will be tied together at the union. This tripod structure will later be used to hold the community Yagé gourd bowl. When the people are ready to drink Yagé, they are not permitted to dip their personal bowls into the pot of Yagé. All people must use the community bowl to dip it into the pot, fill it with brew and then pour that brew into their personal bowl. This is done to prevent any possible harmful or conflicting energy that any person may have during the Yagé drinking ceremony; obviously, this would ruin the cooked brew.

Before sunset, the Cooker and his assistant have already bathed, dressed and decorated themselves in their special Yagé clothing. Then they will wait in the "Casita de Yagé" for the rest of the people to arrive.

The frequency for drinking Yagé is a personal decision. Nevertheless, it would be too strenuous on the physical body to drink Yagé too often, however for a short period of time, the brew can be taken every other night. Whenever a person drinks Yagé, throughout most of the night the four bodies will be actively awake. The following day the four bodies do not feel tired, in fact, they are with tremendous energy, but the person should rest and sleep, trying to recover the lost sleep of the previous night.

Today, the upper Amazonian ethnic natives still practice their religion essentially in the same way as in the past, but there are some changes. For example, they use machine made cotton fabrics as clothes, colorful glass necklaces, and some Cookers use aluminum pots for cooking Yagè. Ceramic pots require more care from breaking, but they are healthier to use, they give a better flavor to the brew and in general a better visionary experience.

Remember as part of your preparation to drink Yagé, at least two weeks in advance you should do a fast of talking, and if you really have to talk, think carefully to choose wisely your words and say only what is necessary, generous and true.

For a non-native person who is on a camping style, I recommend to take to the campsite about 7 liters of pure water without gas, this water you will use during the previous days to drinking Yagé and during the actual days of drinking Yagé. In main towns in the jungle, before boarding the canoe, the water can be purchased. For the actual night of drinking Yagé, you should have two, half-liter plastic bottles of water. Each time you have to open a bottle, purify and bless it yourself using a quartz, a lit candle, your thought, open hands and the energy of Prana.

If you are staying at a lodge or if you finished all the water that you took to the jungle, then accept the water that is available, and before drinking it, purify and bless it.

At least fifteen days before drinking Yagé, as well as throughout the day of drinking Yagé, you should not allow any form of harmful energy to alter your state of tranquility, happiness, honesty, generosity, tolerance, humbleness and unconditional love to all.

On the first day arriving to the jungle, be sure to hire a

responsible native man to provide you for the day of drinking Yagè, with three native cigars, a Mamekoko leaf wand, a few pods of Achiote dye and a thin stick for applying the dye. The Kichwas call this leaf wand Suri Panga, but the Secoyas and Sionas call it Mamekoko. The pleasant sound produced by these shaking leaves is music that pleases and attracts the "People of Yagé". The cigars and Achiote pods should be available by 3:00 pm. The Mamekoko leaf wand may be available by 4:00 pm. Achiote is usually very easy to obtain, practically all native

families cultivate the trees in their gardens. Sometimes it is not possible to find the native cigars because some natives do not cultivate their native tobacco any longer, so that is precisely why as a back up, you have taken cigarettes to the jungle. (The Cooker and his assistant will surely be too busy on the day of cooking Yagé to personally make or get these things for you, so you should find someone else).

I would recommend on one of the days before you drink Yagé, to assure that someone will get for you the Achiote dye and a thin stick, so that you can practice drawing different designs on your face; it will be helpful for you to be acquainted to the dye, the thin stick and the designs. Upon receiving the Achiote pods and the thin stick, check the thin stick to see if the edges are round enough to feel smooth on your skin. Usually the natives enjoy showing their different ancestral designs, so if there is someone who is willing to help you, then take advantage. With sufficient light, your mirror and the thin stick, you can crack open the pod of an Achiote and with a few drops of water you can wet the interior of one of the halves of the pod and start drawing on your face the red vegetable dye tattoos. On the day of drinking Yagé, you should personally paint your own face and body.

Besides the red Achiote dye, which washes of easily with water and soap, in some communities, the people use a black colored dye, which lasts for about six days; this dye is called

Huito, pronounced (we-to). This dye may be applied on the face and body, but it should be applied the day before drinking Yagè, because when you put it on it is practically transparent and with one days time it will become black. If you are interested in using this dye and if it is available, you have to make this arrangement in advance, because it requires a few days to prepare. Unfortunately, the fruit of this dye is not available year

round. Save the same stick that you have been using to practice different designs on your face and body for the day when you will drink Yagé. The Mamekoko palm leaf wand should be made the late afternoon of the day that you will drink Yagé.

Of the hundreds of tourists who I have seen using the Achiote dye, there had only been two people who had an allergic reaction. There was no itching, but on the following morning after washing off the dye, the skin was irritated and signs of the tattoo designs still remained. Consequently, if you have sensitive skin, I would recommend checking with your doctor, to see if you can first put on your face a skin cream or baby oil and then afterwards the red Achiote dye, otherwise you could try putting on your skin a watered down version of only a few Achiote designs.

Since the first day that you arrive to the jungle, it would be better if you eat all your meals using your own personal plate, silverware, and you should wash your own utensils and keep them separate from other silverware or plates. Remember to say grace before each meal.

On the day of drinking Yagé, upon awakening in the morning, light a candle and incense, and as always reaffirm that God is alive in you and because of this, you are a sacred being. Now use your Spiritual energy, your Pranayama breathing exercise and the palms of your hands to activate your internal Spiritual energy. Then, with the force of Prana send off purifying and healing energy to your entire physical, mental, emotional and Spiritual body and to all of the people that are with you.

After this, bless your purgative, drink it slowly and chew it, then you should do your Yoga and Tai Chi exercises, meditate and take your shower. Later in the morning you can have one type of a fruit, like papayas or bananas, pineapple is not advisable.

During this special day you should find an activity which is physically strenuous, like going on a five hour hike or some similar exercise that will make you feel so physically tired, that by the end of the day all that you would like to do is sleep. This I shall explain later, at the actual moment of drinking Yagé.

Around midday, you should eat a light lunch that is easy to digest, like brown rice or potatoes with tomatoes or vegetables, without chili peppers or salt. After eating your light lunch, check with the native man who you hired to obtain the three native cigars and the Mamekoko palm leaf wand. Ask him also to get for you four pods of Achiote. Be sure that this man has at least three hours before sunset to make the wand.

Check all that you will need for the Yagé ceremony. You should have two main nylon bags; bag #1 containing everything that you need to take to the Casita de Yagé, and in bag #2 with personal items that you do not need to take to the Casita de Yagé, this bag may be left back at the Campsite or Lodge.

In your nylon duffle bag #1, you should have: (In a large transparent plastic bag #1a, you will have the following six items that you will need for the next day after drinking Yagé):

1. One set of clean clothes.
2. One pair of cotton socks.
3. Inside a transparent plastic bag; one small, dry towel, preferably of a chamois type, which typically is used by divers and dries quickly.
4. One dry bathing suit in a transparent plastic bag.
5. One roll of toilet paper in a transparent plastic bag.

**6.** Two empty transparent plastic bags for dirty clothes.

(The following items you will need to also have in the    same duffle bag #1, for the night of drinking Yagé.) Some    items may be purchased in Quito, which I shall indicate.

**7.**  Sleeping bag.
**8.** One pair of comfortably white cotton socks which
       may be useful if during the night you feel cold.
**9.** One, 3 cm (1 in.) thick candle and three thick
       incense sticks in a transparent plastic bag. (Quito)
**10.** Hammock with a strong nylon rope at each end and
        with a mosquito netting down to the floor. (Quito)
**11.** One old, white t-shirt.

 (In a light colored, nylon medium size bag #3 with a
 shoulder strap, you should have):

**12.** Flashlight with a medium intensity light.
**13**. Non transparent zip lock strong plastic bag about
        25cm.x 30cm. for spitting into.
**14.** Personal ceramic bowl in a cloth bag and in a
        transparent plastic bag. (Quito)
**15.** 1 roll of toilet paper.
**16.** Two, half-liter plastic bottles of pure water. (Quito)

 (In another smaller nylon bag #4, preferably of a
 different light color with a shoulder strap):

**17.** Three native cigars or a package of cigarettes.
**18.**One small package of waterproof matches.
**19.** A 15 cm. tall plastic jar with a screw top for
        holding water to put out the lit cigars or cigarettes.
        (Quito)
**20.** 6 incense sticks preferably thick. (Quito)
(In a large bag #5, which on the day of drinking Yage you will

put in your backpack, these items you will be using that afternoon for bathing and later for the Ceremonial hut):

21. One transparent empty plastic bag for dirty clothes.
22. One underwear.
23. Yagé jewelry. (Quito)
24. One native style gown. (Quito)
25. One pair of clean, cotton socks.
26. Two, 3 cm. (1 in.) thick candles and a small candleholder. (Quito)
27. Waterproof matches in a plastic bag.
28. Four, thick incense sticks in a plastic bag. (Quito)
29. Swiss army knife or similar.
30. Small mirror.
31. A plastic bottle of purified and blessed water. (Quito)
32. Biodegradable soap in a plastic bag.
33. One small, (100 ml.) biodegradable shampoo.
33. One chamois type of towel that is typically used by divers, in a plastic bag.
34. Crystal quartz wrapped in a cloth, in a transparent plastic bag. (Quito)
35. One roll of toilet paper in a plastic bag.
36. A light colored cotton or linen cloth about 80 cm. by 1 meter (32 in. by 3 ft.). (Quito)
37. One dry bathing suit for bathing that afternoon.

The most appropriate clothes that I recommend for men and women to use for drinking Yagé are loose, thin cotton gowns, similar to gowns that are used by some of the Amazonian tribes in Ecuador, Colombia and Peru. For you, they are the best clothing to use for drinking Yagé. Besides, if you can dress like the ethnic native people for such an important ceremony like drinking Yagé, they will appreciate it, but also the "People of Yagé" will appreciate it and they will assist you more through your Yagé experience. Precisely, this is the reason why the Amazonian natives of each different tribe, dress and decorate their bodies as they do, because after drinking Yagé, they will see the People of Yagé dressed and decorated in that manner. The color black is not a recommended color for the Yagé clothes, because this color is prone to attracting harmful energy.

In Ecuador, the best place to purchase the items for drinking Yagé, signaled (Quito) in your list, as well as Amazonian colorful glass bead necklaces, and posters and lithographs of my Yagè paintings is in a craft shop which together with an Ecuadorian food and vegetarian food restaurant, I shall in the future be opening in Quito. This

shop and restaurant will be called "La Gente del Yagè" (The People of Yagè).

The first ten times that I drank Yagé I was not wearing the colorful glass bead necklaces or a native gown and I had excellent experiences, but if it is possible for you to get these things, your experience would probably be better.

By 3:00 pm., you should be ready to bathe. It would be better for your Yagé experience if you bathe at the bank of a river or lake. It should be safe for you to get to the bank of the river or lake, and the water should not be chemically polluted. Unfortunately, because of toxic wastes from Oil companies, or fungicides and pesticides from African Palm Oil plantations, some of the Amazonian rivers are polluted part of the year. As soon as you arrive to your lodge or campsite, and if you have a river or lake, check with the Shaman or Cooker, if the nearby river or lake is safe from chemical pollution, and if so, then you should bathe in it before the day of drinking Yagè. If you do not have available a river or lake, then probably you have a private shower or an outdoor shower, which will be all right.

Before actually getting into the water of a river or lake, you should spread your cotton cloth on the ground; put your crystal quartz, candle, incense and matches on the edge of the cloth in front of you. Take off your shoes and sit on the cotton cloth in a comfortable Yoga position, now light the candle and incense, pass the open palms of your hands over the flame and place your open palms facing upward, over your knees. Now perform your Yoga Pranayama breathing for a few minutes and then use your thought, your open palms and the force of Prana to bless yourself and the area where you are, including the water. Point your open palms in the direction of what you want to bless. Then get into the water and imagine that the water that is wetting your body is a purifying, sacred light that is coming from God.

After bathing, put on your short or underwear, Yagé gown, socks and shoes, and keep everything else in your backpack. Upon returning to the campsite or lodge, you should check to see if the native man returned with your cigars, Achiote dye, and Mamekoko wand. If not, while you wait for this man to return, you can start organizing your backpack and duffle bags.

Put in duffle bag # 2; the plastic bag with your dirty clothes, wet bathing suit and wet towel. Additionally, put in your backpack the plastic bag (#1a), from your duffle bag #1 that contains the items that you will need for the following day and your Yagè jewelry, if you have. Also in your backpack, you should have a plastic bottle of pure water and a Swiss army knife, or similar.

After this, you should find a place where you can comfortably decorate your face and body. Spread your cotton or linen cloth on the table or ground, take out your crystal quartz, candleholder, candle, incense, matches, Yagé jewelry, mirror, and the thin stick for painting on the Achiote dye. Set all these things on the cloth at one edge in front of you, and leave them there until the native man arrives with the cigars, Mamekoko wand and the Achiote dye. Once the native man arrives and gives you what he brought, put those things together with everything else. By 4:00 p.m., you should light the candle and incense in front of you and bless the cigars, Mamekoko wand, dyes and all of your Yagé jewelry.

Now put on all of your Yagé jewelry and begin to paint designs on your face with the achiote. The ethnic native people always paint their own tattoo designs on themselves, so obviously I recommend you to do the same. You can imitate different native motive designs that you see, or you can invent your own designs, but remember not to imitate any particular designs that you see on Shamans. Under the influence of Yagé, powerful Amazonian Shamans can actually transform them selves into the physical body of a jaguar, and this jaguar will be active during that night in the Spiritual world, as well as also it can be physically active during that night in the material world. Typically, when Shamans are able to become jaguars, they will paint red Achiote lines touching or extending from the edges of their lips or mouths. These special tattoo designs represent the jaguar, by means of its fangs and its ferocious blood thirsty hunting abilities.

All of the facial and corporal tattoo designs used by the ethnic native people are taken from actual designs that they see in the Yagé visionary world. Some of these designs may have also have been tattoo designs painted on the faces or bodies of the People of Yagé. Apart from the face or body tattoos, since centuries ago, the native people have decorated their clay pottery or cotton fabrics with Yagé visionary geometric designs.

Example of some of the Yagè tattoo designs used:

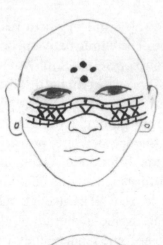
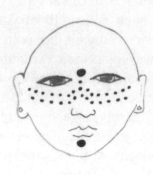

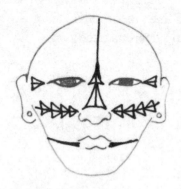

Tatoo designs

Once you have finished decorating yourself, you should pick up the Mamekoko leaf wand and you move your hand freely, feeling the wand as if it were one with your hand, part of your arm. The wand represents a metaphysical open hand belonging to the powerful Spirits of all the plants, trees and People of Yagè. The subtle, rustling sound of the shaking leaves of the wand is music that pleases the Spirits of the plants of Yagé and the People of Yagé, and attracts the presence of the People of Yagé. Additionally, the Mamekoko wand is aiding to control the invisible God-like force of Prana that is in the air. The mild breeze that the wand in motion produces represents the force of Prana, the energy and force of God that is everywhere. The Mamekoko wand also has the power of absorbing any harmful energy, which could be present. Moving the wand, you should think that you are a sacred being and that your Spiritual energy united with the force of Prana is intensely alive in you.

Put in your backpack, your cloth, your candle, your candleholder and your crystal quartz.

Carrying your backpack, your duffle bag #1 and your Mamekoko wand, you should go to the ceremonial hut before sunset. The shoes and cotton socks that you use should fit loosely, the shoes should be easy to take off and put on, so for example if you have shoes with shoestrings, I would recommend once you get to the Ceremonial hut to take out the shoestrings.

As you are walking, keep silent, and mentally ask God and the People of Yagé to bless you and to bless anything that you will touch.

Upon arriving to the clearing of the Casita de Yagé, you should mentally ask permission to the Spirits of the ceremonial hut, the Spirits of the Yagé plants and the People of Yagè to allow you to enter the sacred site and to take part in the Yagé ceremony. Then, entering into the hut, ask the Shaman or leader of the ceremony where you can set up your hammock, and if you have a choice, it would be better for you to be at one of the two long lateral edges of the hut, and not too close to the pot of Yagé. The reason is that during the night, native people that are drinking Yagé will be getting out of their hammocks and going to the pot of Yagé to drink more of the sacred brew. It will be better for you to have the least number of distractions from other people.

After tying your hammock onto the beams of the hut, tie onto the nylon cables of your hammock closest to your reach, as you are in the hammock the following bags: medium size nylon shoulder strap bag (#3) and the nylon shoulder strap bag (#4). These two bags should be of two different light colors like bright lime green for the bag (#3) and bright pink for the bag (#4), or they can be of the same light colors and with a bold black marker, on the outside you can write the names of the contents. This will make it easier for you to distinguish them during the night in case you need to get any of the contents. The nylon material will help to protect the different items that are in the bags from the high nocturnal humidity that is always in the air.

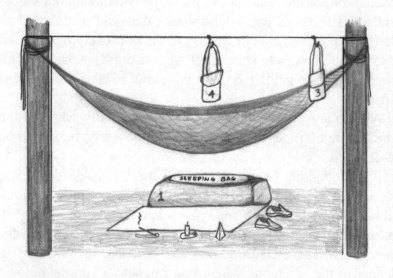

For drinking Yagè, position of bags and items

Underneath the middle of your hammock you can put your duffle bag #1 and in it your backpack. Inside your duffle bag, over your backpack you should have your sleeping bag and your loose, cotton socks, ready to use, for when you feel cold later in the evening.

Before the sun sets, have your Mamekoko wand with you and go with a machete to investigate for the best place where you can walk into the forest. It is almost certain that late in the night you will need a path into the forest to walk a short distance to go behind a tree to use as a toilet. If you see large Conga ants or wasp nests under leaves or branches, do not disturb these animals and look for another path. Once you have found the best path, mark the entrance to the path by pushing a tall stick into the edge of the clearing and tie an old white t-shirt on top of the stick. If a native friend can help you, it will be much better. Check the ground, plants and tree trunks for any thorns, ants or wasp nests. Go back to your hammock, take off your shoes and socks and leave them within your reach, next to your hammock. The only time that you will use your shoes that night is if you have to go out of the Casita de Yagé on to the clearing and to the edge of the forest or into the forest.

Now, you can spread your cotton cloth on the ground next to your hammock and on one edge of the cloth, put a lit candle, two lit incense and your crystal quartz. Sit on the cloth, face the candle, incense and quartz, do your Yoga breathing for a few minutes and using your open palms bless your hammock and all of your belongings. If you are a religious person, pray to God to bless the sacred brew of Yagè, the Casita de Yagè and all the people who are going to drink Yagè. Get out of bag #4 the plastic jar and put in it a little water.

By now it is already sunset and the animal sounds are dramatically changing. Some late diurnal birds are frenetically calling and at the same time flying as fast as they can to reach their nests before it gets dark. Sometimes bats may appear within the clearing of the ceremonial hut as well as in most of the other clearings in the rainforest. Suddenly as the sky blackens, the nocturnal animals with their extraordinary sounds take over the night, the most prominent sounds are of nightjars, nighthawks, owls, tree frogs, toads and the orchestra of crickets. These nocturnal animal sounds are strangely beautiful and set the most appropriate background music for the Amazonian sacred, Spiritual, Yagé ceremony that is about to begin.

Now, with the presence of everyone who is going to drink Yagé, one of the Shaman men is going to lead the Ceremony. He holds in one hand his Mamekoko leaf wand and in the other hand a lit cigar. The Shaman goes to the pot of Yagé, he begins to shake the wand and at the same time, begins to smoke the cigar and blow white smoke at the brew. Humbly and silently, he talks to the newly transformed, powerful Spirit of the brew and almost immediately begins to chant in front of the pot.

After a few minutes, he continues chanting, but takes a few steps past the pot onto the edge of the "Casita de Yagé" on the grass clearing. There he continues chanting but louder and pacing in a straight line, back and forth along the east side of the hut. The Shaman is chanting and shaking the Mamekoko leaf wand towards different directions, but primarily the chanting and shaking of the wand is directed up to the sky. The chanting is repetitive in its phrases and sounds, and its rhythm is very fast. The Shaman is respectfully asking for the almighty, glorious assistance of Gods energy, and asking for the presence and personal assistance of all People of Yagé as well as personal People of Yagé allies that the Shaman may have in the Spiritual world.

After chanting, the Shaman will walk into the hut, put the leaf wand on a bench, get his personal bowl and go to the pot of Yagé. Using the communal Yagé bowl, the Shaman will scoop some of the brew and pour it into his personal bowl, then the Shaman will slowly drink the brew. After this, the rest of the Shamans, Cookers, apprentices and all of the people will likewise drink the brew. After drinking the sacred brew, always the people will walk onto the clearing and throw out the remainder of the brew that settles at the bottom of their personal bowls. Then, most of the people will wash out their mouths with virgin water and may spit out this water onto the clearing or to the edge of the forest.

When it is your turn, get your bowl and go to the pot of Yagé, then use the communal bowl to get the sacred brew from the cooking pot and then put that brew into your personal bowl. Be careful not to touch the brew that is in the pot with your fingers. In some native communities, the Shamans or Cookers do not have a communal bowl, so in that case it would be all right for you to put your own personal bowl directly into the pot. After you have put the sacred brew in your personal bowl, ask the most powerful Shaman or if there is no Shaman, you may ask your friend the Cooker to bless the Yagé that is in your personal bowl.

If the Shaman or Cooker agrees, then give him your personal bowl. He will say or think some special words to the People of Yagé and to the Spirits of the Yagé brew that is in your bowl, and he may blow smoke into the bowl. The Shaman will then put the bowl up to your lips. I strongly recommend for you to wait until all the smoke from inside your bowl has lifted. While you are waiting for the smoke to lift, you can put your two hands together up to your chest and say grace.

Usually, during the blessing of the Shaman or Cooker, they prefer you to drink the blessed brew without you touching your bowl. Therefore, do not touch your bowl; put your hands to the sides. The Shaman will still be holding the bowl up to your lips, slowly drink the sacred brew of Yagé and remember to chew the brew. Keep your lips barely open as you are slowly sipping the brew, so that as soon as you feel the tiny, granulated bits of wooden material or leaves touching your lips, you will be able to quickly close your lips and not drink anymore.

Raise your face, the Shaman or Cooker will understand why you do not want to drink anymore. Then the Shaman or Cooker will hand you your personal bowl. Take your bowl with your two hands and lower your head as if you are bowing, this gesture is to thank the Shaman or Cooker for his blessing. Remember, if you accidentally drink some of the granulated Yagè material, it will be disturbing for your throat and may bother you during the night.

After drinking Yagé, go to your hammock, put on your shoes, get your nylon shoulder bag # 3, your flashlight, your Mamekoko wand and walk onto the edge of the clearing. Remember when using your flashlight, never to direct the light near to anyone's face. Arriving to the edge of the clearing, look at the granulated leftover vegetable material that is inside your bowl and shaking your Mamekoko wand, tell the Spirits of the plants of Yagé that are inside your bowl to go back to Pacha Mama. Then you should throw out the left over brew, into the forest. After this, pour water into your bowl, rinse it out and then again tell the Spirits of the plants of Yagé to go back to Mother Nature. Throw that water out towards the interior of the forest.

Keep your bowl in its cloth and inside its nylon bag. Get your bottle of water and plastic zip-lock bag for spitting, and now rinse your mouth out and spit the water into your plastic bag. It is important for you to remember not to spit on the ground or clearing, only inside the plastic bag. Remember also, never to place your personal bowl or water on the ground. Shamans, apprentices, Cookers and other native people have much more experience with Yagé than you and they will probably be spitting on the ground, but for you as a beginner I do not recommend it. Sometimes, spitting on the ground may not affect some beginners, but why take the risk of jeopardizing your Yagé experience.

Go back to your hammock, light another incense. Remember that bag #3 containing the plastic bag for spitting in, should be within your reach, in case you need to spit again during the night. From bag #4 get your cigars or cigarettes with matches and go to one of the low benches to smoke, if there is a low fire, it is all right to go there. Usually natives are also walking around, sitting or talking. It seems that this activity helps the digestion of Yage. Smoke as much as you comfortably can, stay as long as you want and then go back to your hammock.

Take off your shoes, keep your flashlight in its nylon bag and fasten the nylon bag onto the hammock nylon cable again. Since you have had a long and strenuous day, you should be physically tired. Now lie back in your hammock, close your eyes, and fall asleep.

Your mind is linked to both your brain and to your Spiritual body, and these are the most powerful sources of energy in your body. At this point, your interest is for your Spiritual body to awaken, and for this to happen your conscious mind should not be working. While your conscious, intellectual mind is quiet and resting, then you can sleep, and your subconscious mind can awaken and wander off to dream. This is when your Spiritual body will be more awake and receptive, and precisely this is the state that you are interested in achieving. So remember, do not consciously think about anything, and do not try to control the situation. You should not be at all concerned about when or how your visions will start. On the contrary, if you start using your conscious mind, you will be forcing a situation that is unnatural, and for sure, your experience will not be as wonderful as it could be. Just relax, do not control your thoughts and let your tired body doze off.

Only when the metaphysical chemistry and energy of the Spirits of the plants of Yagé are in your Chakras and Spiritual body, then your Spiritual body will be fully awakened and only then, will your tired, physical, mental and emotional bodies begin to naturally awaken. This may happen after one or two hours, or whenever, this varies with different people and any length of time will be perfectly all right.

You will probably begin to hear animal calls that are louder and you will probably begin to hear a comfortably loud, mystical, beautiful humming sound, this sound is an effect from the awakened energy of your Spiritual body. Now that your physical body has awakened, you may open your eyes and you will see in front of you and all around you the most beautiful, breathtaking scene of your entire life, the fantastic, colorful visions of the Amazonian Spiritual World! Finally, you are in the true world of the Amazon, the Spiritual World.

Eventually, you will begin to feel an incredible amount of energy in you, an energy so powerful like you have never felt before in your lifetime. This is the energy of your Spiritual body that is fully awakened. This energy will make you feel powerful, magnificent, glorious, happy and full of absolute confidence. You are not afraid of anything. This special power, which is now at your disposal, exists because of the fusion of different energies. These energies are from God; the live Spirits of the two Yagé sacred plants that are now rushing in your bloodstream, the eternal glorious force of Prana, and your fully awakened Spiritual body that is now in the Amazonian Spiritual World.

Once again as when your physical body was born, your body is again in perfect balance; this is Spiritually, mentally, physically and emotionally. This is another important reason why you feel so powerful. However, these moments are crucial and you must be careful with this new power. It seems that as you use more your physical body, each cell in your physical body will become more aware of this new glorious sensation, this tremendous power, and your physical body will instinctively want to assimilate all of this power for itself.

If you permit the selfish and greedy instinct of your physical body to take over, yes, you will feel physically powerful, but you will be losing a unique and vital opportunity of strengthening more your Spiritual body and getting closer to God.

Your benefits will be much greater if you control your mind and choose not to use this power in any physical way. Precisely part of one's training as an apprentice to becoming an Amazonian Shaman is that one should always give priority to the awakening and strengthening of one's Spiritual body. Do not allow your physical body to upset the balance that your Spiritual body has finally attained.

Only after months of drinking Yagé, when an apprentice's Spiritual body is very strong can the apprentice afford to give up "some" of her/his Spiritual body energy to perform feats of healing, or other feats that are considered supernatural.

As you are seeing your visions, you should try to remember to give more importance to the awakening and strengthening of your Spiritual body than to the marvelous, colorful visions. However, these visions are so incredibly beautiful, that no one can help, but to admire them. Even though these visions play a secondary role to your Yagé experience, they are also important. Because of the importance of these visions, the ethnic native people would never think of drinking Yagé during the nights of a full moon. With the light of the moon, the quality of the colors, brightness and details of the visions will be poor. The darker that the nighttime sky is, the better that the Yagé visionary experience will be. So for any person who is interested in drinking Yagé, I recommend for you to plan your visit to the Amazon, during the moonless nights. Yes you certainly will admire the overall visions, but do not use your mind to analyze any specific details, just let your subconscious mind and your awakened Spiritual body take you to where they want to go.

After a short while of seeing the visions and assimilating all of this powerful energy and beauty, you should decide whether you want to drink more Yagé or not, obviously by drinking more Yagé, your overall experience will be enhanced. If you do decide to drink more, then you should carefully put on your shoes and get out of your hammock. As you are standing, you should see if you can physically get to the pot of Yagé. The first time that I had my real Yagé visionary experience, I could not walk, so I crawled to where I needed to go. If you can not walk or crawl with complete physical control, then you should get back into your hammock and continue as described later, after *4 paragraphs. But, if you can get to the pot of Yagé without falling or touching any of the other hammocks, then with your shoes on, get your shoulder bag # 3, and your Mamekoko wand. Put the strap of your bag over your head and across your chest and carefully start walking or crawling.

Usually, one's night vision betters with Yagé, so you should have sufficient light within the hut, but if you really need to use your flashlight, it is all right, but you must be very careful with it. Even though, the people who are lying in their hammocks have their eyes closed, you should never direct any part of the light towards anyone's face. The flashlight should always be pointed only towards the ground. (Forehead strap flashlights or headlamps should never be used for drinking Yagé, they are the most unfriendly type of flashlights for the jungle, not only will you disturb the other people and their experiences, but you may cause harm to their eyes. Remember that after drinking Yagé you and everyone else have their eyes dilated.)

Arriving to the pot of Yagé, sit on one of the benches, there may be another person there also drinking more Yagé, remember, it is better if you do not talk. You may see Shamans, Cookers or apprentices talking, but they have more experience and often after drinking Yagé they will sit around the pot of brew, conversing, smoking cigars, walking around, and or chanting.

If you drink a second bowl of Yagé, remember to chew and drink the brew slowly and remember not to drink the granulated material. You may not have the physical co-ordination to walk on the grass clearing to wash your bowl, so tell the left over brew to go back to Pacha Mama and throw the granulated material out to the forest. Put the bowl in its cloth bag and in its plastic bag, then go back to your hammock. Take off your shoes, get in your hammock, wash your mouth with water and spit inside the plastic bag.

(*4th paragraph) Well, here you are sitting in your hammock either you did not go to drink more Yagé or you just got back from drinking more Yagé. Fasten your nylon bag to the hammock cord; now try to smoke another cigar or cigarette. Sit up in your hammock and reach for your bag #4 with cigars. Smoke your cigar or cigarette for as long as you comfortably can. After you finish smoking, put the lit cigar in your plastic jar with water and lay back in your hammock.

In complete darkness, you are seeing and feeling the indescribable, captivating colors and motion of figures and sounds of the Spiritual World, and in reality, you have truly become a part of this World. The powerful, glorious energy of the Spiritual World has actually enveloped you and the entire area of the "Casita de Yagé". You and your Spiritual body are one with God's energy and with everything. You are a sacred being, it is your birthright.

Do not waste these precious moments and this unique opportunity in analyzing what you are seeing or feeling. The following day you shall have plenty of time to recall the beauty of your visions and your glorious experiences in the Amazonian Spiritual World.

Usually, around four in the morning is when the night temperature in the jungle begins to change dramatically and suddenly you will begin to feel cold, then you should reach for your socks, put them on, and cover yourself with your sleeping bag. Shortly afterwards you will fall asleep, which is perfect because your physical body needs to rest.

Generally around 6:30 in the morning is when you will begin to awaken. You will feel very different and will probably want to stay in your hammock for a while longer assimilating your new condition and analyzing your experience of the previous night, but keep in mind that very soon nature will call! So as soon as you can, you should get out of our hammock. Your vision may seem a little blurred and you will probably feel off balance, all of this is completely normal and it should not worry you, after about an hour or so your vision and balance will become normal.

Put on your shoes, get your backpack and put into it, your quartz, candleholder, cotton cloth, and your personal Yagè bowl, and go to the nearest toilet facility. Throughout the rest of the day, remember not to use your special powers, those powers should be stored for your Spiritual body. Do not describe to anyone, any of your Yagé visions. After using the toilet facility, you probably will want to go back to your hammock to sleep, or to recollect your Yagé experience. Eventually, after a few hours of resting, you will probably want to get up and go bathe.

For breakfast, I recommend to first drink slowly a large glass of warm water with drops of lemon, and after a while have one kind of fruit. Later in the morning, you can have something more substantial to eat and remember always to say grace, eat healthy and slowly, chew as much as possible and never overeat.

During this day, do not overexert ourselves, even though you may feel physically very strong. You should have a restful day and not waste your special energy on insignificant feats of physical strength. Your surplus energy should be treated as a precious gift of God, and it should be used only for strengthening more your now awakened holy Spiritual-mental body.

**CHAPTER 8**

When you first start drinking Yagé, your Spiritual-mental body will be able to perceive the true Spiritual world. You will see millions of abstract, beautifully colored geometrical, zoomorphic figures, all of these colors and figures are auras of Spiritual energy that are within Prana, the Amazon Spiritual World and the metaphysical material world. Eventually, after drinking more Yagé, you will also begin to see in a clearer, more physical human appearance, the God sent "People of Yagé", which will appear in this material world as ancestral, very happy, holy Shamans.

Currently, we sometimes see in some forms of contemporary art, abstract art forms similar to the visions of Yagé, but to me what is incredibly amazing is that the upper Amazonian natives as well as the Pacific tropical rainforest natives of Ecuador and Colombia were seeing amazingly abstract colors and images at least one thousand years ago.

At about the same time, in most of Europe, the art was completely different; practically all of the art was non-abstract, conformist to the material world and to the influence of the Vatican and the monarchy governing-class families.

In attempting to better describe the unique and beautiful Spiritual and materialistic Amazonian world, I am presenting photographs of six of my paintings based on my personal visionary experiences in the Spiritual world after taking the sacred brew of Yagé. Through these paintings that I am presenting, my intention is to visually transport the person who sees my paintings directly into the Amazon, and experience an atmosphere of being in the jungle with some of the People of Yagè Shamans.

In this book, for me, it was important not to paint in an

abstract form, so that all foreigners who have never been in the magnificent Amazon can see my paintings and relate to them better, truly feeling as if they were actually being transported into my paintings, into the beautiful Amazon with the People of Yagè.

One of my future projects is to paint much more, exhibit and sell my art. And, eventually, I shall present more colorful, abstract paintings with fantastic forms of the beautiful, glorious Amazonian Spiritual world, which I have been blessed in so often visiting.

Beloved hut of Yagè with two Shamans

A typical clearing and structure of a "Casita de Yagé", within the hut are two Shamans, one is lying in his hammock having his Yagé Spiritual experience, while the other Shaman is about to drink more Yagé. Next to both of them are their Mamekoko wands. Behind the hut at the edge of the forest are many small sacred Angel Trumpet trees with their different white, pink and yellow colored flowers. At the right side of the edge of the forest is a yellow flowering Yagé vine climbing over the canopy of its host tree and other trees. The Yagè plants produce their flowers of yellow, pink or white color. The canopy layer of the trees that are in the background against the skyline are showing many, various animal and human forms, which sometimes appear after I drink Yagé. In this material world, one of the ways in which trees manifest their divine nature as Spirits is by taking on human or animal forms.

One clear star-lit night, after drinking Yagé, I was inside an open thatch roof native hut, sitting in my hammock looking out at the wondrous jungle. At one side of the hut was a small river and at the other three sides was virgin forest. As I looked out at the nearby vegetation, I could feel a vibrant energy radiating from the vegetation. Then I remembered what my Shaman friends had always told me and what I had always felt since I started drinking Yagé, God created everything, including plants and trees with their own Spirits.

In the distance, beyond a giant Kapok tree I noticed a dense group of clouds coming nearer to the area where I was, then I felt an unfamiliar breeze arriving to the entire area of the hut. Suddenly from within the nearby forest about 12 meters (37 ft.) away, I distinguished a strange spot of fog that was lifting from a group of plants. To my amazement, this rising fog quickly took the shape of a "People of Yagè" Shaman. This Spirit Shaman had come to me from the Amazonian Spiritual world. He was smiling at me and his eyes reminded me so much of my first Shaman friend and teacher Don Piwali.

When I saw this vision, I was not afraid of it. The Spirit Shaman was friendly. In one hand, he was shaking a bundle of Mamekoko leaves and in the palm of his other hand; he was holding an iridescent green magical "Tsentsak" dart. Then it occurred to me that the Spirit Shaman wanted to give me his green magical dart. At that time, I did not know enough about these darts, I had heard that they were powerful magic helpers, which could be beneficial to have, but also I had heard that they could be dangerously evil. Therefore, I was hesitant, and eventually decided not to accept the gift.

The color of the Spirit Shaman's body was the same color of the beautiful clouds, until his body was completely formed, then his skin became a natural dark brown color and his ornaments changed to gorgeous bright, glowing colors. The Shaman extended his hand with the dart forward towards me, but I decided not to take his gift, soon afterwards the vision faded away. On the following morning, I regretted not having accepted the dart. However, learning more about the magical darts, I knew that I had made the right decision.

All of the upper Amazonian tribes have used these darts, but especially famous is in the southern Ecuadorian Amazon with the Shuara (Jivaro), Achuara and Shiwiar tribes. These tribes call the darts Tsentsaks. It is believed that the only way for an apprentice to acquire her or his first magical darts is by receiving them directly from a powerful Shaman, and when one receives these darts, one has to swallow them, keep them in one's stomach and feed them in order to strengthen them. Powerful Shamans may have hundreds of these magical darts inside of them; these darts can be used for protecting one from harmful energy, or witchcraft, or for attacking one's enemies. Unfortunately, between the Shuara and Achuara tribes there has been a long history of hostility, which has forced the two tribes into becoming more aggressive and war-like. Inclusively, they both practiced shrinking enemy human heads and in the past, they performed a lot of witchcraft.

When an apprentice or Shaman has these darts inside of their stomach, they have to be very careful, because the devil is constantly tempting that person to use the darts in an evil way, in which case, one could use the Tsentsak magical darts through witchcraft to harm and or kill people.

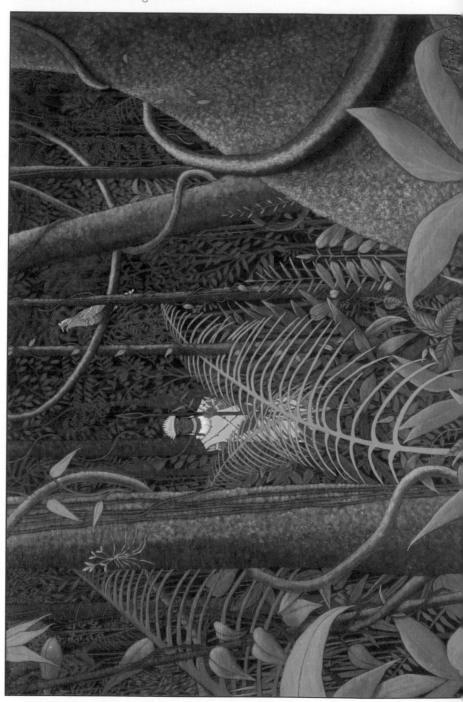

One of the most typical and most beautiful animal sounds in the Amazon is the call of a nocturnal nighthawk named in English the "Common Potoo." Personally, I feel that this bird should have a name more deserving of its unique and beautiful call. All through the Amazon, millions of these nighthawks will call out only on a full Moon or near full Moon nights. (Within the cosmology of most of the ethnic natives, the Moon is a divine, female star.)

During one of my Yagè visionary astral flights I met a Shaman from the Spiritual world of Yagè in the middle of the forest, he was of the Cofan tribe and was wearing a jaguar fang necklace, a seed necklace with four whistling trumpet Yagè seeds, also he was holding a bamboo spear and next to him was a Common Potoo perched on a liana, singing. The Shaman welcomed me and together we went deeper into the forest to hunt, I saw and heard many animals, including many Common Potoos. At one point I asked the Shaman Spirit about the origin of the nighthawks, and then he told me the following story:

Since the beginning of time, the full Moon has always been the brightest and most beautiful star in the night sky. Many years ago, one night, there appeared in the sky a new star that was also beautiful; this star was almost as big and bright as the Moon and it was a distant brother-star of the Moon. Impressed with the extraordinary beauty of the full Moon, hopelessly the male star began falling in love with his sister. Eventually, the Moon also fell in love with her brother. Their love was strong, but especially so, during that time of the month when the Moon was full. One full Moon night, their passionate attraction to each other was so great that they made love.

God discovered their forbidden act; they had performed incest and because of this God decided to punish them, so God banned the male star from the sky. The male star began falling from the sky down to earth; finally, after a long dreadful journey, it crashed right in the middle of the Amazon, there was a tremendous explosion, which sounded throughout the forest and made the ground tremble. From this great explosion, there were millions of sparks, which dispersed in the four main directions of the jungle, and from each one of these sparks was born a "Common Potoo" nighthawk.

Seeing the fate of its past love, the Moon began to weep. The tears of the Moon fell throughout the Amazon as rain. These tears fell on each nighthawk and transformed the Common Potoos feathers to a mottled gray-white color, almost identical to the colors of the Moon itself. The millions of newly born Common Potoo nighthawks did not know what to eat; the jungle was dark and filled with dangerous animals. Considering this terrible misfortune, the Moon pleaded with God to help the Potoos. Therefore, God made their mouths larger and instructed them to eat flying nocturnal insects.

Since that night, during the daytime, the Potoos sleep on ends of broken, dead tree branches, which camouflage perfectly with the unusual mottled gray-white color of their feathers, and during the nighttime, they awaken to feed on flying insects. Strangely enough, only on full Moon nights and sometimes, on near full Moon nights, these unusual nighthawks will call out their song. They perch on vines and branches, they look up to the Moon and sing their song, and afterwards they go up to the sky above the canopy layer to catch flying insects. Later they land somewhere else within the forest where again, they will
rest, and then they will look up to the Moon, make their call again, and so on, throughout the entire night.

During the full Moon nights, the Common Potoos will more easily catch flying insects. The reason being that nocturnal flying insects are naturally always attracted to light, and during a full moon, the light emitting from the Moon is the most powerful light in the jungle nights. Therefore, most of the flying insects are up in the sky trying desperately to reach the Moon.

The call of the Common Potoos is one of the most beautiful Amazonian animal sounds and it is the most melancholic of the birdcalls.

If you are not interested in drinking Yagè, and you are visiting the Amazon during the full Moon nights, you should be attentive to the beautiful calls of these nighthawks. Their song is a series of up to six lamenting notes; the first note is loud in pitch and volume, and then the following notes drop in pitch and volume.

Jaguars are the strongest animals and best hunters in the forest, they are a physical representation of a divine being; a powerful Spirit which controls all land domains. This Spirit represents a powerful force of unique energy which if a person learns of this energy, they could use it. Black jaguars are believed to be more dangerous than the spotted yellow and black jaguars and because of this, within the Yagé world, black jaguars are more often seen. One of the major steps in becoming an upper Amazon Shaman is to meet the jaguars of the Amazon Spiritual world. For the advanced apprentices, this meeting is essential and it takes place after drinking Yagé.

Let us imagine that you are an advanced apprentice and you have just drunk Yagè, the moment when you meet the jaguar you should remember that none of the Yagè animals will hurt you. However, the vision of these animals is so real that many people are afraid of encountering such a ferocious beast. When this vision appears, the jaguar will growl and it will attack you with its claws and fangs, you will feel the actual weight and power of the animal, you will smell the animal's body and its breath and you may see your flesh being torn and blood gushing out. Nevertheless, you have to control your mind and emotions and not show fear; you should demonstrate your courage by fighting back. Only in this way will you gain the respect of the jaguar of Yagè, and of the Spiritual-mental energy within the Amazonian Spiritual World.

As soon as this happens, the jaguar will stop attacking you; your bleeding wounds will stop hurting and will immediately start healing, and from that moment on, this particular jaguar will become your life long friend and one of your important allies. Anytime afterwards, that you drink Yagé, you may summon your jaguar ally and it will always appear. As friends and allies, the Yagé jaguar and you will travel together through the Spiritual and material worlds and the jaguar will teach you all that it knows, inclusively how to transform your  physical human body into the physical body of a jaguar! By doing this, you will be able to see and feel the Spiritual and material worlds through the eyes, and senses of a real jaguar. Obviously, this energy and relationship with this Spirit jaguar are so important, that it becomes a vital step to becoming a powerful Shaman.

When eventually you learn how to transform your physical body into the physical body of a jaguar, you have to be very careful because the devil is dangerously present. The devil will tempt you to use your recently acquired powerful jaguar energy in an evil way. If you are not attentive to the devil's presence and if you do not control your mischievous mind and constantly affirm Gods holy energy in you, you will have an uncontrollable urge to use your jaguar animal instinct to kill and not only to kill other animals but also to kill people. This important step in becoming a powerful Shaman is dangerous because some apprentices will fall into the temptation of the devil, they will kill and consequently become evil Shamans.

There is a special species of Yagé Oko called Llai Yagé, (pronounced Jai Jagè) which means Jaguar Yagé. By drinking this admixture with Yagé, the female Spirit of the plant that one ingested will instinctively be calling the Yagé jaguars and consequently Yagé jaguars will appear to the person. The first times that I drank Llai Yagé I was working with different tour groups, obviously the tourists never knew that I was drinking Yagé. After they retired to sleep in the camp house, I would take my duffle bag, hammock and cooked Llai Yagé into the forest for about 400 meters (1,300 ft.) away from the camp-site.

Completely alone in the forest I would find two trees safe from Conga (bullet) ants, Army ants and wasps, there I would set up my hammock. (In Chapter 11, I shall explain Conga and Army ants). I would light two candles, burn incense, put on my Yagé jewelry, pray, meditate, and then drink Llai Yagé. Later in the night, after my visions began, I would hear in the nearby forest, the moaning and growling of a jaguar. On the following mornings, usually the tour groups would comment on the loud growling animal sounds which during the previous night, they had heard from the forest. Our staff that was native had also heard these animal sounds and confirmed to the tourists that these were sounds of a jaguar.

If during one night, I had been drinking Llai Yagé and the tourists had not heard jaguars that night, it was almost certain that on the following morning, if we walked into the forest near to where I drank LLai Yagè, we would find fresh jaguar tracks on the ground.

Amazon ethnic natives believe that whenever jaguars killed humans, it was because these jaguars were evil apprentices or evil Shamans who had allied with the devil.

Don Fernando's sister Matilde a woman in her seventies once told me that as a teenager, she was an apprentice to becoming a Shaman and she was already in the process of learning how to transform her human body into the body of a jaguar. She could still remember this transformation. After drinking Yagé, when her Yagé jaguar ally appeared, she would get down on the ground and her body would slowly begin to change, she could remember each part of her body changing, including her face; she could even feel her jaws and fangs growing.

Observing the beautiful archeological pottery from the Pacific tropical rainforest of Ecuador, we find throughout all of the different cultures many human-jaguar figures. For at least a thousand years, throughout all of the tropical rain-forests of Ecuador, the native tribes were drinking Yagé and the powerful Shamans learned how to transform their physical bodies into the bodies of jaguars.

Often, besides seeing and confronting Yagé jaguars, some of the apprentice's will also see and confront Yagé anacondas. The anacondas are the best hunters, strongest, most feared and respected animals in rivers and lakes; they are a physical representation of a divine being, a powerful Spirit, which controls all water domains. As the jaguar, the Anaconda Spirit also possesses great knowledge and a unique powerful force of energy.

Another important animal for the Shamans is the Yagè Harpy eagle. The Harpy eagles are the largest and most powerful eagles and birds of prey in the world; they represent a powerful Spirit, which controls all the sky domains. In the past, Harpy eagles were abundant in the Amazon and the Pacific tropical rainforest in Ecuador and Colombia, and in the Central American tropical rainforest.

As with the Yagè Jaguar, when the Yagé Anaconda or the Yagè Harpy eagle appears, the apprentice should not show any sign of fear. However, if the apprentice cannot control the mind and emotions, and becomes afraid of the vision, it means that probably the apprentice will run away from the Yagè jaguar, Yagè anaconda or Yagè Harpy eagle. Consequently, the next time that the apprentice considers drinking Yagé, she or he may not want to confront the vision of these Yagè animals again. This situation could be a terribly difficult obstacle to overcome. Precisely because of this reason, some natives may give up their Shaman apprenticeship.

Shaman with Kapoc Tree

The Kapok tree is the largest and one of the most beautiful trees in the Amazon. It is an emergent tree; it grows above the canopy layer of the forest. For the Amazon Shamans, the tree is a physical representation of a divine Spirit that symbolizes old age-maturity, wisdom and strength. Since millennia, Shamans of certain tribes have selected it for special ceremonies. At nighttime, after drinking Yagé, is when these ceremonies take place.

One night after I drank Yagé, I had an astral flight, flying over the jungle seeing the forest, the rivers, animals and millions of beautiful, colored geometric figures, eventually I saw a small clearing and in the middle of the clearing I saw a thatch roof hut, getting closer I realized that it was a "Casita de Yagé". At one end of the hut, I saw the dim light of firewood, so I knew that at that moment it was in use. Coming down to the hut and looking inside, I saw a "Person of Yagé" from the Shuara tribe sitting on a low stool, playing a flute. He stopped playing his music, looked up at me and asked whom I was and what I wanted? I told him my Yagé name (different to Patricio) and told him that I was interested to learn from him. He smiled at me, put down his flute, picked up his Mamekoko wand, stood up, looked at me and went into the forest. However, he was not walking; he was floating about 50 cm. (20 in.) above the ground. I followed him, and soon he arrived to a giant Kapok tree.

He stood in front of the huge buttress root structure of this enormous tree and looking at the tree, he began to shake his wand of Mamekoko leaves, at the same time he chanted loudly and beautifully. I imagined he was chanting to God and to the Spirit of the tree. Then getting closer to the root structure of the tree, he bent down and moving aside some dirt, he picked up from the ground a flat, round, white colored rock. He then began to chant another song to the Spirit in the rock. The rock acquired a faint, lime-green color. Suddenly he began talking to the rock and blowing air at it, then he closed his hand and walked about twenty meters (65 ft.) away from the tree, he turned around looking at the tree and began to shake the Mamekoko wand. In a louder tone, looking up at the sky, he continued chanting.

After a few minutes, I heard a distant wind traveling through the forest. The wind sound was gradually getting louder. Looking towards the direction of the wind, the Shaman and I saw the forest swaying, then we saw nearby trees and branches desperately moving, as leaves, fruits, and dried branches were falling to the ground. As the full force of the wind reached me I looked back at the Shaman and saw him with his arms stretched outward, his face was looking up to the sky and his long hair was blowing in all directions.

Looking at the Shaman and the giant tree behind him, I noticed that the posture that the Shaman had assumed was similar to the physical appearance of the Kapok tree, with its branches spread outward and its vertical trunk standing upright. After a while the wind calmed down, the Shaman put his arms down to his sides. In one hand, he was still holding the wand of Mamekoko leaves and he slowly began to open his other hand, then I saw the rock radiating its green color stronger than before. At that moment, he said something to the rock, closed his hand again, turned sideways and moved his hand with the rock in it as far back as was possible, and with one swift, movement, he threw the rock as hard as he could at the tree.

The bright green colored rock flew rapidly through the air and like a powerful magnet, which seemed to be attracted to the Kapok tree; it hit the exact centre of the trunk. Upon impact, I saw a beautiful, great explosion full of phenomenal colors and tiny zoomorphic, Yagé-like figures flying out in all directions, at the same precise moment of impact; I heard the comfortably loud, beautiful sounding explosion, like thunder echoing through the forest. At the same time, the tree had blown up in millions of pieces. Afterwards, the forest was calm again and I saw the tree once again whole. Then, the entire vision gradually faded away and I awakened in my hammock.

The following day I told this vision to one of my dear Shaman friends and he explained that this special ceremony can be performed only after drinking Yagé. Depending on the destructive power of the explosion, the Shaman will be able to self evaluate her or his level of Yagé-Spiritual energy, and the level of power of the Shaman's "Tsentsak" magical darts. If after the Shaman throws the rock to the Kapok tree, she or he sees the tree being shattered into millions of pieces, it means that her or his Spiritual energy is excellent. If however, the Shaman sees a small explosion and no damage occurs to the tree, it means that the Shaman's Spiritual energy level is low.

At times during a Shaman's life it is essential to know exactly how strong ones Yagé Spiritual energy level is. This may be necessary if the Shaman needs to heal a patient of a severe spell of witchcraft. Or else also, if a God-like Shaman needs to confront a powerful evil Shaman, in this case, it becomes vital because usually this sort of confrontation will end with one of the two Shamans dying.

My wife Lily, daughter Michelle and
Anaconda energy next to canoe

In 1990, my wife Lily and daughter Michelle accompanied
me with a British tour group on an adventure camping tour
into the Amazonian national park of Cuyabeno. Each day
while we were there, we had canoe rides on the different lakes
and rivers and always I would be searching the banks for
Anaconda snakes. In the past, in this lake reserve, I had spotted many Anacondas. To see an Anaconda in the wild is an
impressive experience, which of course I wanted my wife and
daughter to witness. While we were traveling in our canoe, I
was using my thought control with Prana and my Spiritual
Yagè energy to summon an Anaconda to appear, but no
Anaconda ever appeared. On our last afternoon in the reserve
we were canoeing back to our campsite, so I decided to take a
last photograph of my wife and daughter, I took the photo-

graph from the bow of the canoe, my wife was sitting at the front while our daughter was sitting all the way at the back, on one side in front of the pilot of our canoe. His name was Rogelio Criollo, a good friend of mine from the Siona tribe.

Returning to Quito I had the roll developed and looking at this photograph, I clearly noticed that something very strange was in the water next to the canoe, something like a long tube of water on the water. What puzzled me even more was that the photograph was taken in the middle of the "Cocha Grande" lake, far from the Amazonian Acacia trees that are growing in the water and far from the bank that is in the background. Examining the photograph closer suddenly it dawned on me that the strange tube-like form that was next to the canoe could be the effects of a large adult Anaconda, which at that precise second was underwater!

To confirm what I suspected, the next time that I went to the jungle I took the photograph with me and showed it to my Shaman friends. Without telling them what I thought, I asked them to look at the photograph to see if there was anything unusual. Almost immediately, as they started to look at the photograph all of the Shamans including Don Fernando smiled and pointing at the water tube-like form, they said that there was a large Anaconda under the water!

Don Fernando told me that years ago, before outboard motors and pollution arrived, during astral flights, he sometimes saw large Anacondas in the rivers attacking people in their small canoes. He said that the animal would get under the canoe and swimming in a circle would create a whirlpool and radiate an invisible force, which he saw as waves in the air. Without possibility of escaping, the people and the canoe would be trapped in the Anaconda's field of energy. The faces of the people and the canoe were distorted within these intermittent waves. Then the stern of the canoe would start to sink as if it were being pulled underwater by the invisible force.

Quickly, the canoe would disappear into the depths of the river or lake, where the Anaconda would hunt the people that were in the water.

This special field of energy that the Anaconda produces is undetectable to the human eye, but through the energy of Yagé it becomes possible for the Shamans to see this phenomenon. I was fortunate, at that time, I had a lot of accumulated Yagé energy in me, and the camera that I had in my hand was able to perceive and record this unique Anaconda energy.

Anacondas as well as all other reptiles are cold-blooded animals, they cannot produce heat in their bodies as birds and mammals can. They depend almost entirely on the sun for their body heat and energy. Typically during the day they will find a safe place where they may absorb the heat from the sun and also during the day they may hunt for food, but at night time is when they are much more active hunting for food. In the jungle, the temperatures on land and in the water change radically during daytime and nighttime. For reptiles, during the daytime, the temperature on land is warmer than the temperature in the water and during the nighttime, the temperature in the water is warmer than the temperature on land. This is the main reason why Anacondas and other water reptiles spend most of the day on land and they will be in the water during most of the night.

The native people find that bathing in the rivers or lakes is most comfortable between 6:00 until 6:30 in the evening; they feel that at this time, the water temperature is warmest and still safe. They know that the Anacondas and other water reptiles will be moving into the water around 6:45. Because of this, the ethnic natives will never navigate the rivers or lakes in their small paddle canoes at nighttime, unless it is an emergency.

In relation to Anacondas, I have an interesting story to tell. About fifteen years ago, I had a group of tourists on a camping style tour to the Amazon. We arrived by bus in the late afternoon to a small river called Aguas Negras where two large motor powered native canoes were supposed to meet us, but no one was there, we waited for one hour but still no one arrived. Maybe the natives who our company had previously contracted forgot the date or had a problem, in any case I had to find a solution, so down the road there lived five mestizo families, which had the same river passing behind their houses. I paid one of the families to allow us to set up our tents on their property so that the tour group could spend the night there. Our cook Carlos Segovia stayed with the group, together with plenty of food supplies. Quickly I asked around to see if someone had a canoe, fortunately I found a nice Colombian man called Miguel who had a small canoe. I paid him to paddle with me down the river in his canoe. My plan was to paddle down river to the native people who we had contracted, and this way, be sure that the two large motor canoes would arrive to the tour group, early the next morning to continue with our tour.

Before leaving, we stopped at a small neighborhood grocery store to buy extra batteries and light bulbs for our flashlights, and then Miguel said that I should buy many cigarettes. I did not smoke and of course assumed that he was a heavy smoker, so I bought him twenty packages of cigarettes. He took a small nylon duffle bag in a plastic bag with him, his machete and I took my backpack, rain-poncho and my machete.

It was about 5:45 pm. when we left, the small river was about 14 meters (43 ft.) wide. Miguel was at the stern (back) and I was at the bow (front). Our tiny dugout canoe was about three meters (9 ft.) long. After about an hour it got too dark to continue, so we stopped the canoe, and then Miguel took out of his small bag, two long rubber strips made from an old tire inner tube, we used these rubber strips to tie our flashlights onto one side of our heads. Afterwards Miguel said "Well Patricio, now for the rest of the journey, we're going to have to start smoking and puffing the smoke to the banks." Surprised and at the same time, confused to hear this, I asked him why? Then Miguel said, "Only with Gods help and sufficient smoke will we be safe from all the Anacondas that live in this virgin river and jungle." I could not believe what he had just said, and even though I had quit smoking years ago, of course, I quickly took up smoking. I blew out smoke to the left bank and he blew out smoke to the right bank. With the light of my flashlight towards the forest, I could see hundreds of orange-red color eyes looking at us, these eyes were not necessarily of anacondas but yes of different animals like nocturnal monkeys, snakes, iguanas, frogs, nocturnal birds, caimans, rodents, insects, etc… On four occasions, we heard a loud noise, similar to an outboard motor turning on; these sounds were of angry Anacondas.

Eventually after eight long hours of paddling, we finally arrived to the native community. Miguel and I were exhausted, we were met by my native friends and taken to one of their homes, we were fed a delicious hot piraña fish soup with yuca bread. (This tropical plant is a tuber; also known in English as cassava, when refined it is called manioc or tapioca. Yuca is the staple of the Amazonian ethnic diet, prepared in different ways it represents about sixty per cent of the food. The bread of Yuca is similar in shape, texture, thickness and size to a large pizza without the ingredients. It is broken into pieces and used to scoop up the soup or other food and is eaten together with that food, it replaces the use of silverware. The scientific name of the bitter cassava is Manihot utilissima and of sweet cassava is Manihot aipi).

That fish soup served in a simple gourd was one of the best meals that I have ever had in my life. Immediately afterwards we were given hammocks to sleep in. After a few hours of sleep we were awaken, our small canoe had already been placed inside one of the two big motor canoes and with my native friends; we traveled up the river to pick up the tour group.

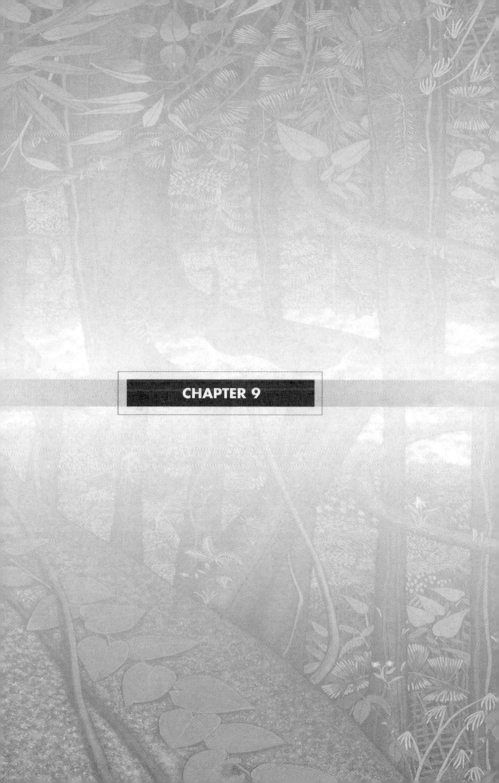

**CHAPTER 9**

In 1956, five U.S. Protestant-Evangelical missionaries in their small plane were reported to be missing in Ecuadorian Amazonian Huaorani native territory. Shortly afterwards, from the U.S. military base in Panama a few planes and military parted and soon arrived to Quito. Together with Ecuadorian military they flew over the Andes and descended into the Amazon where they landed at the Protestant-Evangelical missionary air strip and base of Arahuno. Upon arriving, the U.S. military personnel interviewed the wives of the lost missionary men. With the use of a few planes, an aerial search party was immediately organized. Later, by radio it was notified that other Protestant-Evangelical missionaries who were flying over the jungle had sighted the missing aircraft. The plane had been spotted on a sand bar near to one of the Huaorani communities, in Huaorani territory. The wings of the plane had been manually destroyed!

Quickly a rescue operation comprised of U.S. and Ecuadorian military, fellow Protestant-Evangelical male missionaries, Quichua native porters with supplies and Quichua native scouts left the Arahuno base by means of four planes, one helicopter and three canoes. After two days of traveling, eventually the rescue team arrived to the sandbar. Within the nearby forest and in the small Curaray river were found the dead missionaries with 3 meter (9 ft.) long Huaorani spears sticking out of their bodies.

This incident made the front-page news all over the world and anyone who had heard this story was shocked! Of course from modern societies, the general public opinion was that clearly these Amazonian ethnic natives were savages, they killed the very same people who were trying to help them.

Supposedly, missionaries were good, generous people; they were giving up the comforts of living in a first world nation to go to a third world nation to teach the natives about God and how to be civilized!

There exist different articles, books and even film documentaries about this significant South American Native historical event and the information that has been available has come from two "official" sources, first, from the missionary organizations and secondly, from the Ecuadorian military and government. This is fine, but what about the Amazonian ethnic native's point of view?

At that time, the native inhabitants of my country were about 70% and unfortunately, they did not have equal citizenship rights as the rest of the Ecuadorians, obviously they did not know how to read and write and their word had no credibility in relation to the word of whites, mestizos or foreigners.

In this chapter, my intention is for everyone who is interested in the South American Native history and in the Amazonian ethnic native cultures to have a more clear understanding of the ethnic native's desperate situation concerning invasive Protestant-Evangelical missionaries. In addition, my intention is to defend the human rights, cultural rights, and ethnic religious rights of all the ethnic groups in my country, Latin America and anywhere else in the world where the religious, cultural and land rights of
ethnic people are under attack by "civilized" modern civilization.

One of the main goals in life for all humans throughout the world and during all times has been to find happiness. For the Amazonian ethnic natives, happiness was blessed on a person when that person was successful in obtaining four objectives; first, enough food for one, one's family and community, secondly, peace and a harmonious, loving relationship within ones family and community, thirdly, good health, and last, a true awakening and strengthening of ones Spiritual body! Well for centuries, the ethnic Amazonian natives have been successful in obtaining happiness in their simple, but fortunate lives, without the "guidance" or approval of foreign missionaries.

Throughout the human history of our planet, stronger civilizations have always taken advantage of the weaker civilizations in order to steal their treasures, land and colonize and or exploit them. During centuries, the dense vegetation of the Amazonian tropical rainforest has always acted as a natural protection for the native tribes towards the outside world. But gradually, within the last sixty years with modern technology and capital in the hands of the stronger modern civilizations, this virgin tropical rainforest became vulnerable and quickly began to dissipate, giving way to a form of conquest which modern civilization officially labeled as "progress".

Everyone likes "progress", but curiously enough, the ancestral native inhabitants of the Amazon who had been living there for more than two-thousand years were not going to benefit from this progress! This Amazonian "progress" would become economically favorable in thousands of millions of U.S. dollars for first-world nation Oil companies, Logging companies and the foreign missionary organizations, also benefiting from this "progress" on a lower economic level were unscrupulous anti-patriotic local government officials, military, local companies and mestizo merchants.

Unfortunately, for the majority of the millions of Amazonian native families what this modern civilization "progress" really meant was a hypocritical, systematic invasion of their ancestral territories. This resulted in native tribes losing their land, contamination of rivers and lakes, deforestation, spreading of deadly foreign diseases, and destruction of their ethnic religion and culture.

Regrettably, for the Amazonian aborigines, they have always lived in a giant tropical rainforest, which is unbelievably rich in raw materials that are economically valuable for modern civilization.

The first scientific observation from modern civilization concerning the richness of South America's tropical raw materials was around 1740 when a native Shaman in Ecuador's north Pacific tropical rainforest showed the French scientist Charles Marie de La Condamine an unusual tree. The scientist was so impressed with this tree that he recorded it in his notes; "A tree called Heve grows in the province of Esmeraldas, with a single incision it secretes a milky-white fluid that gradually hardens and darkens on contact with air!" Charles Marie de La Condamine became the first person to collect samples of rubber for scientific investigations and introduce rubber to Europe. By 1850, the first world nations demanded huge quantities of rubber for their new bicycle tire industry, as well as also for other latex industries. Years later, there was much more demand of rubber for the automobile tire industry. With these fresh markets, the Amazon "Rubber boom" began and continued growing rapidly for sixty years.

The Brazilian city of Manaus on the Amazon River and in the middle of the Amazon jungle became the commercial center for this precious raw material. Tons of freshly tapped rubber arrived to Manaus and from there rubber was loaded onto ocean cargo ships to travel down the Amazon River to the Atlantic Ocean to cover the world market. For its time, Manaus became one of the most modern, luxurious cities in the world; Manaus had 16 kilometers (10 miles) of electric trolleys while in Boston they still used horse cars. Thousands of tons of rubber were exported to the industrialized nations and throughout this time, from first world nations, all eyes were on the rich, South American Amazon tropical rainforest.

Around 1890, a group of British botanists had illegally smuggled thousands of rubber tree seeds out of the Amazon to England! Eventually these seeds were transplanted to the

British colony of Malaysia. It took about twenty years for those small seeds to become adult trees and to begin to produce rubber. The harvested rubber from the jungles of Malaysia was less expensive to market than the Amazonian rubber. The collapse of the Amazonian "Rubber boom" occurred in 1910. Suddenly Manaus was living its worst economic nightmare as companies were declaring bankruptcy, and foreigners and mestizos were desperately boarding ships to abandon the city.

For hundreds of thousands of Amazonian natives the collapse of the Rubber boom was an answer to their prayers, because during the past sixty years, the majority of them had been enslaved to tap rubber trees and many of them had been brutally mistreated and killed.

Ten years later, in 1920, once again we see an interest by first world nations in the Amazon. Standard Oil Company, Royal Dutch Shell, Texaco, Gulf Oil Corporation, Mobil Oil and other oil companies are signing work contracts with local governments. In 1922, a tremendous quantity of oil is discovered in the basin of the Maracaibo Lake in Venezuela. If so much oil was found in Venezuela, well obviously there must be plenty of more oil in Colombia, Ecuador, Peru and Brazil. Suddenly South American oil, as well as timber and other possible raw materials become very important for the powerful first-world nation Oil companies, as well for local South American governments, and governing class economic groups.

At that time in Ecuador and other South American countries, public or private institutions lacked the technology or the capital to invest in the regions economic mineral development, so obviously foreign companies were more than glad to fill this need. The Amazon was at that point in time one of the main unexplored frontiers left in the world.

Together with the local governments, the foreign companies began planning their strategy of work, but there existed one "minor" problem. The problem was that there were millions of native people living in many areas of the Amazon and of course these native tribes considered this land to be theirs and in fact historically and morally speaking, yes this land was theirs. Their ancestors were the first humans to live on this land since thousands of years ago. Also of deep concern for the governments and investors was the common belief that the Amazonian tribes were hostile.

In general, the Amazonian ethnic native tribes have always been a gentle and friendly people, but since many years ago, most of the communities or tribes have become unfriendly towards foreigners and there are more than enough reasons for this behavior. They had suffered countless, criminal attacks, first it was the Spaniard and Portuguese Conquistadors and then it was the infamous Rubber Boom.

The native people have always had the tradition of passing down from generation to generation the verbal history of their tribes and obviously the countless frightening stories that they have in regard to foreigners, instinctively had made the Amazonian native tribes more suspicious and fearful towards all white or mestizo strangers!

Foreign Protestant-Evangelical missionary organizations began their activity in South America around 1930 and at that time, more than 75% of all the Amazonian native tribes in Ecuador, Colombia, Peru and Bolivia were still practicing their ethnic religion.

By 1950, the influence of the traditional Catholic Church missionaries in Latin America was quickly being replaced by a new wave of modern, economically wealthy, high-technology missionaries who were primarily arriving from the United States. The foreign missionary work was mainly concentrated in the Amazon and in Ecuador and Colombia's Pacific tropical rainforest. At least 200 foreign Protestant-Evangelical missionary sects have operated throughout all of Latin America.

These missionary organizations "apparently" operated independently and carefully maintained this appearance, but in reality the great majority of them were and are still today working under the surveillance of a powerful umbrella organization, which is controlled by two main Protestant-Evangelical missionary organizations; Wycliffe Bible Translators-Summer Institute of Linguistics and New Tribes Mission. Also working with these two main missionary organizations were Missionary Aviation Fellowship together with Jungle Aviation and Radio Service which provided U.S. pilots and small planes to facilitate the missionary work throughout the South American Amazon, the Pacific tropical rainforests of Ecuador, Colombia and throughout the rest of tropical Latin America. Of vital importance for the overall communication throughout Latin America was World Radio Missionary Fellowship-(Voice of the Andes-H.C.J.B.)

Supposedly, the "official" function of the Summer Institute of Linguistics was to write down the languages of the ethnic native tribes; usually this was done with the assistance of a previously converted tribe. Typically all of the tribes know at least one other native language which would be of one of their neighboring tribes.

According to the Ecuadorian Governments and in the eyes of Ecuadorian society, the work of the Summer Institute of Linguistics was to help "civilize" the native tribes in an academic-educational sense. However, after learning the language of an ethnic tribe, the linguists who in reality were missionaries would use the native language to make contact with the tribe and eventually begin their evangelization program by interpreting from "their point of view" different stories from the missionary Bible into the native language.

The system that the Protestant-Evangelical missionaries applied for "converting" the Latin American tropical rainforest tribes has been done in a totalitarian manner, without the most minimum respect for the traditional religion, customs, legends, social values and ancestral land rights. Using underhanded tactics, the missionaries imposed on the Amazonian ethnic natives a foreign religion, which was based on a warped interpretation of the Bible, which of course according to these missionary organizations, their interpretations are the only official "Word of God."

Obviously, this foreign religion had a tremendous impact on the entire native society; there was absolutely no aspect of the native's daily life, which would not be affected by this new religion. Therefore, within a few generations, the result of "conversion" was an imposed political, social, and economical structure, which were for the political and economic benefit of these missionary organizations, foreign and local companies and of course the corrupt, irresponsible and anti-patriotic Ecuadorian Government officials.

But, how was it possible that the ethnic natives would accept to replace their powerful traditional religion which was so effective for awakening and strengthening a person's Spiritual, mental, emotional and physical bodies for the Protestant-Evangelical religion? There are three reasons for this: First, was the dishonest tactics that the foreign missionaries used to confuse, trick, manipulate and divide the native communities. Second, was a terrible weakness, which all of us as humans have, and this is that every day of our lives we are vulnerable to the pleasures of our flesh. In modern societies, industries have flourished precisely to fill this demand and consequently we find an amazing assortment of objects, which satisfy our pleasures and make our physical duties a lot easier to perform. The missionaries presented unique "gifts" as bait to seduce the native people. The Third reason was that some natives who had been victims of Amazonian malevolent witchcraft were frightened of evil Shamans, so they saw the foreign religion as a refuge.

Without giving any gifts, if the Protestant-Evangelical missionaries would have presented to the ethnic native people the best of their religion so that the native people could objectively compare the foreign religion to their ethnic religion, it is certain that the natives would have never replaced their effective and powerful religion for the Protestant-Evangelical religion. Of course, the missionary organizations knew this and precisely this is why they used an "old trick" which had worked hundreds of years ago in Latin America. The first time that this trick was used in the Americas was in 1492 with the famous Italian navigator and explorer Cristoforo Colombo, who together with the Spaniard Conquistadors and clergy of the Vatican, arrived to San Salvador Island in the Bahamas.

After the native leaders received gifts from the Protestant–Evangelical missionaries, by the time that they realized what the consequences of these gifts were, it was already too late, the missionaries had obtained total control over the native community, which means control over their land and their future.

The missionaries that were in the Ecuadorian Amazon in 1956 were using as a base a few abandoned buildings and an airstrip, which had previously been used by the Shell Oil Company. This relationship between the Royal Dutch Shell Oil Company and the Protestant-Evangelical missionary organizations is most suspicious and is one of many evidences of a close working association between missionaries and multi-national companies for a common purpose. According to the "official" report and the press, the abandoned Shell Oil base of Arahuno was on the edge of Huaorani territory. This is false; the truth is that the base of Arahuno, used by Shell Oil Company and later by the Protestant-Evangelical missionaries was located on the southeast side of the Arahuno River, which is within the boundaries of ancestral Huaorani native territory.

Obviously, this was a dishonest and direct act of provocation against the Huaorani tribe.

At that time in history, the Huaorani people and all of the

other ethnic tribes in the Amazon considered outsiders from modern civilizations who would enter into their territory as enemies and everyone knew this, including the missionaries. That is why, immediately upon occupying the base, the missionaries set up an electric fence; they set up their radio communication system and always had loaded weapons ready, just in case Huaorani natives would attack.

"Operation Auca" is how the missionaries named their plan for "converting" the noble Huaorani tribe. In the language of the previously "converted" Ecuadorian Amazonian Quichua tribe, the insulting word Auca means savages. In the language of the Huaorani tribe, the word
"Huaorani" means "The People". For all of the Amazonian tribes, the name of their tribe in their language means "The People", but it seems that whenever the missionaries encountered tribes that fought against "conversion," the ancestral names of these brave tribes would be replaced with an offensive word meaning savages.

World Radio Missionary Fellowship-Voice of the Andes-H.C.J.B. missionary organization had invested a lot of money to build in Ecuador, one of the most advanced and expensive transmitting antenna electronic communication systems in the world. This communication system-radio station was strategically located in Quito, high in the Andes, and close to the equatorial line. Daily evangelical programs were transmitted on the strongest AM signal to all Ecuador, Colombia and Peru, including special Protestant-Evangelical programs that were translated into native languages of all the converted tribes living in the Pacific tropical rainforest regions of Ecuador and Colombia, as well as the entire South American Amazon region. In addition, they used standard short wave bands to transmit Protestant-Evangelical programs throughout all of Latin America. Furthermore, Protestant-Evangelical programs were translated into 30 other languages and sent all over the world, including at that time the Soviet Union and other

Communist or Socialist countries.

Obviously, from this radio station in Quito, communication was available with all of the Protestant-Evangelical missionary bases in South America, including the Amazon and the missionary base of Arahuno. This radio system was vital for the logistics and the success of "Operation Auca" and all other Protestant-Evangelical missionary "Operations" throughout Latin America.

The general opinion from the people of Quito and Ecuador was that the "apparently" small radio station together with a modern, well-equipped missionary hospital was part of a charitable community service, which was provided by the "generous" gringitos. This was true, but what the Ecuadorians did not know was what the true economic-political activities these powerful missionary organizations were contriving in South America.

With a medical staff of U.S. and local professionals, the hospital in Quito and the hospital in the Ecuadorian Amazon at Shell Mera provided good medical service for a fee, which was in accordance with one's economic status. Believers received special consideration, which evidently enhanced the attractiveness of joining the Protestant-Evangelical religion. Besides offering medical service to all local people, the hospitals also gave medical service to the many U.S. missionary families that were working in this country as well as other U.S. that were working in Ecuador.

By 1955, the Protestant-Evangelical organizations already had at least five different missionary bases with air strips actively at work, frequently flying planes over the ancestral territories of the Kichwa, Yumbos, Alamas, Cofan, Secoya, Sionas, Shuara, Zapara, Achuara, Shiwiar and Huaorani tribes. Within the northern Pacific area of Ecuador' tropical rainforest, the foreign missionaries were also active "converting" the Awa and Chachis tribes. Unfortunately, for all of the ethnic aborigine tribes and for the virgin jungle and wildlife, the apocalyptic wheels of greed and "progress" from modern civilization were gradually but surely turning in a diabolic plan to exploit and destroy the pre-historic, virgin, paradise tropical rainforests of South America. This ecological devastation would not only be a tragic loss for all of the indigenous tribes, but also in years to come for all of the new generation South American people.

The Protestant-Evangelical missionary organizations were already successful in "converting" the Kichwa, Alama and Yumbo tribes, and they were almost finished with their evangelization of the Cofan, Secoya, Siona, Zapara, Shuara, Achuara, and Shiwiar tribes. Geographically speaking the Huaorani tribe living in their small communities was further east from the Kichwas, Alamas and Yumbos, deeper in the Amazon and next in line to being "saved" by the foreign missionaries.

Of course, the Huaorani people must have felt threatened and terrorized. They knew that their ancestral territory was gradually being invaded by strange beings who were flying in the sky in frightening, noisy objects. Inclusively, these aliens were already building strange structures with electric fences, on their land.

Out of desperation, on many occasions, as courageous warriors, the Huaoranis fought with wooden spears against the invaders of their land who were armed with shotguns and rifles. Many times, Huaorani men attacked missionary bases, Oil camps, cattle ranches, and loggers, killing mestizos, foreigners and "converted" Kichwa natives.

The missionaries that worked at the base of Arahuno would fly their small plane over Huaorani territory practically every day until they soon spotted the clearings of Huaorani villages. The missionaries would then mark these different villages on their maps and fly back to their base. After planning their strategy, two missionaries would fly their plane once a week to the village that had been first selected for "Operation Auca." The plane would circle over the village at low speed and low altitude. Then, using a loud public address system, the missionary man that was accompanying the pilot would call out different Huaorani phrases like; (We want to be your friends). Then the same man would reel out of the plane a long line, and at the end of this line, loosely attached was a large aluminum pot filled with gifts. After the pot hit the ground, the pot was automatically released from the line and the line was reeled back to the plane.

After a few months of making daily flights to the village, one day as the missionary was reeling in the line; he saw that there was a head-crown of feathers tied onto the end of the line, one of the natives had presented a gift to the missionaries! Clearly, this same strategy of presenting and exchanging gifts had worked in the past with practically all of the other native tribes throughout the tropical rainforests in Latin America. However, on this occasion, the missionary system of exchanging gifts was going to fail.

On the morning of January 6, 1956, a small propeller plane with five missionary men left the base of Arahuno and after a short journey landed on a long sandbar adjacent to the Curaray River, in Huaorani territory, just a few kilometers to the Huaorani village, where the missionaries had been dropping gifts. The missionaries named the sandbar "Palm Beach"; they set up camp and waited for the natives to visit. After a few days of dropping more gifts at the native village and announcing through their loudspeaker system to go to the Curaray River, one day three Huaoranis suddenly appeared on the sandbar, they were a middle age woman, a young woman and a young man whom the missionaries decided to name "George". The three Huaoranis stayed with the missionaries throughout the remainder of the day communicating in sign language and receiving gifts, before nightfall, the three Huaoranis went back into the jungle.

The next morning as usual, the plane with two missionaries left the sandbar to the village to drop more gifts and as the plane was returning to the sandbar, the pilot spotted ten Huaorani men walking along the bank of the river in direction to the sandbar where the rest of the missionaries were. Upon arriving to the sandbar, the pilot and co-pilot excitedly informed their companions of the Huaorani men that were coming; the missionaries were content and waited impatiently to receive their guests. After a few hours, from the dense vegetation of the virgin jungle, the ten Huaorani men appeared onto the sandbar and finally as the missionary organizations wanted, contact was finally made. At that meeting, nobody knows what happened, but during the afternoon of that same day, suddenly the radio in the plane stopped working.

The five missionaries had concealed guns and according to the official reports; the weapons had not been used. After the rescue teams eventually located the lifeless sandbar, a camera belonging to one of the dead missionaries was found containing some photographs.

At that moment, the economically powerful and highly technical teamwork of these missionary organizations had suffered an unexpected loss, but they knew that it was just a matter of time until they would be triumphant in "converting" the Huaorani tribe and all other Latin American tropical rainforest tribes.

In order to understand how the actual missionary evangelization occurs in a native community, let us imagine that after presenting many gifts by plane, a few Protestant-Evangelical foreign missionaries have just been accepted into an ethnic native village. Obviously, they would arrive with more gifts, and immediately they would carefully analyze the social structure of the community in order to destroy it. (Once the missionaries are able to destroy the traditional social structure, this will give them a great advantage to conquer the weakened community).

The missionaries would identify the more influential leaders, as well as how responsive each one of these leaders is to the gifts. The leaders that are more receptive to the presence of the missionaries will receive a more privileged relationship with the missionaries, based on special and more quantity of gifts. Evidently, the community will follow its leaders who are blinded by the unique and practical gifts.

The great majority of the leaders and people will always accept the gifts, nevertheless, sometimes one or a few of the leaders are suspicious, they don't like what they are seeing and try to convince the other leaders to organize their people with the purpose of expelling the foreigners from their community or quickly migrating deeper into the jungle. However, the majority of the leaders and people do not want to move away from their source of gifts. The few leaders who are against the missionaries may decide to stay on in the community and make the best of this new situation or they would decide to migrate with their families to go deeper into the jungle. For the ethnic natives, this last alternative is tragic because families are separated and the number of ethnic native families that migrate and form a new community are always few.

After a few months when there is more friendship and trust, which of course is based on more gifts, and there is no direct opposition by the native adults, the missionaries show their bible and little by little start teaching specific Biblical stories from their "point of view". Through their interpretation of the Bible, the missionaries gradually replace the ethnic native religion for the Protestant-Evangelical religion and begin to mold a completely new social, moral, economical and political lifestyle for the community. Afterwards, the missionaries will choose a group of young adult men to teach how to read and write. From this group, a few of these young men will be selected and sent to the S.I.L. centre at the Limoncocha missionary air base in the Ecuadorian Amazon, or to the "Centro Linguistico" (Summer Institute of Linguistic centre) in Quito. In these two missionary centers is where all of the selected young native men from Ecuador will receive their intense training to become Protestant-Evangelical preachers for their communities.

Apart from these few young men who have been selected, none of the other adults is taught to read and write. Clearly, this discriminating system eliminates any possibility of the older generation to have any say or leadership role in the future of the newly "converted" communities. The elderly generation is the only direct link that still exists between the younger generations with their ethnic religion, philosophy and culture. By not permitting the elderly generation to have the same educational opportunity as the future preachers, they as well as the rest of the people will be completely dependant on these Protestant-Evangelical native preachers.

Meanwhile the one or two foreign missionaries that are still living in the community are indirectly playing the leadership role for the community through the system of giving gifts to a few of the elderly, Shaman leaders. The only objects that are still given as gifts are candy. All other objects which before were given as gifts now have a price, for example: building a house for the missionaries, building a runway near the community, cooking food for the missionaries, building a chapel which will be used for the weekly sermons, etc...

The most common gifts and trade-objects that missionaries gave were; aluminum pots and pans which the natives prefer to their traditional pottery because these will never break, steel machetes, steel axes and steel knives that are much more efficient than the traditional hardwood machetes and stone axes, steel fish hooks, nylon fishing lines and nets, mirrors, salt, sugar, candies.

There were other objects that were more expensive and required harder work or more valuable Amazonian objects for trading, for example, I have many friends of different tribes who 40 years ago wanted shotguns and chainsaws from the Protestant-Evangelical missionaries. Typically, the price for a shotgun was about ten Jaguar skins, ten Ocelot skins, five Anaconda skins and five Caiman skins. Like my friends, there must have been thousands of other native men, from all over the Amazon who would kill animals for their skins to trade with the missionaries. Was all this killing and shedding of blood a God-like behavior? What kind of a religion would promote this massacre? What were the missionaries doing with thousands of animal skins? This repulsive business of trading skins with the missionaries lasted for many years. Today the modernized "converted" natives do not trade skins with missionaries anymore, but they continue hunting animals for skins, which they sell to mestizo merchants.

Strangely enough, there was a special ethnic native item, which the foreign missionaries gladly accepted as a trade object and this was the sacred Yagé jaguar-fang necklaces, which the people traditionally used when drinking Yagé. These necklaces were highly valuable, it took about eight dead jaguars to make one necklace and to hunt a jaguar with a spear was dangerous and required great courage. Thousands of these unique, valuable, beautiful necklaces were traded for a few aluminum pots, knives and fishhooks. By publicly giving up these jaguar-fang necklaces, which was their most prized decoration for the Yagé ceremony, the ethnic native people were spiritually and physically breaking off with their traditional ethnic religion, this was one of the first expected steps to accepting the Protestant-Evangelical religion.

In practically all of the native communities where shotguns were introduced, the native hunters preferred this modern weapon instead of there traditional spears and blowguns. Amazonian blowguns are admirable weapons that are testimony to the wisdom of the ancestors of the ethnic culture. By smearing the native curare poison with it's paralyzing effects or the deadly poison of one of the tiny poison-arrow frogs of the Dendrobates or Phyllobates genera onto the tip of a dart, and then fitting that dart into the blowgun, we have one of the most lethal and silent weapons in the world. The natural, chemical poison that is on the skin of one Colombian Phyllobates terribilis poison-arrow frog is so potent, that one drop can kill at least forty people. In the past, the ethnic native hunters would go into forest with their blowguns and silently kill many animals without the other animals realizing what was happening. However, hunting with shotguns in a tropical rainforest is terrible because sound travels much louder and further than in temperate forests. Each time that a shotgun is fired, the blasting noise is heard more than three kilometers away, obviously most of the animals in the area will be stressed, they will temporarily hide and eventually they will move away.

The reasons why the "converted" natives preferred shotguns to their traditional blowguns are because first, at that time, there were still plenty of animals in the forest and the hunters did not realize the impact that the explosion of a shotgun caused on the frightened animals. Secondly, while the natives were hunting for wild boars or tapirs and these animals were hiding behind thick vegetation, it was sometimes difficult for the spears to pass through the dense foliage to hit the animals. The same occurred when using the blowgun and shooting the darts at birds or monkeys that were up in the trees, hiding behind leaves or branches. Therefore, because of these reasons, each native man wanted to have his own shotgun.

When the Shaman leaders first accepted the foreign missionaries and their gifts, and later accepted for a few young native men from their community to go study at the Limoncocha missionary base, they really did not understand what was behind all of this. Inclusively, they were not concerned because they were receiving gifts and throughout that entire time, they had not witnessed any harm or threat. Then suddenly one day, after about one year, the young native men return to the community, they are well groomed and well dressed and they even wear shoes just like the foreign missionaries. Not only have they learned how to read and write in their native language, but they have learned how to read, write and speak in Spanish.

These few young native men are the only people in the community who know Spanish, and this gives them a tremendous advantage over the Shamans or any of the other adults. The reason is because this community will gradually begin to have contact and be more dependent on the growing, modern mestizo and white civilization that will eventually take over the Amazon.

Of these young native men, one of them has already been assigned by the missionary organizations as the main preacher for the community, and the other young native men will work as secondary preachers and assistants to the main preacher.

The first day that the native preacher gives his first passionate sermon on one of many captivating stories from the Bible, only at that moment seeing the enthusiastic response by the people, do the Shamans and the other elders of the community realize what has really happened. However, unfortunately at that point, they have already lost their leadership role in their community. It is too late to go back to how things were before.

The foreign missionaries will officially present the native preachers to the community as their representatives and publicly entrust the leadership of the community to these young men, after this, the foreign missionaries will leave and probably never return. The native preachers will represent the community before the government, Oil Companies or other Companies from modern society. Apart from this strategic and important duty, the other duties of the preachers are to use their weekly sermons and influence to control their community, to defend the best economical and political interests for the missionary organizations, to work against the few ethnic communities that still exist, and to spread their Protestant Evangelical religion to other nearby communities. In exchange for their work, the preachers and their assistants will be economically well compensated by the missionary organizations.

Constantly the preachers will deliver a general idea to the community, which is that practically everything that their ancestors did in the past was either wrong or immoral. With this persistent message, all of the people will start to feel shame, guilt and rejection towards their ancestors and their traditional culture. These teachings will have a life-long damaging psychological effect on the self-identity and self-pride of the native people.

Once an ethnic community becomes "converted", the Shamans and other leaders will quickly lose the high respect that they traditionally had from their people, they will feel stressed and helpless and as time passes things just get worse. Less and less natives accompany the Shamans to drink Yagé and no young people want to become Shamans. The Shamans and other leaders feel terrible with this new situation but they realize that they cannot do anything, so they continue living in the communities with their "converted" families. They dare not say anything against the Protestant-Evangelical religion, missionaries or preachers and secretly they try to continue drinking Yagé and practicing their ethnic religion.

However, in such a small society, the majority of the "converted" natives realize that the Shamans are still drinking Yagé. Under this circumstance, what typically happens is that one day the Shamans will discover that the sacred cultivated vines of Yagé and other sacred plants have been destroyed and the "Beloved Casita de Yagé" has been mysteriously burned to the ground. After this, no one in the community will ever drink Yagé again.

Inclusively because of the hate-induced teachings of the preachers, many "converted" natives cut down the beautiful, giant Kapok trees, simply because in the past, Shamans used those ancient trees for a special ethnic religious ceremony. The "converted" natives actually believed that those trees, as well as also all sacred plants were instruments of the devil and consequently had to be destroyed.

With support from the missionary organizations, after a couple of years, the preacher will petition to the Ecuadorian Government funds in order to finance the construction of a government school and a government medical dispensary for the community. After obtaining the funds, then the preacher will purchase the materials and the community will build the school. In addition, the government will supply basic medicines and will train the nurses and pay the salaries of the teachers and nurses.

What is most suspicious concerning the education in the "converted" native schools is that these missionary organizations are in charge of selecting and training young native men to become the future schoolteachers! This system exists thanks to an agreement signed many years ago between the Ecuadorian Ministry of Education and these foreign missionary organizations.

The selection for schoolteachers will be from amongst the older boys who have just graduated from these same native secondary schools (high schools) and most importantly those boys who have stronger convictions concerning the Protestant-Evangelical religion! The boys that are chosen will be sent to a special teacher-training boarding school in the Amazonian missionary base of Limoncocha.

A Protestant Evangelical native preacher (left), and of the Summer Institute of Linguistics, is a native teacher (right). Behind the teacher, is Emilio, one of my dear friends. Copyright: William T. Vickers, 1975.

( A Protestant Evangelical native preacher (left), and native teacher (right) of the Summer Institute of Linguistics. Behind the teacher, is Emilio, one of my dear friends.
Copyright: William T. Vickers, 1975. )

This unjust system of allowing foreign missionary organiza-

tions to select and train future teachers is a manner of perpetu-
ating the narrow-minded political, economical, and social
philosophies of these missionary organizations in "converted"
native communities. In addition, this system combined with
the Protestant Evangelical preachers assures the foreign missionary organizations to maintain a political and educational
control over the future generations of the "converted" communities.

Before the missionaries arrived, the relations between the
families were healthy and there was as much harmony and
happiness as could be desired by any human social group.
These people did not have the
economical luxuries that exist in modern society, but they did
not need them either, they were completely self sufficient,
they had plenty of food from the virgin forest and rivers, they
lived as one big family, as one clan.

However, with the Protestant-Evangelical missionaries, the
concept of one big, united, harmonious clan, gradually began
to crumble. This happened because the communal society,
which the wise native ancestors had developed during hundreds of years, was under attack, and was quickly being
replaced by a "civilized" society, which was based on individualism, corruption and all the material objects that money can
buy.

The Protestant-Evangelical missionary organizations have
always had an absurd way of looking at the noble native tradition of "communal living". They were convinced that the
communal lifestyle of helping one another, sharing with one
another and living all of the families in the same equal condition was a serious threat to the First world's Capitalist system.
Supposedly, the "communal" society that existed within ethnic communities in second and third world nations could lead
to communism!

Consequently, for these missionary organizations it becomes
important to destroy the native tradition of communal

lifestyle, a true God-like behavior that has its basis on helping one's fellow human beings. The ethnic native communal philosophy had lasted for at least two thousand years and had created a constructive atmosphere of harmony and unity among all the families and community. Precisely, it was the unity in the ethnic society that the missionaries did not like. By eliminating                                               the community harmony and unity, it was going to be easier for the missionaries to control the people on an individual basis. Divide and conquer is another old trick that has been often used throughout the History of our planet.

The missionaries and preachers teach the "converted" natives that individualism, selfishness and Capitalism is the true Christian way of living, and even though the native people have never heard of the word "communism", suddenly they are being taught about the "evils of Communism" and its affinity to the devil and to hell.

Traditionally in the past, the Amazonian tribes lived in a state of nudity or semi-nudity, simply because this was the most practical and healthiest way of living in a tropical rainforest. By wearing clothes, the skin cannot breathe as well and moisture cannot evaporate as effective. The rays of the sun as well as oxygen cannot come into direct contact with more of the skin surface, and this daily contact of the sun and oxygen with the skin is very important, because these two elements are natural, powerful germ killer agents.

In the Ecuadorian Amazon, there is an average of 5 mtrs. (17 ft.) annual rainfall, and an average of 90% humidity. This environment is ideal for the growth of fungus, which will collect on a person's damp clothes and will affect the person's health. At the beginning, the missionaries were giving away second hand clothes, but after "conversion", the clothes had a price in money or trade-objects. Living in a humid jungle, clothes gets dirty quite quickly, so this means that the family clothes have to be washed every day. This terrible daily chore requires a lot of time, hard work and soap. The missionaries taught the native communities that it is the women's "role" to do the washing of the clothes for the family; unfortunately, this is the custom in the mestizo settler's, unjust, male-dominating society.

A few times, I have heard missionaries say that clothes was given to ethnic natives to protect them from insects. Obviously, I recommend mestizos or foreigners who are visiting a tropical rainforest to use clothes as a protection from insects, but if a person is born in a jungle, it is crucial to develop a strong defense system. Precisely this has been one of the keys to the successful survival of the Amazonian native tribes who have lived in the Amazon with millions of insects for at least two thousand years.

In reality, there are four main reasons why the missionaries convinced the "converted" ethnic natives to wear clothes. First, because according to the missionaries the past ethnic natives were immoral, they were living in sin because they were publicly exhibiting their semi-nude body or nude body. Secondly, in order to make the "converted" natives look "civilized" like the missionaries, preachers and other "decent" people from modern societies. Thirdly, to make the traditional native dress, traditional culture, ancestors, Shamans and elderly generation leaders look primitive and inferior, and the fourth reason was to make the native tribes abandon their ancestral self-sufficient lifestyle and rely as much as possible on money and the Capitalist system.

After "conversion", the missionaries convinced many tribes to abandon their ancestral land and migrate to other areas, without the natives knowing, the reason why this was done was to facilitate Oil exploration.

Gradually mestizo settlers, military personnel, mestizo merchants, and Oil and Logging workers will begin to appear. Some mestizo merchants in large canoes start making weekly visits to all of the converted native communities. They sell items like: machetes, chainsaws, shotguns, ammunition, steel fishhooks, nylon fishing lines, plastic ware, rubber boots sugarcane liquor, knives, toys, mirrors, tools, etc…They prefer money, but they will accept cash crops, lumber or exotic animal skins.

Clearly now, if the "converted" native people have allowed for activities of logging and or Oil exploration to occur in their territory, it is because they had already lost their traditional religious philosophy concerning the sacred relationship that their wise ancestors have always had with Pacha Mama. For the traditional ethnic natives, Pacha Mama and all of the animals, plants and minerals are also children of God and consequently have a Soul. Because of this is why they would never think of killing trees unless it was really necessary, for example to build a house, bridge or canoe. In contrast, when loggers look at a tropical rainforest, all that they are looking at is the economic value of the timber. When ethnic natives see an oil well or the effects of an oil spill, they believe that the crude oil is the actual blood that comes out from the interior of Pacha Mama.

Since long ago, these missionary organizations realized the existence of this sacred relationship that the ethnic tribes had with Pacha Mama. Consequently, this became another reason for these organizations to separate the Latin American tropical rainforest tribes from their ethnic religion and consequently from their Spiritual relationship with Pacha Mama. After "conversion", the modernized natives will never be emotionally or spiritually disturbed by activities of logging or Oil exploration.

Within the "converted" communities, the preachers and their families are the wealthiest families, then the teachers with their families are the next wealthiest and then the great majority of the rest of the people live in a permanent, hopeless state of poverty, often waiting to be hired by the preachers to work in their homes or on their fields. At one time or another, most of the "converted" native men have worked for Oil companies; clearing the jungle for building trails, shelters and oil campsites.

After Oil exploitation and Logging there will be very little game left in the forest and very little fish in the rivers or lakes. In order to obtain more protein for their families, the natives are breeding pigs, chickens or fish. Additionally, they cultivate cash crops to raise money in order to purchase modernized food and items. What is also becoming common is that out of family economical distress, many young native women will go to mestizo towns looking for work to make money and regrettably, some will be recruited into prostitution or will find dishonest mestizo people who will mistreat them.

Because of the astonishing success of "conversion" by the Protestant-Evangelical missionary organizations and because they prohibit "converted" natives to marry ethnic natives, the ethnic aborigine communities in the Amazon are few and small. Thanks to these foreign missionaries, within the ethnic native communities, the genetic pool is becoming dangerously small and too much intermarriage within the same bloodlines is a serious problem. Today less than 5% of the Upper Amazonian natives in Colombia, Ecuador, Peru and Bolivia are still practicing their true ancestral ethnic religion. I suppose that the Protestant-Evangelical missionary organizations must be very proud of their victorious "conversion" in the Amazon and in other Latin American tropical rainforests. It took them less than fifty years to destroy practically all of the tropical Latin American ethnic native religions. The Vatican with the Spaniard Conquistadors did basically the same in the Andes and throughout other areas in Latin America, but that was five-hundred years ago when supposedly we as humans were still living in backward, barbaric times.

As an intelligent person, I cannot believe that these two historical first-world missionary activities (the Vatican five-hundred years ago and modern day Protestant-Evangelical missionary organizations) would "generously" invest so much money, time and energy for the sole purpose of saving the souls of millions of Latin American natives.

In all honesty, the only reason why the foreign Protestant Evangelical missionary organizations invest so much money, time and work to "convert" tropical rainforest ethnic tribes is to control the political ideology of the indigenous tribes, and economically gain part of the profit from the raw materials that exist on the indigenous ancestral land. Of course, they will never admit to this truth. Conveniently, they say that God "ordered" them to convert the entire planet, "Go ye and preach the gospel to every creature." I think that any church or religious organization that makes this ridiculous affirmation is working for a world dominance political-economical motive. I do not think that it's a coincidence that since Colonialism-Imperialism began in our planet, missionaries from first-world nations began racing to second and third world nations to "convert" and "save the souls" of the same people that they were killing, enslaving, stealing their land and raw materials. Today, imperialism is still very much alive and more desperate than ever before. Unfortunately, in this hypocritical, economically unjust material world: greed, dishonesty, corruption, military force and the power of money will always play a major role in controlling our planet and its raw materials. Since many years ago, the two most profitable businesses in the world have been Oil and the manufacturing of war weapons. Many wars have been fought throughout the world over Oil interests and many anti-patriotic dictators or anti-patriotic puppet governments have received bribes by powerful first world nation Oil companies to sign work contracts whereby these corrupt governments would practically give away their nation's rich Oil reserves to the foreign companies.

One of the big problems that most Latin American governments have always had is that they have often been pressured by some first world nations to sign treaties allowing Protestant-Evangelical missionary organizations to work in their countries. Using the international policy of "freedom of religion" some first world nations have forced weaker nations to sign these treaties. If the governments of the second or third world nations do not sign or renew old treaties, then usually economical, commercial sanctions will be applied.

I think that any person in their right mind would agree that an honest relationship between two people or between different groups of people should be based on honesty, mutual respect and equality. Well, by applying this basic conduct of human relations, I have the following observation to make. If missionary organizations from first world nations can easily obtain permission to enter into second and third world nations to work; then likewise, missionary organizations from second and third world nations should also be able to easily obtain permission to enter into first-world nations to work.

However, would the embassies of the first world nations easily give visas and work permits to thousands of second and third world "missionaries" to go to preach their different religions in the first-world nations? I do not think so.

No country has the right to impose its religion or culture on another country, however, in this modern world, if the second and third world governments really have to sign these treaties with any first world nation, then the people of the second and third world nations should at least demand this equal condition. This would be reciprocal, fair and true "freedom of religion."

# CHAPTER 10

The Amazonian Shamans of the past have not only been wise, Spiritual leaders, but since centuries ago, they have also been incredibly intelligent chemists. After discovering Yagè, and after learning how to correctly use this sacred plant, the enlightened Spiritual body of the Shamans would communicate with the Spirits of the plants, and these plant-Spirits would reveal to the Shamans what medicinal properties or other qualities they each had. Likewise, it is believed that special People of Yagé could tell the powerful Shamans the chemical values that are found in certain plants.

Apart from Yagé, which is the most important plant discovered by the upper Amazon Shamans, there are at least one-hundred other medicinal-chemical plants used by Shamans. I am just going to mention six medicinal plants and one example of ancestral Amazonian Shaman chemistry.

**1)** Since hundreds of years ago, ethnic Amazon natives discovered the potent chemical of the Curare liana plant. With the sap of curare, the natives would make a powerful deadly poison, which they put on the tips of their darts for hunting with blowguns. The concentrated chemical of curare would act as a muscle relaxant, which would force the lungs of the wounded animals to contract so much that, the animals would die of suffocation. In modern medicine, the synthesized, vital chemical-drug of Curare is "tubocurarine" which is used in general anesthesia, also it is used as a muscle relaxant and in some cases of paralysis.

**2)** Kurarina is the Kichwa name of a small under-story tree found in the primary forest. Its valuable leaves are collected for making a bitter tea which is drank as one of the best natural medicines for curing poisonous snakebites, obviously the people cultivate this and other important medicinal plants in the nearby forest or within their cultivated food crops, near their houses.

3) The Cofan and Secoya ethnic natives have a special brew which they use as a unique method of birth control. Typically, soon after an adolescent girl begins to have her period, her parents will collect different plants and prepare a brew which she will drink every day for ten days. After this, even if she has sexual intercourse she will not get pregnant.

Parents do not approve of premarital sex, but very intelligently they know that it can happen and if it does, their daughters will not get pregnant. A few years later, that same girl would become old enough to get married. After she marries, her parents, elders or one of the Shamans would prepare another brew for her to drink for about ten days, and then she would become fertile again and get pregnant. Usually the Upper Amazon ethnic natives do not like to have more than six children. So normally after having the fifth or sixth child, the married woman will drink again the first brew for about ten days, and after that, she will never get pregnant again.

I have told this story to different tour groups and occasionally one of the tourists will ask why the big laboratories do not know about this fantastic natural drug, and if so, why don't they make a permanent birth control medicine from the plants. My answer has been that this natural drug as well as all other Amazonian brews has to be taken fresh and to synthesize natural medicine is not easy: sometimes by changing its form, often the desired results will change. In addition, maybe the big laboratories are not interested in manufacturing a permanent birth-control method. In all probability, they make more money by selling a birth-control method which a woman has

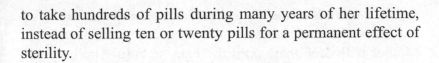

to take hundreds of pills during many years of her lifetime, instead of selling ten or twenty pills for a permanent effect of sterility.

**4)** One plant that Don Fernando told me about is used by all pregnant women. A special brew is made from the plant and this brew is drunk by the expecting Mother, the natural chemicals in the plant together with the metaphysical energy of the Spirit of the plant would act in the woman's body to help position the baby correctly before the actual time of being born. This brew can be drunk periodically, a few months before it is time to give birth, also when it is time to give birth, the woman will drink another brew from a different plant which will dilate her vagina.

On the subjects of pregnancy and giving birth in ethnic communities, I will give some interesting information:

As soon as a woman realizes that she is pregnant, she and her husband will not have any sex until after the baby is born. The ethnic natives believe that having sex during pregnancy is disrespectful for the baby and for the Mother. The expecting Mother does not eat armadillo meat or she will have difficulty giving birth. She does not eat monkey meat or the baby's umbilical cord may wrap around the baby's neck and she does not eat peccary, wild boar, or quail meat, in general, it is better if the only meat she eats is fish.

After the sixth month of pregnancy, the expecting Mother will not do anymore cooking or house chores; the husband with older children will do the everyday cooking for the family and the house chores. The wife will not have any physical contact with any family members who drink Yagé, and during the day and night the expecting Mother will be staying in the adjacent hut that is normally used during menstruation. At the same time a group of women, which are family to the pregnant woman will build a very small thatch roof hut about 50 meters (164 ft.) from the expecting mother's house, within the virgin forest. The walls of the hut are made of palm leaves and once the hut is finished building, the pregnant woman with her Mother will sleep there until the baby is born. The husband, family and friends, who visit, will sing special songs to the baby that is still in the Mother's womb, telling the baby to get ready to come out safely.

When it is time to give birth, two or three other women like Grandmothers, aunts and or sisters will accompany the expecting Mother in the little hut. In the majority of ethnic communities, the husband never accompanies his wife while she is giving birth. During this special moment, it is considered important for the metaphysical female Spiritual energy of Pacha Mama to assist the pregnant woman in the vital and precious act of giving birth. Mother Nature represents life, fertility, Motherhood, wisdom and the glorious Prana energy of God. Other women can be present, but a man's male-energy presence could interfere

with the overall, powerful, female energy. However, some ethnic communities have slightly different beliefs and permit the husband to be present with his wife while she is giving birth.

In any of both cases, the woman would give birth in the middle of the small hut, in a semi-standing squat position. A horizontal, strong, smooth, wooden pole which is about 1 meter (39 in.) long hangs from the ceiling by two ropes, or another method is that the pole be placed on two strong v-shape tip sticks that are vertically stuck deep in the ground. In either of two methods, the pole is at about 76 cm. (30 in.) from the ground so that as the pregnant woman places her underarms over the pole, her legs would be in a comfortable open squat position. Underneath her body, in-between her open legs, is a hammock about 15 cm. (6 in.) from the floor. Standing behind the woman is her Mother, aunt or her husband holding the woman's elbows for support. Next to the pregnant woman, on one side, kneeling on the floor is another woman who is holding the hammock open. And on the other side, kneeling on the floor is another woman who is ready to guide the baby as it comes out, so that the baby would gently slide into the soft, open hammock.

If the husband is not present, after the baby is born, the husband will be immediately notified. After the husband hears that his baby has been born, he races to the little hut and arriving he will see his wife laying in her hammock, he takes the baby from one of the women and takes a sharp-edge strand of a palm leaf to tie around the umbilical cord to cut it off, as he is doing this, he sings a song so that the cord will never unfasten, then he or one of the elderly women bathe the baby in warm virgin water. The husband spends the night there to sleep with his wife and baby, and in the majority of cases on the following day, the three will go to their house and continue with their normal lifestyle, or the three will stay in the little hut for more days until the Mother and baby are ready, then they will go to their house.

After birth or during the following months, if the Mother, Father, elders or Shamans detect that the baby is mentally challenged, visually impaired or some other physical problem, the baby will be taken deep into the forest, the baby will be put to sleep and will be buried. This unpleasant, but necessary chore is performed by the Father.

Because of such harsh conditions in the Amazon with insects, animals, fungus, etc…, the infant mortality rate has always been elevated; this high risk of dieing is until the baby is about one year old. Because of this, many parents will not name their baby until after one year; this is in order for the parents and family not to get too emotionally attached to the child. The infant mortality rate can be about 10%, which is very high for modern civilization standards, but let us remember that all living species of our planet have always had an infant mortality rate and as painful as this is to accept, it is one of the natural mechanisms that Mother Nature has always relied on in order to maintain a healthy numerical balance among different species and not overpopulate an ecosystem or the planet. It is "modern civilization's conventional medicine" that desperately tries to lower the infant mortality rate to zero.

**5)** There is a large tree in the Upper Amazon region called Drago, by making a small incision into the tree early in the morning, almost immediately the deep red color sap of the tree will drip out. The local people call this liquid "The blood of Drago." For years, this liquid has been commercially marketed in Ecuador, to cure stomach ulcers. If you rub this liquid on your skin, a cream will be formed which can be used on small cuts to stop bleeding, prevent infection and to heal quicker any wound.

The scientific name of the Drago tree is Croton lecheri Fortunately, this tree grows in secondary forests, so its commercial use does not threaten primary forests.

**6)** Another unique and remarkable Amazonian plant which for centuries has been used in Ecuador and Peru, is a woody liana called Uña de gato. The powerful alkaloids and other chemicals in this plant are used to strengthen the blood, making the blood healthier and richer. This provides a general, immune stimulating effect to the body. Due to its major anti-inflammatory properties, it is used to treat different sicknesses like arthritis. Research has also shown that the chemicals in this plant successfully reduce several types of harmful viruses. In 1980, the U.S. National Health Institute performed anti-cancer studies on this plant and discovered that Uña de Gato has vital tumor-inhibiting properties.

The scientific name of Uña de Gato is Uncaria tomentosa. The literal translation in English is "Cat's claw".

7) Years ago, when I led camping tours deep into the Amazon, I would drink Yagé during a few nights of each tour. From Quito, I would always take with me a large nylon tarp. After the tour

group went to sleep, I would take my hammock, nylon tarp and duffle bag faraway into the forest. There I would set up my hammock between two trees and I would tie the nylon tarp about one meter (39 in.) over my hammock, between the two trees, to form a roof for the rain, and then I would drink Yagé. In the Amazon or any other tropical rainforest, you can never tell when it can rain. However, on one occasion that I had a tour to the Amazon, from my house in Quito I could not find my nylon tarp. Arriving to the jungle, when I met my native friends, they asked me if I was going to drink Yagé, I told them that I would like to, but that I did not have my nylon tarp. The native owner of the canoe then offered to lend me a large sheet of thick plastic to use instead of the nylon tarp. Gladly I accepted his offer.

That afternoon upon arriving to the campsite, after organizing everything and while the tour group was resting, I took the folded, large plastic sheet with a long nylon cord and put it under one arm, with my other free hand I picked up my machete and went into the forest. Eventually after walking on a narrow hunting path, about
200 meters (650 ft.) away from the campsite, I found two appropriate trees, which I could use that night for setting up my hammock. I tied onto the trees the plastic sheet forming an inverted V shape roof. After finishing, I went back to the campsite.

That night after dinner and after the last person of the group had gone to sleep, I took my backpack with the bottle of Yagé inside it, and my hammock, duffle bag, machete, flashlight, and I went into the forest. Eventually when I reached the plastic tarp, I set my things down and tied up my hammock to the two trees, underneath the tarp.

After preparing everything, I drank Yagé and had a wonderful experience, which lasted for about seven hours, but suddenly at about three in the morning I began to feel a strong breeze moving my hammock. Shortly afterwards I began to hear a forceful wind, trees swaying and torrential rain approaching. Dried leaves, branches and ripened fruit were falling on the ground until finally the rain arrived. I love it when it rains at nighttime, there is so much live energy around you and it gets comfortably cooler, which is great especially when you are under a roof and in your warm hammock.

Everything seemed perfect, I was enjoying the pouring rain, but suddenly because I was using a hard plastic roof, the rain-drops that were pounding on it were making such an unbear-able loud sound that I felt that my ears begin to ache. I quick-ly reached under my hammock into my duffle bag and pulled out two t-shirts, which I quickly put against my ears to block the noise. Supporting the terrible noise, I eventually fell asleep. The following morning I woke up early and saw that it had already stopped raining, then I looked up at the hard plas-tic roof and thought about how well it protected me from the rain, but unfortunately because of its hard surface, the rain-drops had made an earsplitting racket.

Upon returning to Quito, during my first night, while I was in my bed ready to sleep, I began to hear an unusual disturbing sound, ringing in my ears. I had never heard this sound before; it was so annoying that I had difficulty in falling asleep. The next morning with my wife, we went to an ear specialist who diagnosed that I had damaged my eardrums. To be sure of this diagnose, we went to other doctors, but they all coincided that from the raindrops hitting the hard plastic roof, I had severely injured my hearing. The doctors named it tinnitus and said the damage could be permanent and that there is no cure for it; in any case, they prescribed pills, which I was taking but did not help in any way. During the day, because of all the sounds of different activities, the sound was not noticeable, but at night-time, because of the silence of the night the unusual static sound was really annoying.

Fortunately, after one week I had another tour to the Amazon, I was looking forward to going to the jungle, because I was sure that my Shaman friends would be able to cure my tinnitus. Once in the Amazon, I told my Shaman friends what had happened to my hearing, they smiled and said not to worry, because they could cure my problem.

The following day, the tour group, my two Shaman friends and myself, went on a four-hour walk into a primary forest. After about an hour, suddenly the Shamans told us to stop; they had found a column of a special type of ants, which they needed to cure my hearing. One of the Shamans looked around the area and found a small tree and after analyzing its leaves; he selected one large leaf and gently twisted its stem, breaking it off the branch. It was a smooth, almost round, shiny leaf about 25 cm. (10 in.) in diameter, he laid it flat on one of his open hands, then with the fingers of his other hand he pushed it down in the center, forming the flat center of the leaf into the shape of a cup. Meanwhile the other Shaman squatted next to the column of ants and carefully started pick-ing certain ants from the column; he put those ants in the cen-ter of the leaf. The ants were about one cm. long and were frantically trying to get out, but could not because the leaf sur-face was slippery and they were constantly sliding back to the center. After there were about six ants in the center of the leaf, the Shaman raised the outer edges of the leaf to the top, form-ing a type of hollow bag, and then he brought the edges together and twisted them tightly so that the ants, which were inside the hollow space, would not get out.

The Shaman then passed me the leaf and said, "Patricio, hold the leaf firmly along the edge so that the ants will not get out." I held on to the leaf and asked my friend what else I should do, and then he said, "Now, put the leaf up to one ear and listen to the ants." I thought that I had misheard him or that he was jok-ing, so I started laughing and at the same time I said, "What did you say?" The two Shamans smiled and they said, "Listen to the ants." I put the leaf up to my left ear, and started listen-ing. To my surprise, I could hear their tiny feet scratching the surface of the leaf as they were trying to find a way out, but also I could hear a strange squeaking sound, which I guessed was a vocal sound that they were making among themselves. Supposedly, ants communicate only with their antennae. The two sounds together were not loud, but they were quite clear, obviously, the type of leaf surface and its hollow space in the center was just right in order to create the proper echo and clarity of sound. We continued walking in silence through the primary forest until about half an hour later, then one of the Shamans told me to stop and change the leaf to the other ear and to continue listening to the ants.

I estimate that after about half an hour, again the Shaman told me to stop listening to the ants. Therefore, I moved the leaf away from my ear and asked him what I should do with the leaf. He then said that we were going to make a loop and return to the same colony of ants. Arriving to the colony of ants, we put the six ants back in their original column, and obviously, the tour group was amused and skeptical of this unusual form of medicine. For about an hour after listening to the little ants, my two ears did feel something strange, they felt warm and a little numb. Those nights in the jungle, with so many animal sounds, I never heard the uncomfortable static sound of tinnitus.

During my first night in Quito, I lay back in my bed, turned off the lights and heard absolutely nothing! Yes, my Shaman friends had cured my tinnitus, in an unusual, unconventional manner, but easy and very effective.

That event became another interesting story for me to tell my tour groups. In one group I had an elderly man who after listening to my story said that he would like to listen to the ants to see if it could help his hearing problem, he had been in World War II and because of so many bomb explosions, he had lost his hearing and used especially strong ear-aids. The tour group, my Shaman friends and myself, went into the same primary forest and we followed the same procedure. We found the ants, put them in a large leaf and he listened to them, but it was not until the following day that he told the rest of the group and me that his hearing had improved! Going back to Quito, he again reaffirmed that his hearing was better.

On one occasion, after telling this story to a British tour group, there was a woman doctor in the group who said that in Great Britain, they were testing different sound frequencies in order to cure hearing problems, and that probably the Amazonian Shamans had discovered just the right sound to cure tinnitus and other hearing problems.

The majority of medicines that we use in our modern civilization have originally come from tropical rainforests. These medicines from the jungles have been available to laboratories, pharmaceutical firms and to our local pharmacies, thanks to important information provided by tropical rainforest Shamans or Healers.

Healers are quite different to Shamans. In the past, before Catholic or Protestant Evangelical missionaries arrived to Latin America, only Shamans existed, the Shamans were the Spiritual leaders of the people and also the Shamans had the best knowledge of the plants. Shamans can cure their people of practically any Spiritual, mental, emotional or physical sickness.

In "converted" Protestant Evangelical communities, the natives are more fundamentalist so they generally do not allow for Healers to exist, but in "converted" Catholic native communities the people are not so fundamentalist, so generally they allow for Healers to exist.

The main differences between Shamans and Healers is that Shamans are much more powerful than Healers, Shamans are the Spiritual leaders of the native ethnic religion, they frequently drink visionary brews made of sacred plants, they perform many astral flights, and they have the best knowledge on medicinal plants. Shamans prefer to perform their religious or healing ceremonies at nighttime. Healers prefer to perform their healing ceremonies during the day. Healers only use conscious mind here in this material world, where as Shamans use conscious and unconscious mind as well as energy from the material and Spiritual world. Shamans are more powerful and effective. In "converted" communities the Healers have the best knowledge on the medicinal plants, they perform "cleansing" ceremonies using a leaf wand and smoking a cigar. The cleansing ceremonies help to balance a person's energy and physical health which is fine, but healers do not practice the ethnic religion, they do not drink sacred brews, they do not perform astral flights and they do not have supernatural powers like Shamans have.

If someone were to organize a group of 100 of the best botanists and chemists from the top universities in the world and send them into the Amazon jungle for one year to find new natural medicines, without any assistance from Shamans or Healers, most certainly these experts from modern civilization would fail in their mission.

There are different reasons for this, but one of the main reasons is because tropical rainforests are the most complex ecosystems of our planet, producing the greatest biological diversity of plants and animals in our planet.

More than 80% of the world's plants come from tropical rainforests. In a temperate forest, there may be a few hundred co-existing species of plants and animals, while in a tropical rainforest there may be tens of thousands of co-existing species of plants and animals. In the Amazon there are more than 10,000 different chemical compounds found in the plants, and even in the animals we find extraordinary chemical richness, for example there is one species of a poison tree frog from the Brazilian Amazon, which contains more than 300 chemical compounds. Precisely, because of the complexity of a tropical rainforest is why pharmaceutical corporations from first-world nations prefer to rely on ethnic native Shamans and Healers for information.

Since 1990, the first-world Biotechnology (technology of Biology) has become a growing multi-billion dollar industry. Considering that none of the first-world nations have tropical rainforests, obviously, the regions of our planet that primarily interest the pharmaceutical and chemical corporations are the rich, tropical rainforests that exist in developing countries. Consequently, some first-world governments have passed an absurd and unfair law in their countries, known as "International Intellectual Property Patenting," which gives their multinational corporations the International legal right to patent any natural life-form from any foreign country of the planet. This includes native medicinal information, genetic material, cell lines, animals, plants, insects, micro-organisms, and even blood samples, saliva samples and hair samples of native people. Usually it is in the foreign missionary hospitals where these samples of the indigenous people are collected, without even their knowledge or consent.

In all honesty, the laboratories which have used information provided by native Shamans or Healers, and or have taken specimens of plants, insects or animals out of the Amazon or other tropical rainforests, should give to these Shamans or Healers and to their tribes a just economic compensation. The best form of economic compensation is by means of purchasing land in the tropical rainforests for creating ecological reserves whereby the same native tribes can be the guardians of the reserves.

Unfortunately this does not happen, for me it is disappointing and offensive that corporations from first-world nations, through their biologists take advantage of the Amazonian natives. The indigenous people are so poor, naive and trusting, that in exchange for a few dollars and a friendly smile, they will reveal to foreign biologists all possible information concerning their ancestral natural medicines. The indigenous tribes simply have no idea of how valuable their ancient, ethnic, natural, chemical recipes are to multi-national corporations.

To make matters worse, first-world governments are persuading second and third-world government leaders to sign treaties of "Free Trade" officially accepting the absurd "International Intellectual Property Patenting law. The most important terms are that first-world biologists and chemists may go to developing nations to collect as many samples of any life form, plants, animals, information, etc..., and patent them, and likewise, second and third-world biologists may go to first-world nations for the same purpose. But surely, all of the few hundred chemicals found in the plants and animals that exist in the temperate forests in the first-world nations have already been patented by the first-world corporations.

Apart from this, the rich diversity and number of species of plants, trees, animals and natural chemistry in tropical rainforests (developing nations) far exceeds the, diversity and number of species of plants, trees, animals and natural chemistry in temperate forests (first-world nations). Just the tiny country of Ecuador, which is about the size of the state of Colorado in the U.S., or twice the size of England, has far more species of plants, trees, insects, and animals than all of the United States, Canada and England together. To mention a few examples: in Ecuador there are more than 1,560 species of birds compared to 930 species in all of North America, in Ecuador there are more than 125 hummingbirds compared 20 species in all North America. In Ecuador there are more than 460 species of amphibians compared to 197 species in all North America. Ecuador has more than 2,000 native trees, more than 20,000 native plants, more than 4,400 species of orchids, more than 700 species of reptiles, more than 2,200 species of butterflies compared to 678 species in all U.S.A. And if we add to Ecuador's fantastic biological wealth, the fabulous diversity and richness in flora and fauna of Venezuela, Brazil, Colombia and Peru we realize that these tropical South American countries together have one of the richest biological-chemical areas of our planet.

This International Intellectual Property Patenting law cleverly designed by the first world, allows first-world corporations to "legally" steal ancient tribal information, or natural genetic or chemical substances from second and third-world nations, and patent them as exclusive property of the corporation. Consequently, these first-world corporations will be assuring for themselves an international monopoly of medical, agricultural, chemical and military industries worth thousands of billions of dollars. This new invention by the first world to steal life-forms and ancestral indigenous information from second and third world nations is deceitful and disgraceful. Rightfully so, instead of being called "Bio-Prospecting," it is often called "Bio-Piracy."

As usual, the problem of course is greed and dishonesty, where first-world corporations do not want to pay a just economical price to the second and third-world nations for information or natural genetic or chemical substances; they prefer to obtain higher economical profits by using underhanded methods.

Fortunately there are some first-world pharmaceutical corporations, working in second and third-world tropical rainforests, which are practicing Bio-Prospecting in an ethical and reciprocal manner. This is the case with Shaman Pharmaceuticals, a U.S. biotechnology corporation, and the U.S. based pharmaceutical firm Merck & Co., which in 1991, signed a mutually beneficial economic agreement with the National Biodiversity Institute of Costa Rica. The National Biodiversity Institute agreed to contribute 10% of the upfront payment from Merck and 50% of any royalties to help conserve tropical rainforest national parks; furthermore, Merck will provide technical assistance and training to the institute, for drug-chemical research in Costa Rica.

This type of Bio-Prospecting between these two first-world corporations and developing nations is a mutually respectful, honest and correct manner of working in the tropical rain-forests of the developing nations. Hopefully these two examples would be imitated by all first-world governments and first-world corporations.

**CHAPTER 11**

- Amazon Ethnic Religion- Shamans
  Foundation and Tourism

If nothing is done to help the ethnic native communities, I am certain that within the next 12 years, they and their ancestral, ethnic religion will have perished. Precisely, in order to prevent this from happening was my main motive for writing this book, and in order to help the ethnic communities, I have different projects in mind.

As soon as I can get enough money together, I am going to create a Foundation and organize different projects, which will assist the Amazon communities that are still practicing their God-like ethnic religion and culture. For the last fifty years, modern civilization has forced these ethnic communities to migrate deeper into the jungle. The ethnic communities are small in population, few in number and they desperately need help.

Some ethnic communities may not be interested in working with this or any other Foundation, they are most likely not interested in having any contact with modern civilization and obviously, this foundation will always respect their privacy and never disturb them. However, I am sure that the majority of the ethnic communities will be very much interested in working with this Foundation.

The Foundation will economically support different projects to better the quality of education, health, and raise the standard of living of the ethnic communities. For the native families it is important to have a regular, sufficient supply of protein, so the Foundation will provide technical training to increase their production of farm animals like chickens, pigs, breeding their own fish in large ponds, breeding capybara rodents and or tapirs.

In addition, for those ethnic communities that are interested to receive tourists and where it is viable, the Foundation will build small native style eco-tourism lodges near the communities. Those native communities that are interested in working with tour groups will receive appropriate training to attend the tourists at the lodge as well as in the guiding services. Tourists that visit these lodges will not only have an opportunity of visiting the Amazon, seeing pristine forest and its wildlife, but also a personal, first-hand experience with ethnic Amazon natives and Shamans who still practice their true ethnic religion and culture.

Another important purpose of this Foundation is to promote the conservation of their primary forests and if possible purchase land to protect the forests by establishing reserves.

Of all industries, tourism is considered the cleanest, and Eco-tourism is the best form of tourism, because it is the most ecologically minded. Eco-tourism tour operators, take tourists to visit natural ecosystems and or cultural sites and assure that those visits will cause the least impact possible to the ecosystem, as well as to the local people living there. In addition, true Eco-tourism tour operators should directly support the conservation of the ecosystem it is visiting as well as the well-being of the indigenous people that live in the area.

By you visiting an Amazon eco-tourism lodge, part of the money that you have paid for your tour will be used to protect the virgin forests, animal life and help the indigenous people that live in the area.

Unfortunately, there are many tour agencies or lodges, which say they practice Eco-tourism, but in reality, they do not. A true Eco-tourism lodge has to act completely responsible concerning different issues like investing the necessary amount of money to deal adequately with the treatment of garbage, pollution and sewage. In addition, supporting conservation programs and purchasing forests to protect as reserves, and supporting different community projects so that the native people in the area may be able to live a more dignified life.

To finance the Foundation and its projects, I shall depend on the sales of my book, posters and silkscreen replicas of my artwork. Additionally, I will open a tour company in Quito offering tours throughout Ecuador, as well as Amazon Spiritual, Shaman, cultural tours to ethnic communities, and other type of Amazon tours to reserves or National parks. Also, in order to obtain money for the Foundation, I shall rely on private donations from generous people around the world who want to be a part of saving the upper Amazon ethnic religion from extinction and helping the Amazon ethnic communities to find a more balanced, dignified and healthy life. As soon as possible, I shall have a web site under the same name as the title of my book giving more information on the Foundation, its projects and Amazon tours.

• **Museo de Arqueología del Banco Central, (Government Archeological Museum).**

Avenida Patria, between Avenida Seis de Diciembre and Avenida Doce de Octubre.
Tue.-Fri. 9:00-5:00
Sat. and Sun. 10:00-4:00
Tel. 222 3258, 222 3259

This museum is the best Pre-Inca Archeological museum of all South America. Among its displays are the 5,800 yr. old. Valdivia Culture, which is the oldest pottery so far discovered in all North, Central and South America. Within the same museum is the gold section, where you will see the first platinum metal work ever made in the world, here in Ecuador with the 2,500 yr. old La Tolita Culture. This museum will give you an excellent introduction to the country, History and first people of Ecuador.

• **Museo-Fundacion Capilla del Hombre, (Modern Art Museum of the artist Oswaldo Guayasamín).**

Calle Mariano Calvache and Calle Lorenzo Chavez.
Tue.-Sun. 10:00-5:00
Tel. 244 6455, 246 5266

The multi-talented and renowned artist Oswaldo Guayasamín was Ecuador's best and most famous artist, also he is considered as one of the best artists in all Latin America and the world. A visit to this fine museum will be a worthwhile, most unforgettable experience, which you should not miss.

# • Jardin Botanico de Quito, (Botanical Gardens of Quito)

Avenida Shyris, within Parque La Carolina
Mon. 9:00-12:30
Tue.-Sun. 9:00-5:00.

Because of Ecuador's unique and plentiful biodiversity with its flora, this botanical garden is considered one of the best in Latin America. On display are more than 1,000 species of orchids, as well as unique plants from Ecuador's tropical regions, Cloud forests and the high altitude Paramo region.

# • Teleferico, (Pichincha Volcano Cable Cars).

From this new, modern complex, you will be at different altitudes to get spectacular views of Quito, as well of the beautiful surrounding Andes. For hikers, there are paths to climb up to the crater of the volcano, and for other visitors who do not want the rugged exercise; there are horses that may be rented. If you take the cable car to the highest station, you will be at 4,100 m. /13,450 ft. from where you will get the best views, but if you have a heart condition, I do not recommended to go so high, otherwise, there is no problem. Within the complex, there are many small restaurants.

# • Itchimbia,

From the top of this hill, you will get the best view of Colonial and modern Quito and of the impressive Pichincha Volcano. On this hill is a large, beautiful metal structure, built around 1886, in Alexandre Gustav Eiffel's famous workshop in France.

# • Iglesia La Compañia de Jesus, (Jesuit church)

With more than 5 tons of gold leaf decorating its interior, this exquisite church in Colonial Quito is considered the richest and one of the most beautiful churches in all North, Central and South America. This visit is one of the most important sites to see in Colonial Quito.

Mon.-Fri. 9:30-5:30, Sat. 9:30-4:00, Sun. 1:00-4:00. Sometimes, on Sunday afternoons there are special religious services during which, tourists will not permitted to visit the church. From April 20 until April 30 are the annual religious services in honor to the Virgin of La Dolorosa, during these days the church is closed to tourists.

Tel. 258 0612

## • Museo de la Ciudad, (The Museum of the City)

Calle Garcia Moreno 572 and Calle Rocafuerte
Tue.-Sun. 10:00-5:00
Tel. 228 3882, 228 3883

The main theme and display of this museum is the Colonial History of Quito. The museum functions in a beautiful Colonial Spanish-style building, where originally operated the first European-style hospital in all South America, built in 1565.

## General advice for Amazon travellers

**(What to bring).**

* Loose fitting, light-weight, cotton clothing, preferably of earth colors; shades of dark greens, browns and dark greys. Do not take "blue jean" pants, shirts or jackets.

* Do not take leather hiking boots, if these get wet, they will never dry. Most lodges supply knee-high rubber boots, which are the best footwear in the jungle, but you should take shoes

like high top sneakers with a good grip sole for muddy trails, just in case you do not find rubber boots of your size.

* Long cotton or wool socks, so that you may tuck your pants in the socks. Do not take ankle socks.

* Raingear. Always when you leave your lodge or campsite take it with you, you can never tell when it will rain.

* Bathing suit.

* Biodegradable soap and shampoo.

* Binoculars.

* Wide brim hat, for strong sun.
* Insect repellent, if you bring spray repellent; never use it near other people, sometimes a breeze may blow it onto the eyes of others. Never put repellent near your eyes, nose or mouth, and never put it on your forehead. It will last longer on your clothes, than on your skin.

* Light-weight, long sleeve shirts are more practical than t-shirts to protect you from mosquitoes or other insects.

* Before walking on sandy banks, always put on insect repellent to protect you from sand flies.

* Chiggers are always present within grass clearings of native homes or gardens of lodges. If you have to walk on grass, tuck your pants in your socks and spray insect repellent on shoes, socks and pants.

* Never step on fallen Palm trees, if the tree has recently fallen, the thorns on the trunk are still strong and they may pierce through your sneakers or boots.

* Before bathing in a lake or river, ask your guide to check the area of the bank, so that there are no fallen palm trees around the bank or in the water. Most palm trees have nasty thorns which would be dangerous if you are barefoot.

* Snakes are rare to find, they are not considered a problem if you follow your guide. In case you decide to walk on a path into the forest alone, never get off the path. If you get off the path, it is quite easy to get lost and not find your way back to the path, and chances of encountering snakes are much higher. More of a problem than snakes are ants, always look first before you touch something in the forest and even within your lodge, look carefully before you touch hand rails, and never lean against any tree. Ants have poor eyesight; they will never sting you unless you touch them.

* If you are setting up a hammock in the forest, always check first the trees for ants; never tie your hammock to trees with ant nests, too much ant traffic, or large ants, about 3 cm long / over one inch long called Conga ants. (Scientific name is Paraponera clavata). These ants live in small colonies; typically their nests are in the ground against tree trunks. Conga ants carry a nasty sting with a powerful venom, which is terribly painful. Never disturb a Conga ant, they can be dangerous.

* If you take snacks, after eating these in your room, seal the bag or package tightly and keep it in your luggage, or the food will attract insects.

* At the end of the day after your activities, clean your camera and binoculars and keep these in your closed luggage, this will protect these items from night air humidity.

* During all walks in the forest, especially if you are near other people, please keep silent, you will get a better feel for

the forest and its natural sounds and you will have a better opportunity of hearing and seeing animals. Only when your guide stops to explain something, then you may ask questions.

* Never pet or play with native or mestizo dogs.

* Never dive into a river or lake, you can not see what is under the surface of the water, there may be a tree with its pointed branches. Get into the water slowly.

* Some guides catch Caimans with poles or their hands, this is not in accordance to Ecotourism; it disturbs the animals, stresses them and eventually will force them to abandon their living area. Please mention this to your guide.

* Please do not take part in fishing activities, this is not in accordance to Ecotourism, the native families rely on fish for their families.

* Regardless of what type of Amazon tour you are on, please collect all of your old, used batteries and plastic packaging, or empty plastic bottles and put them in a plastic bag into your luggage, to take this bag out of the Amazon to Quito or any other big city where you can dispose of these items in the garbage. In this way, you will be helping with Ecotourism, to create less of an environmental impact on the forest and the native tribes.

*Walking through any primary forest, I always recommend my tour groups to be in complete silence in order to listen to the forest and its animals. Likewise, during a night walk,
It is recommended to keep silence and at some time during the walk, stop and all people turn off their flashlights and in silence listen to the forest for a few minutes.

**General travel advice:**

* On all your travels, you should carry on you a good quality, loud whistle; it can be useful for many types of emergencies in the jungle or even in the cities with pickpockets. Walking on your own in Quito or other cities in Ecuador, wear it on a string around your neck, under your shirt, sometimes there are groups of small native children, that are selling candies and unfortunately they will aggressively surround tourists. In reality they are trained pickpockets, so never buy candies from groups of children and never permit these groups of children to get too close to you. If after you tell them to back away; they still come violently towards you, hold on tightly to your fanny packs, valuables or possessions and quickly start blowing your whistle, or if you do not have a whistle, scream out loud "Policia, Policia." Until they leave.


**General advice:**

* The safest way to protect your passport and money from pickpockets is by carrying these valuables in a neck pouch, underneath your shirt or t-shirt.

*Never drink water from the faucet.

*Never have drinks with ice, unless your guide guarantees that the ice is made from pure water. Otherwise when you order your drink, specify "Sin hielo."

*The general rule is to eat only what has been peeled or cooked; never eat grapes, strawberries, or Mora (blackberry) juice or Fresa / Frutilla (strawberry) juice.

*Never eat lettuce or the skins of tomatoes, unless your guide guarantees that it is safe.

*Remember, before eating, always wash your hands.

*Please do not give money to beggars, some hotels have donation boxes for Charity organizations, this is the best way of helping poor people.


**Recommended Reading:**

Culural Adaptation to Amazonian Habitats:
The Siona-Secoya of Eastern Ecuador.
William T. Vickers.    1976

Tropical Nature, Adrian Forsyth and Ken Miyata
ISBN: 0-684-18710-8

Savages, Joe Kane
ISBN: o-679-41191-7

The Amazon, Past, Present and Future Gheerbrant Alain.
ISBN: 0-8109-2860-4
Discoveries, 1988.

The Jivaro, Michael J. Harner
ISBN: 0-385-07119-1

The Healing Power of Illness, Thorwald Dethlefsen and Rudiger Dahlke MD,
ISBN: 1-84333-048-2

Satchidananda, Yogiraj Sri Swami.    Integral Yoga Hatha
ISBN: 0-03-085089-4

Chakra Therapy, Keith Sherwood
ISBN: 0-87542-721-9

The Complete Book of Tái Chi, Stewart McFarlane
ISBN: 0-7607-3040-7

The Hidden Messages in Water, Masaru Emoto
ISBN: 1-58270-114-8

# BIBLIOGRAPHY

Chapter 6

Axel Rudin.

Sherwood, Keith.    Chakra Therapy-for personal growth and healing. Llewllyn Publications, 1988.

Satchidananda, Yogiraj Sri Swami.    Integral Yoga Hatha Holt. Rinehart and Winston of Canada, Limited, 1970

Sant Rajinder Singh.

Chapter 9

Vickers, William T.    Culural Adaptation to Amazonian Habitats: The Siona-Secoya of Eastern Ecuador.Ph.D. dissertation, Department of Anthropology, University of Florida, 1976

Is God an American?    International Work Group for Indigenous Affairs, Survival International.  Edited by Soren Hvalkof and Peter Aaby, 1981

Gheerbrant Alain.   The Amazon, Past, Present and Future Discoveries, 1988.

Elliot, Elizabeth.    Through Gates of Splendor. Wheaton, Ill.:Living Books, 1988.